MOMENTS OF IMPACT

Moments of
IMPACT

INJURY, RACIALIZED MEMORY, AND RECONCILIATION IN COLLEGE FOOTBALL

JAIME SCHULTZ

University of Nebraska Press · Lincoln & London

Acknowledgments for the use of previously published material appear on page xiii, which constitutes an extension of the copyright page.

Library of Congress Cataloging-in-Publication Data
Names: Schultz, Jaime.
Title: Moments of impact: injury, racialized memory, and reconciliation in college football / Jaime Schultz.
Description: Lincoln: University of Nebraska Press, [2016] | Includes bibliographical references and index.
Identifiers: LCCN 2015020835
ISBN 9780803245785 (cloth: alk. paper)
ISBN 9781496211767 (paper: alk. paper)
ISBN 9780803285033 (epub)
ISBN 9780803285040 (mobi)
ISBN 9780803285057 (pdf)
Subjects: LCSH: African American football players—Iowa—History—20th century. | Iowa State University—Football—History—20th century. | Drake University—Football—History—20th century. | Collective memory—Social aspects—Iowa. | Memorialization—Social aspects—Iowa. | Racism in sports—United States—History—20th century. | Simmons, Ozzie, 1914–2001. | Trice, Jack, 1902–1923. | Bright, Johnny, 1930–1983.
Classification: LCC GV959.52.I6 S35 2016 | DDC 796.332/6309777—dc23 LC record available at http://lccn.loc.gov/2015020835

Set in Dante MT by M. Scheer.

For my parents, Robert Gordon Schultz and Deborah Tauber Schultz

CONTENTS

ILLUSTRATIONS

ACKNOWLEDGMENTS

In the fall of 2002 I taught a class at the University of Iowa titled "Inequality in Sport." It was there that one of my brightest students, Jessman Smith, related the "real" story behind the Floyd of Rosedale trophy, for which the Iowa and University of Minnesota football teams play each season. It stemmed, he told me, from a 1934 contest between the two schools in which an African American player named Ozzie Simmons had been injured. The anecdote inspired me to do a little digging. That initial excavation uncovered two additional incidents involving black football players at Iowa schools—Jack Trice at Iowa State University and Johnny Bright at Drake University. I am forever indebted to Jessman for starting me down the path that led to *Moments of Impact*.

A number of graduate school mentors including Bonnie Slatton, Shelton Stromquist, and Stephen Wieting were instrumental in helping me see this project to fruition. I was especially lucky to benefit from the wit and wisdom of my primary advisers, Susan Birrell and Tina Parratt. Additional thanks to all the faculty and students at the University of Iowa who helped me in this endeavor.

I have been fortunate and humbled to receive recognition for this work. I am grateful to the North American Society for Sport History for its Graduate Student Essay Prize, the Sport Literature Association for its Lyle Olsen Graduate Student Essay Award, the North American Society for the Sociology of Sport for its Barbara Brown Student Paper Award, and the International Society for the

History of Physical Education and Sport for its Reinhard Sprenger Junior Scholar Award. In addition, a grant from the State Historical Society of Iowa allowed me to devote my time to delving into state and local archives.

At these and other archives, special collections departments, and libraries, I have encountered amiable and resourceful librarians and archivists. I offer particular thanks to the staffs at Drake University (especially Claudia Frazer and Bart Schmidt), Iowa State University (Laura Sullivan and Whitney Olthoff), Minnesota Historical Society, Oklahoma State University, University of Iowa (Kathryn Hodson), University of Minnesota (Jennifer Torkelson and Erin George), and the *Des Moines Register*. I am also indebted to the late Dick Bolin, Tom Emmerson, Adam Gold, Bill Kunerth, the late Eutopia Morsell-Simmons, and Charles Sohn, all of whom consented to interviews. Professor Emmerson was especially helpful, both with his experience in the campaign for Jack Trice Stadium and his continued backing of this project.

I am indebted to copyeditor Vicki Chamlee for her careful reading. From the University of Nebraska Press, I thank associate acquisitions editor Courtney Ochsner, associate project editor Sara Springsteen, and senior editor Rob Taylor. Rob also secured an amazing team of reviewers for this manuscript. Michael Oriard is, without question, the preeminent scholar of football and cultural studies. His comments on my initial proposal helped immensely. Daniel A. Nathan wrote, among other excellent works, *Saying It's So: A Cultural History of the Black Sox Scandal*—the gold standard for work on sport and memory. His help was invaluable. And David K. Wiggins is without peers when it comes to the scholarship on African Americans and sport history. He reviewed each phase of this project and offered important insight throughout. In addition to their expertise and keen judgment, each of these scholars has been consistently kind, generous, encouraging, and influential.

The same is true for several other people who helped me at different stages of writing this book. Allen Guttmann took the time to help me improve my writing and clarify my ideas. He truly is a gentleman and a scholar. With his encyclopedic knowledge of college sport, Ronald A. Smith helped me to get things right. Maureen Smith shared her knowledge on sport, race, and commemoration. Mark Dyreson is a wonderful colleague and mentor who has helped me without fail. And I surely put Paul Hefty's brilliant football mind and seemingly infinite patience to the test with questions about terminology, statistics, and logistics of the game.

Finally I thank my family for its unwavering support. I thank my grandmothers, Marcella Schultz and Bee Tauber, who passed on their love of language and passion to learn. I dearly wish they were here. Thank you to my brothers, Rob and David, whom I adore. Thank you to my parents, Deb and Bob Schultz, to whom I dedicate this book. And thank you to the newest and most precious branches on my own family tree—Paul D., Nella Bee, and Sylvie Lee—for putting it all into perspective.

An earlier version of chapter 1 previously appeared as "The Legend of Jack Trice and the Campaign for Jack Trice Stadium, 1973–1984" in *Journal of Social History* 41, no. 4 (2008): 997–1029.

An earlier version of chapter 2 previously appeared as "'Stuff from Which Legends Are Made': Jack Trice Stadium and the Politics of Memory" in *International Journal of the History of Sport* 24, no. 6 (2007): 715–48.

An earlier version of chapter 3 previously appeared as "'A Wager Concerning a Diplomatic Pig': A Crooked Reading of the Floyd of Rosedale Narrative" in *Journal of Sport History* 32, no. 1 (2005): 1–21.

An earlier version of chapter 4 previously appeared as "Photography, Instant Memory and the Slugging of Johnny Bright" in *Stadion* 32 (2006): 221–43.

MOMENTS OF IMPACT

Introduction

Telling Exceptional Tales

Jack Trice Stadium, the Floyd of Rosedale trophy, Johnny Bright Field—each originates with an African American man seriously injured while playing Iowa college football. Iowa State University's Jack Trice died in 1923 following a match with the University of Minnesota. Seventy-four years later, his alma mater dedicated its stadium in his name. In 1934 Minnesota players' attacks against the University of Iowa's Ozzie Simmons initiated Floyd of Rosedale, the bronze pig that has come to define the schools' rivalry. The intent behind creating the trophy was not to remember Simmons or the brutality he endured but rather to distance them from public attention. In 2006 Drake University officials memorialized Johnny Bright, arguably the best athlete to ever represent the school. Before they dedicated the field in his honor, they sought an official apology from Oklahoma State University for a 1951 incident in which an Aggie player shattered Bright's jaw and ended his college career.

In each episode, the injuries came at the hands of white opponents. This is not surprising, for Trice, Simmons, and Bright played football during an era in which whites overwhelmingly manned sport, higher education, and, indeed, most American bastions of institutionalized power and privilege. The three men were, therefore, *exceptional* in several regards. They were racial exceptions on campus and on the gridiron. They were also exceptional athletes, superlatively talented. This has led to consistent debate about whether race or prowess played the preeminent role in such adversarial motivations to violence. Most likely it was an ugly combination of the two. The regularity with which black gridders found themselves in the crosshairs of white opponents strongly suggests that the assaults on Trice, Simmons, and Bright were *unexceptional*. Yet although these three incidents occurred within a relatively short time span (1923–51), in a state where the black population has never exceeded 2 percent, the popular media failed almost unilaterally to connect the three violent acts.[1] Instead, most journalists represented them as discrete phenomena, as exceptional occurrences.

The final element of exceptionalism that characterizes the biographies of Trice, Simmons, and Bright is that they are all associated with some form of material culture: a stadium, a trophy, and a football field. The central questions in *Moments of Impact* concern why, when, and how these memorials came about. These are questions about cultural memory—that is, the processes and politics associated with communities' efforts to remember and to forget the past.[2] Over time those efforts have become increasingly *racialized*. In other words, those who remember and explain have infused the three stories with racial character and, especially, have identified racism as motivation for the abusive incidents in ways that earlier narrators did not. This is not to suggest that one version of history is more "correct" than another. Instead, considering the ways that these histories change reveals a particular type of cultural memory—*racialized memory*—a communal form of remembering imbued with racial meaning and, like all forms of cultural memory, one that is inevitably influenced by the sociohistorical context in which it takes place.[3]

In different ways racialized memory manifests in Jack Trice Stadium, the Floyd of Rosedale trophy, and Johnny Bright Field, particularly within what legal scholar Roy L. Brooks characterizes as the "age of apology."[4] At the turn of the twenty-first century, an unprecedented number of civic, educational, and political leaders began to express regret for their communities' historical sins. A significant share of these apologies was for crimes committed against racial and ethnic minorities by a dominant (usually white) power structure. This trend did not escape the world of sports.

In this era of reconciliation, restitution often comes in the form of commemoration. A number of these tributes include a tacit acknowledgment of past wrongs as well as an explicit celebration of hard-won triumphs during difficult times. They can also have congratulatory effects that praise American society and its various institutions for "having come such a long way" since the days of Jim Crow. In the process commemorative efforts risk reducing racism to isolated incidents and suggest that talent, hard work, determination, perseverance, and an abiding social conscience are enough to overcome seemingly insurmountable odds. This neoliberal view tends to minimize the structural and ideological problems that continue to plague society, resigning racism to a relic of the past and distracting collective attention from the work that remains to be done.

Black Athletes in White College Sport, 1900–1950

To begin with a brief overview of early twentieth-century black college athletes, mainly black college football players, at predominantly white colleges and universities (PWCUS) admittedly starts this investigation down a certain path; it sets the racialization process in motion. Locating the careers of Trice, Simmons, and Bright within a narrative of sporting and societal racism risks obscuring more nuanced understandings of the injuries they sustained in the 1920s, 1930s, and 1950s. While none of the episodes is quite so definitive, this interpretation foregrounds race as a motivating factor. Historians not only analyze narratives about the past; they also create them. Even by organizing this chapter in a particular way, I am complicit in racializing the memories of Trice, Simmons, and Bright.

This narrative starts in the nineteenth century, when only a handful of black students went to college, and the vast majority of them attended segregated institutions. From 1826 through the 1890s just thirty African American students graduated from PWCUS; by 1910 less than seven hundred had earned their degrees from such schools.[5] In addition to black codes, inadequate school-ing, and other racist traditions, the 1896 *Plessy v. Ferguson* verdict legalized racial apartheid in public spaces and contributed to the dearth of black students at majority-white schools. The infamous decision encouraged many states to establish racially separate and ostensibly equal schools, including historically black colleges and universities (HBCUs), rather than integrate their white institutions.

Around the time of World War I, racism, a lack of opportu-nity, and the possibilities for employment and education brought about a "great migration" of blacks from the South to northern, industrial centers. This movement augmented the number of Afri-can Americans at PWCUs, which rose from 1,400 students in 1924 to 2,538 students in 1932. Still in 1933, 97 percent of the more than 38,000 black collegians matriculated to segregated institutions.[6]

African Americans began to appear on predominantly white intercollegiate football teams in the 1890s.[7] Early pioneers took to the gridirons at schools stretching from small New England colleges, through the Ivies of the East, into parts of the Midwest, and over to the Pacific Northwest and Southern California. These institutions typically maintained unofficial quota systems, allow-ing only one or two African Americans per squad. Most north-ern schools failed to field black athletes before the middle of the twentieth century, with "conspicuous" absences at some Catho-lic universities, at Princeton, and at West Point and Annapolis.[8]

In 1915 two stars, Paul Robeson of Rutgers College (now Rut-gers University) and Frederick Douglass "Fritz" Pollard of Brown, became, as Arthur Ashe assessed in *Hard Road to Glory*, the "legators of future generations of black [football] players at white schools."[9] But they, like other black citizens, found themselves in difficult circumstances. The same year Robeson and Pollard made their gridiron debuts, for instance, white audiences flocked to *Birth of a Nation* (or *The Clansman*), a film that celebrated, among other things, the rise of the Ku Klux Klan during the era of Reconstruc-tion and the "heroic" lynching of an African American character (played by a white actor in black face). "Particularly around 1915," writes film scholar Michele Faith Wallace on the topic of lynching, "huge, festive crowds, including women and young children, often turned out to witness these hangings, in which victims were sometimes tortured, slowly burned alive, or castrated, their body parts distributed among the crowds as keepsakes."[10] These atrocities, like the popularity of *Birth of a Nation*, speak volumes about the racial tenor of the time.

That same year many Americans rejoiced as boxer Jack Johnson lost his boxing title in Cuba to Jess Willard, who was just one in a series of "great white hopes" intent on dethroning the first black heavyweight champion of the world. In 1913, five years after Johnson first won the title, a Chicago jury had convicted the boxer of violating the Mann Act (or the White Slave Traffic Act), a statute that "forbade the transportation of women in interstate or foreign commerce 'for the purpose of prostitution or debauchery, or for any other immoral purpose.'"[11] Widely recognized today as a "racially motivated criminal conviction," it was a trumped-up charge, prompted both by Johnson's athletic prowess and his unabashed romantic relationships with white women.[12] Johnson lived in exile for seven years before returning to the United States and serving a year's time in the Leavenworth, Kansas, penitentiary. His persecution loomed as a formidable warning to those African Americans who failed to "know their place."[13]

Like Johnson, African American men who made their way into majority-white sports during the epoch of Jim Crow racism (there is almost no evidence to suggest that African American women joined their white peers in analogous competition) had to show exceptional talents.[14] Whereas white football players "may get on through fraternity politics," wrote Ed Nace in a 1930 piece for *Opportunity* magazine (published by the National Urban League), "a colored star must qualify through sheer ability."[15] Woody Strode, a luminary in the backfield for the University of California at Los Angeles (UCLA) in the late 1930s, reminisced that a "Negro had to be a good athlete. There was the old supposition if I was going to play on your team, then I had to be twice as good as anyone else."[16]

Off the field African American student-athletes suffered what sport historian David K. Wiggins calls the "twin terrors of academic neglect and social isolation."[17] Demonstrably beginning in the 1920s, a number of black sportsmen, unprepared for the rigors of academic life at PWCUs, found themselves funneled into college courses that kept them eligible for sport but did little to advance them toward a degree.[18] White administrators and students—the very same people who cheered the black superstars' talents on game day—denied African Americans access to fraternities, school parties and dances, and other communal activities.[19] As historian Donald Spivey puts it, black college athletes found themselves "simultaneously scorned and loved" at predominately white schools.[20]

Interracial dating was strictly taboo, and accompanied by few African American coeds, the athletes were often lonely and longing for companionship. A handful of heartrending anecdotes give some insight into their exclusion from restaurants, movie theaters, businesses, and social functions in their respective college towns.[21] Even as late as 1953, halfback J. C. Caroline of the University of Illinois found that he could not get his hair cut in Champaign. "Ironically," wrote the *Pittsburgh Courier*'s Wendell Smith, "in the window of that same barber shop was a picture of Caroline, blasting the opposing football team's line in All-American style. He couldn't crash the color-line in the barber shop, however."[22]

Living conditions compounded this sense of alienation. Until the 1950s and 1960s most northern colleges denied African American students on-campus housing, consigning them to live in boardinghouses, in black fraternities, or with local black families.[23] All things considered, remarked Dan Kean, an athlete at the University of Michigan in the 1930s, "I'd have to say black students were AT the University but not OF it."[24]

"If sports indeed related something of the character of the country between 1919 and 1945," wrote Ashe, "then football was a less than satisfactory commentary on American life."[25] In the post–World War II era, though, attitudes began to shift, if only slightly, and pressures to desegregate the military, education, professional sports, and other facets of social life began to mount. "Although

6

few people realized it," writes scholar Richard M. Dalfiume, "the war was working a revolution in American race relations."[26] The hypocrisy of fighting against Nazi totalitarianism was not lost on American civil rights leaders, who used the occasion to poke holes in U.S. theories of racial superiority that seemed "uncomfortably like the unscientific Nazi doctrine of Aryan supremacy."[27] The National Association for the Advancement of Colored People (NAACP), the National Urban League, and allied groups promoted a "Double V" campaign, calling for victory in the war abroad and victory over racism at home. Activists argued that if African American servicemen were good enough to fight and die on the battlefields for their country, they were good enough to take to the ball fields alongside their white brethren.[28]

Even so Jim Crow governed much of their military lives, and once mustered out of the armed forces, African American servicemen did not enjoy the full advantages of citizenship. Education was one aspect of social life that remained a bastion of white privilege. A 1944 study found that "in seventeen states and the District of Columbia, Negro children are compelled by law to attend separate schools."[29] It was not until the 1954 *Brown v. Board of Education* decision that the courts struck down legalized Jim Crowism, though for decades many stonewalled the decision "with all deliberate speed."

In 1946, one year after the end of World War II, President Harry S. Truman formed the Committee on Civil Rights. The distinguished committee's report, published the following year, called for "the strengthening of the machinery of civil rights, the right to safety and security of the person, the right to citizenship and its privileges, the right to freedom of conscience, and the right to equality opportunity." Standing out among the group's position statements, writes renowned historian John Hope Franklin, was its "rejection of racial segregation, highly controversial in 1947, and its call for an end to lynching."[30]

President Truman also established a Commission on Higher Education, charged with examining the nation's postsecondary schools. Among the commission's many findings was evidence that the educational system severely disadvantaged people of color and that the "present policy will make it an instrument for creating the very inequalities it was designed to prevent." At the time African Americans made up only 3.1 percent of all college students, and 85 percent of them attended segregated institutions.[31] Thus commission members determined, "Discrimination in the admission of college students because of an individual's race . . . is an antidemocratic practice."[32] This finding echoed the thesis of Gunnar Myrdal's 1944 *An American Dilemma: The Negro Problem and Modern Democracy,* the massive, influential project that identified the ways in which racial inequities stood in stark opposition to the nation's foundational values of liberty, equality, and justice for all.[33]

Following the war African Americans, particularly those benefiting from the Servicemen's Readjustment Act of 1944 (or G.I. Bill), attended PWCUS in greater numbers, and many joined the schools' varsity sports programs. By then, observed scholar Rufus Clement, "it was no longer an oddity to see a Negro athlete trotting out on the gridiron, being cheered, second-guessed, booed, criticized, hoisted upon shoulders, just as any other athlete of the period was treated."[34] Clement overstates the racial tolerance of the era. The late 1940s and 1950s did usher in what Wiggins classifies as the "romantic era" of desegregation, but while high-profile black athletes increased in the amateur and professional ranks, inequalities persisted.[35] Consequently, writes historian Adolph Grundman, 1950s college sport did not "mark the triumph of equalitarian ideals in American society," but it did indicate a move toward integration.[36]

Coaches did not necessarily desegregate their teams because of a sense of moral correctness; rather, as Grundman contends, the "galloping professionalization of collegiate sports after World War II, particularly football and basketball, made the recruitment of black athletes especially enticing." Many athletic programs saw this untapped source of talent as a shortcut to national recognition. Consequently universities outside the South were in the enviable position where they could build their athletic programs and claim that they were advancing the cause of race relations in America. The media, in turn, pointed with pride to collegiate sports (as well as professional sports) as a model for race relations in American society.[37]

As PWCUs improved their sports programs with black athletes, they simultaneously improved their image as racial progressives even though the athletes suffered in the process.

Benchings, Slights, and Violence

"Gentlemen's agreements" were among the many indignities that African American football players endured in the first half of the twentieth century. These were tacit accords between administrators, as opposed to de jure forms of segregation, but there was nothing gentlemanly about arrangements that kept blacks out of contests against teams from southern and former border states. Not all such institutions insisted upon segregated competition, and several northern schools refused to comply with requests to that effect. Nonetheless, wrote the historian and educator E. B. Henderson, "Few coaches seem to have the fortitude to treat their colored players with the regard due them in cases of this sort."[38]

There were various arguments for maintaining segregation in athletics. For staunch bigots, taking the field with a black player might extend him a sense of dignity that they were not ready to concede. In this opinion, "gentlemen's agreements" kept African Americans "in their place." In 1957, for example, Georgia legislators proposed a law prohibiting interracial competition. As Georgia senator Leon Butts explained, "When Negroes and whites meet on the athletic fields on a basis of complete equality, it is only natural that this sense of equality carries into the daily living of these people."[39] Some school administrators were so opposed to squaring off against black opponents that they opted to forfeit contests rather than lower their racist barricades.

Northern administrators justified submitting to these agreements by claiming either respect for their southern comrades or concern for the well-being of their black athletes. Harvard University's William Matthews may have served as a cautionary tale in this regard. In 1904 Yale officials requested that Harvard with-hold him from competition. The reason, explains football his-torian Raymond Schmidt, was that an African American on the gridiron "would be considered an affront to the southerners who attended Yale."[40] Harvard coach Edgar Wrightington rejected the appeal and sent Matthews into the game. Before long the Elis "kicked and hammered" the black athlete "nearly into insensi-bility."[41] He, like other African American athletes, paid a heavy price for the seemingly simple though hugely courageous act of taking the field.

Concerns over the "respect" for southern opponents and poten-tial violence against black athletes played out thirty years later when "athletic authorities" at the University of Michigan insisted Willis Ward should not play because "1) it would be discourteous to Georgia Tech; [and] 2) he might be injured," *Time* magazine reported in 1934.[42] Decades later Ward still felt the sting of rejec-tion. "It was not the fact that I was not made captain of either the football or track team that destroyed my will," he recalled. "It was the fact that I couldn't compete in the Georgia Tech game. . . . That Georgia Tech game knocked me square in the gut. It was wrong. It will always be wrong, and it killed my desire to excel."[43]

Ward referred to yet another injustice of the era: white coaches and teammates habitually failed to elect deserving African Amer-icans as captains of their squads. The same was true when it came time to name the teams' most valuable players, an honor denied to Ward and other black contemporaries. Outside their respective universities, athletes of color seldom made college All-Star games or registered on prestigious all-conference and All-American lists. Between 1889 and 1925 Walter Camp, "the father of football," named African Americans such as William H. Lewis, Paul Robeson, and Duke Slater to his mythical All-American squads. When journal-ist Grantland Rice took over Camp's duties, he selected just five black All-Americans over the next twenty-eight years. Between 1924 and 1937 no black football player made the All-American first team though, without question, the performances of several of these men warranted their inclusion.[44]

Such was the case for UCLA's Kenny Washington, who, along with Strode, Bill Willis, and Marion Motley, later reintegrated professional football. Washington's omission was a glaring oversight, considering his statistics, his contributions to his team, and his impact on the college game. "It's unfair," he said on being passed over for the college All-Star game. "It's because I am a Negro that they don't want me to play."[45] This says nothing of the tremendous talent at HBCUs, where, as William G. Nunn of the *Pittsburgh Courier* explained, "only the color of their skins and the fact that they matriculated to Negro schools kept their names out of the daily sport page headlines."[46]

The exceptionalism of black athletes of this era—both in terms of talent and race—made them prominent targets for gridiron brutality. *Opportunity* observed that "color aids [the African American athlete] by marking him conspicuously in the course of the activity, but frequently it identifies as the bull's eye for the shafts of the opposition."[47] So did the player's ability. When Princeton opponents ended Dartmouth's Matthew W. Bullock 1903 football season, most observers assumed that Princeton, which had "a strong Southern sentiment," fielded players who deliberately broke Bullock's collarbone for racial reasons. Pressed on the issue, however, the Tigers' quarterback protested, "We *didn't* put him out because he is a black man. . . . We're *coached* to pick out the most dangerous man on the opposing team and put him out in the first five minutes of play."[48]

In a sport that values aggressive play and hard hits, injuries occur with alarming regularity. Excessive violence was so pervasive in college football that President Theodore Roosevelt intervened in 1905 after 159 college players suffered serious harm and another 18 died from football-related incidents.[49] Despite a series of rule changes designed to make the sport safer, between 1906 and 1946 more than 500 football players died from on-field incidents, and injury rates remained high.[50] "You're out there trying to beat each other up," reasoned Woody Strode. "How do you know when a guy's trying to hurt you because you're black?"[51] Regardless, there can be no denying that African American footballers found themselves disproportionately targeted by white opponents for particularly injurious hits.[52]

In 1892 the Purdue crowd reviled Michigan's George H. Jewett with chants of "kill the coon" until Boilermaker players knocked him unconscious. Purdue fans then cheered as trainers removed Jewett's limp body from the field.[53] In the 1910s and 1920s high school, college, and professional opponents attacked Fritz Pollard often enough that he devised strategies to keep opponents from piling on after a play by rolling onto his back and kicking his legs. On other occasions he would "curl up like a turtle" for protection. Despite these tactics, he endured multiple injuries, including a "kick in the back" that was severe enough to make him miss the following game.[54] The question remains: were they black athletes who were hurt or were they athletes who were hurt because they were black?

This issue cannot be easily sorted out. When members of the University of North Carolina team assaulted New York University's star Ed Williams in a 1936 match, he was "carried off the field unconscious and was ruined as a football player."[55] Mauled in the first quarter of the 1938 Duke game, Wilmeth Sidat-Singh, the outstanding quarterback from Syracuse University, did not return.[56] In 1944 Claude "Buddy" Young of the University of Illinois was "seriously injured on the last play of the first half" after Notre Dame opponents "kicked [him] in the head." He sat "dazed on the bench" for the remainder of the game, reported the *New York Times*.[57] In all three cases the victims were black, and the opposing teams and their respective institutions maintained segregation; yet none of the incidents engendered public speculation about racism.

It was not just white opponents who brutalized black college football players but also, incredibly, the players' own white teammates. The novelist John Saxon Childers dramatized the phenomenon in his 1936 *In the Deep South* when, on the first day of practice, a white player pummeled a black player to the ground. Childers made clear the assailant's motives: "When everyone else was taking things easily, [the white athlete] felt constrained to prove his racial superiority and his individual disdain by putting the Negro in his place."[58] Undoubtedly scores of real-life situations echoed this fictional scene. In 1915 Paul Robeson's compatriots at Rutgers "directed scrimmages against [him] until his nose was broken, his shoulder dislocated, and one finger nail taken out by the roots by a player's cleats."[59] Robeson later recalled, "I was attacked by twenty-one guys. All the guys on defense, and all the guys on my team. They put me in the hospital for two weeks."[60]

Once game day came around, critics speculated that whites failed to block for their African American teammates, leaving them susceptible to particularly brutal hits.[61] In fact, several analysts believed that Ozzie Simmons's fellow Hawkeyes were guilty of this very practice. Once tackled to the ground, players were vulnerable to further dirty tactics: kicking, punching, scratching, gouging, pinching, biting, raking, and other maiming efforts that the mass of bodies shielded from the officials' view. "The refs would call it if you piled on a white player," Simmons told a reporter in 1989, "but they were not as quick to blow the whistle if you were black."[62]

Athletes of color were loath to openly discuss the problems they encountered. During this time, writes John Behee in his history of African American athletes at the University of Michigan, "racism so permeated American society that blacks who took issue with it were quickly branded misfits."[63] He understates the issue. Black athletes were undoubtedly worried about more than the misfit label; instead, voicing their frustrations raised threats of expulsion from their teams and institutions and the potential for additional verbal, social, and physical violence.

When it seemed as though Illinois's J. C. Caroline would fight for access to Champaign's segregated barbershops, members of the Athletic Department ordered him to "drop the issue. He was coerced and threatened," detailed the acclaimed African American sportswriter Wendell Smith. "He was . . . told that if he insisted on fighting for his rights—for the right to get a haircut in a white barber shop—his athletic scholarship might suddenly disappear. Then where would he be? Where would he go to school? How would he get an education?"[64] Caroline complied with the administrators' request. To "have made an issue of racism at the time," maintains historian John M. Carroll, "would have raised the specter of Jack Johnson."[65] If authorities could incarcerate the heavyweight champion of the world on little more than cooked-up charges, there was no telling what might happen to a relatively obscure college football player.

The physical violence that black athletes sustained also contributed to the segregation of professional football in the 1930s and 1940s. By 1933 Ray Kemp (Pittsburgh Pirates) and Joe Lillard (Chicago Cardinals) were the only African Americans playing big-time professional football. The following year National Football League (NFL) owners released the two men and failed to sign another black player to their rosters until 1946. Cardinal coach Paul Schissler explained that Lillard "was a marked man, and I don't mean that just the Southern boys took it out on him either; after a while whole teams, Northern and Southern alike, would give Joe the works, and I'd have to take him out. Somebody started it, it seemed, and everybody would join in." That "wasn't the worst of it," the coach continued. "It got so my Cardinals were a marked team because we had Lillard with us, and how the rest of the league took it out on us! We had to let him go, for our own sake, and for his, too!"[66]

At the same time one should not think of the violence against black athletes as confined to the context of sport. Racially motivated gridiron brutality was part of "a long reign of organized terrorism" against African Americans that included rape, lynching, whitecapping, and similar abominations.[67] Sport may seem trivial in the larger scheme of things, but it provided a prominent platform on which whites might exercise their racial animus.

The Symbolic Importance of Black Athletes

In spite of all the obstacles and inequities black footballers faced in the first half of the twentieth century, their successful performances did important cultural work for local, regional, and national African American (and white) communities. The "black press"— those publications created by and specifically aimed at African

American readers—regularly praised their "sepia sports stars" who "shown in the heavens . . . with satellite brilliancy."[68] The men inspired "race pride" and became popular "symbols to nucleate group sentiment."[69] Indeed, as Ed Harris of the *Philadelphia Tribune* observed, "Many a colored fan took the long trip up to the stadium and came away very much satisfied" with the exploits of their gridiron heroes.[70] The athletes' achievements, wrote Evelyn Cunningham for the *Pittsburgh Courier*, "makes us mighty proud of them and makes us go to the ball game feeling kinda proud about being colored ourselves."[71]

Beginning with the first "Negro college game" in 1892 (Biddle University against Livingstone College), African Americans showed great enthusiasm for and allegiance to those who played for HBCUs. The contests became social events of the highest order, and fans revered the gridiron greats. Unfortunately, wrote one reporter, "nobody ever heard of a chap from a Negro college getting on the All-American team. Hence, when we discuss prospective Negro All-Americans we have to scan the ofay [white] sports and pluck out their copper colored stallions."[72] As a result African Americans likely heard more about, and perhaps celebrated more ardently, the exploits of black gridders at PWCUs.

Part of this enthusiasm was due to the belief that achievement in sport translated to other facets of American life. This sense of "muscular assimilationism," to use historian Patrick B. Miller's term, demonstrated to white Americans that, if given a chance, men and women of color had much to contribute to society.[73] Even those who disparaged sport as crass or frivolous had to admit that "the beautiful breasting of a tape by Jesse Owens and the thud of a glove on the hand of Joe Louis [carried] more 'interracial education' than all the erudite philosophy ever written on race."[74] Thus, as Henderson wrote in 1949, those "Negro boys battling on the striped gridirons are rendering a social service not to be overlooked as a force of great power in establishing the Negro in the hearts of his brother Americans."[75] The visibility and significance of college football has held, and continues to hold, seeds of social change.

For these and other reasons, Iowa makes a unique case study. First, Iowans tend to invest a great deal into their collegiate sports, especially college football. It may have to do, at least in part, with the lack of a professional franchise in the state. It may also have to do with historian Benjamin G. Rader's contention that "citizens in states without a conspicuously significant history, great civic monuments, or remarkable physical scenery not only frequently formed powerful emotional bonds to their state university's football team but also found in a team an important sense of personal identity."[76] Though Iowans (myself included) may take umbrage with the deficiencies Rader suggests make football an important rallying point, the fact remains that we pour considerable affect and devotion into our college "elevens." They even become symbolic of larger struggles. "Iowa football reflects the mores of the greater community which is all of Iowa," remarked one resident. "There are striking similarities between the uphill fight of the Hawkeyes to win football recognition among the toughest foes . . . and the uphill fight of the state itself to become a positive factor among the community of states."[77]

Second, Iowans take pride in their early athletic integrationist history, holding up men such as Archie Alexander (University of Iowa), Joseph Collins (Coe College), and Edward Solomon "Sol" Butler (University of Dubuque) as exemplars in a legacy of racial tolerance. Comparatively speaking, Iowa colleges and universities were ahead of the curve when it came to desegregating their football teams. Frank "Kinney" Holbrook played football for the University of Iowa in 1895, just six years after William Lewis and William Tecumseh Sherman Jackson first broke the color line at Amherst College. Iowans maintain that Holbrook is important for "proving the Hawkeyes were among the nation's first to decree skin color had no bearing on whether a person could represent the school in athletic competitions."[78]

These types of comments, however, aggrandize Iowa's racial activism, for systemic inequalities at Iowa schools and in their surrounding communities persisted. The small contingent of African American students at Iowa colleges and universities between 1868 and 1945 were part of a practice of "tokenism," and as scholar Hal S. Chase found, "*de facto* segregation contaminated Iowa higher education until the end of World War II."[79] Outside the ivied halls, determined historian Dorothy Schwieder, several Iowa towns enforced housing covenants and sundown laws and allowed hate groups, including the Ku Klux Klan, to establish a presence in the state.[80] With African Americans making up only about 1 percent of Iowa's total population for most of the twentieth century, black athletes—though celebrated on the gridiron—likely found themselves isolated, alienated, and denigrated in Iowa. These matters notwithstanding, the idea that the state provided a "safe haven" for black students is a story that Iowans like to tell themselves about themselves.[81] It is a story that commemorations such as Jack Trice Stadium and Johnny Bright Field tend to bolster.

Finally, and although Trice, Simmons, and Bright are exceptional individuals, their experiences are representative of what other contemporary black athletes endured. As Willis Ward once told an interviewer, "Much of the racism Michigan men experienced, during the first half of [the twentieth] century, as they worked, studied, socialized, and competed for their school, was typical of the Midwest and much of the nation outside of the 'solid South.'"[82] The same can be said of Iowa. Trice, Simmons, and Bright all found themselves in unique circumstances during their college days, but at the same time, their experiences were not uncommon to other African Americans at PWCUs during the early to mid-1900s.

Chapter Organization

It is within the larger arc of athletic triumph and tragedy that the collegiate careers of Jack Trice, Ozzie Simmons, and Johnny Bright unfolded. Adulation, celebration, discrimination, and, notably, violence marked each of their lives in different measures. Chapter 1 outlines Trice's short life, his death in 1923, Iowa State students' subsequent disregard and rediscovery of his legacy, and their push in the 1970s to dedicate Jack Trice Stadium. Integral to the initiative was re-narrating and, specifically, racializing the "legend of Jack Trice." Chapter 2 picks up the story's resurgence in the 1990s, when Iowa State administrators finally bent to student requests and named the football facility for Trice. Driving the decision, though, was not a sense of fairness or a respect for students or even the life and legacy of Trice. Instead, Jack Trice Stadium became a conciliatory gesture designed to offset charges of the university's racial insensitivity.

"Any study of Memory," insists theorist Thomas Butler, "has also to take into account *forgetting*."[83] This is the case with Ozzie Simmons and the Floyd of Rosedale trophy in chapter 3. A bet between the governors of Iowa and Minnesota, in an effort to gloss over the injuries Simmons sustained in 1934, virtually wrote the athlete out of the trophy's origin story. In effect, they de-racialized the rivalry between the two schools, stripping it of larger political inflections.

Chapter 4 tackles the 1951 "Johnny Bright incident," the photographs of which made it almost impossible to deny that a white athlete intentionally attacked Drake's unsuspecting black star. Still contemporary audiences tended to frame the event in terms of corruption in college sports and the adulterated ethos of fair play on American playing fields. It was only within the last decades of the twentieth century that powerful and passionate indictments of racism emerged. Consequently, the final chapter in *Moments of Impact* represents my attempt to understand what it was about the late 1990s and early 2000s that encouraged the racialized memories of, and subsequent memorial ardor for, these and other transgressions against African American athletes.

What develops is a skeptical analysis, a cynical investigation. Commemorative efforts, whether they come in the form of an official apology, a celebration, a statue, or a place name, can resonate from sincere, even altruistic motives. At the same time individuals and groups make their own meanings out of those commemorative efforts—meanings that are polysemic, contested, subjective, and contextually situated. Certainly noble incentives were behind all the memorials examined in this book, and to suggest otherwise is grossly unfair and woefully obtuse. But political motivations also lurk behind the scenes when it comes to the memorial efforts for Trice, Simmons, and Bright. Ultimately it is better to remember them than to forget them. I do not mean to suggest otherwise. But my intent is to question the racialization of memories, the political appropriations of those memories, and the historical circumstances that evince those appropriations.

1

Resurrecting Jack Trice

Life, Death, and the Campaign for Jack Trice Stadium

"It seemed to me," remarked *Des Moines Register* columnist Donald Kaul in 1984, "that the story of a young black man who literally gave his life in the service of Iowa State football was the stuff from which legends are made."[1] Indeed, since his death in 1923, Jack Trice's story has reached legendary proportions. Over time members of the Iowa State University (ISU) community have remembered, forgotten, and resurrected their memories of Trice, re-narrativizing his legend according to contemporary circumstances.

"It is impossible to overstate the significance of *narrative* in cultural memory," asserts cultural theorist Annette Kunh, for the ways that collectives remember the past is dependent upon their scripting of history.[2] In creating narratives, Hayden White contends, historians emplot, or fashion particular kinds of stories, according to a series of four archetypal forms: romance, satire, tragedy, and comedy.[3] Critic Peter Burke extends White's theory to argue that emplotment "is to be found not only in the works of historians, but also in attempts by ordinary people to make sense of their world."[4] From the time of Trice's death to the student-led efforts to memorialize him fifty years later, the changing emplotment and, especially, its racialization have been central to the ways in which the Iowa State community remembers Jack Trice.

The initial, romantic version of the tale glorified Trice's "transcendence of the world of experience, his victory over it, and his final liberation from it," to borrow from White.[5] Before long, however, this interpretation began to fade, as did memories of the fallen athlete. When students rediscovered Trice in the 1970s, they resisted the romantic imaginings of the past. No longer a noble hero exalted in death, Trice had become a wretched victim in a racialized drama. Administrative resistance to memorialize him, students argued, compounded the racism that cut short Trice's life. Thus, the Jack Trice Stadium initiative sought to reimagine his story as a tragedy so that there could be a "gain in consciousness for the spectators" when it came to issues of race, sport, and institutional memory.[6]

The Legend of Jack Trice

In the near century since Trice's death, the same preliminary, expository "stuff" has stayed relatively constant in this protean tale. In 1902 John G. "Jack" Trice, the grandson of slaves, was born in Hiram, Ohio, a virtually all-white, rural town. His father, a member of the all-black U.S. Tenth Cavalry, fought in the Indian Wars and, in 1909, died of a sudden heart attack. Jack's mother, a woman of reported "wisdom and dignity," was left to raise her only child.[7] As Jack prepared to enter high school, Mrs. Trice insisted he live with his uncle in nearby Cleveland, wishing, according to one of his elementary schoolmates, "to get him among people of his own kind, to meet the problems that a negro [sic] boy would have to face sometime, and to give him an opportunity to make social contacts with people of his own race."[8]

In Cleveland Trice attended East Technical High School. Although his mother hoped the environment would be racially diverse, he was the only African American football player on the squad (fig. 1).[9] Recognized as "one of the best linemen ever graduated from the school," he was a standout athlete on an excellent team.[10] In his 1919 sophomore season, the East Technical football team lost only one game. The next year it ranked as the best team in the Midwest, setting up Trice and his compatriots for the national championship against the Pacific coast titleholder, Everett (Washington) High School. (Everett won 16–7.) In Trice's senior year, East Tech went undefeated, but while coaches from

Notre Dame and similar schools recruited his white teammates, most northern football teams maintained their tacit policies of racial segregation.[11]

During Trice's senior year of high school, his coach, Sam Willaman, accepted the head football position at Iowa State College of Agriculture and Mechanic Arts (now Iowa State University).[12] Willaman convinced Trice and several white teammates to attend the land-grant institution in Ames, a central Iowa town with a population of a little more than six thousand residents, nearly all of whom were white.[13] It is reasonable to surmise that because of his race it was the only offer Trice received to play the sport at a PWCU, though his talent, size, and speed should have made him a highly desirable recruit at any school in the country (fig. 2).

That Trice had few postsecondary options was sad but not surprising, considering the tumultuous state of race relations in 1920s America. Around the time of World War I, more than 900,000 African Americans moved from the South to northern cities, hoping to find jobs and escape the grinding racism that met them at every turn. Although the northern industrial centers offered greater freedoms, they were not bastions of racial tolerance. Segregation, both de facto and de jure, characterized black lives. It was a period of racialized violence, and riots, beatings, and murders plagued the era. In the first half of the decade, mobs lynched more than 250 people; African Americans made up all but twenty-three victims.[14]

Paradoxically it was also a time of racial progress with the emergence of the "New Negro" movement and the Harlem Renaissance that highlighted the rich intellectual and artistic talents of African Americans. Activist groups including the NAACP and the National Urban League waged campaigns to improve the lives of black Americans, and early civil rights leaders, such as Marcus Garvey and W. E. B. Du Bois, rose to prominence. The circulation of black newspapers and magazines expanded, providing outlets to herald black achievement as well as "to attack, expose, to marshal public opinion against all wrongs and injustices, all discrimination and inequality, but especially those adversely affecting the

1. Jack Trice in an East Technical High School letterman's sweater. Jack Trice Collection, Special Collections and University Archives, Iowa State University Library, Ames.

2. Jack Trice in Iowa State uniform, 1923. Jack Trice Collection, Special Collections and University Archives, Iowa State University Library, Ames.

aspirations of the Negro."[15] These publications regularly extolled the exploits of black athletes, though it would take another decade for journalists to consistently assail sport's racial injustices.

Chief among these offenses was a lack of opportunity for African American athletes in the 1920s. The vilification and incarceration of boxer Jack Johnson in the previous decade effectively served to ban black fighters from title shots. A series of organizational policies, bylaws, and "gentlemen's agreements" set in place in the early 1900s excluded black athletes from the League of American Wheelmen, the Jockey Club, the United States Lawn Tennis Association, the United States Golf Association, Major League Baseball, and other white-governed sports leagues. The leaders of professional football had not yet drawn the color line, but less than a dozen African Americans took the field in the twenties. And while football began to flourish at HBCUs, predominantly white institutions allowed no more than a handful of black players to join their squads. Jack Trice therefore found himself an outsider, even while a rising star in the college ranks.

The makeup of Iowa State's student body must have magnified Trice's feelings of isolation. He began his schooling there in the fall of 1922 as one of only "10 to 15" African Americans among 4,500 total students.[16] He was the university's first black student-athlete, though in 1891 noted scientist George Washington Carver had preceded him as the school's first black student. Trice was apparently ill prepared for the rigors of the college classroom and struggled academically, but as often noted in the legend of Jack Trice, he quickly caught up and averaged higher than 90 percent in his classes.[17] He majored in animal husbandry and, as Carver had, planned to use his degree to assist southern black farmers, an element that melds the legacies of two noble men of color at the predominantly white institution.

Playing in the era before athletic scholarships, Trice supported himself by working on the "bleacher gang" in the school's gymnasium and as a custodian in a local office building. In Ohio his mother took on a second job to help pay her son's tuition. At the time the National Collegiate Athletic Association (NCAA) banned freshmen from varsity programs, but as one of ninety members on the Iowa State freshman football squad, Trice's 6-foot, 200-pound frame and obvious skill impressed the coaching staff. He also showed talent in track and field, placing first in the shot put and second in the discus event at the Missouri Valley Conference freshmen track meet.

Jack Trice returned to Ohio in the summer of 1923. He worked for the Highway Department and trained nearly every day for the upcoming football season. Most accounts claim that he married Cora Mae Starland during this time (though they may have been married in 1922). At summer's end the two made their way to Iowa State, where Cora Mae began taking courses in home economics.[18] Trice reported for preseason practice and continued his schooling.

So begins the exposition of the "legend of Jack Trice." At this point in the narrative the hero has already overcome quite a bit—positioned in a way that highlights his strength of character in the face of adversity. Against the odds Trice managed to play college football in Iowa. He rose above his humble beginnings and seemingly subpar preparatory education to achieve academic excellence, which he intended to direct toward a worthy cause. A supporting cast of characters, including his widowed mother and his young bride, soon to be widowed herself, add additional heartbreaking elements to the story. This is not to imply that these aspects are not real or are undeserving of admiration or compassion; rather, they serve to draw attention to a particular characterization of Trice—one in which his determination and valor set the stage for his subsequent heroism.

Trice's athleticism contributes to this narrative. Coaches, peers, and the media touted his physical size and defensive talents when he joined the Cyclones' varsity program in 1923 (fig. 3). Before he even stepped foot on the field, Iowa State's student newspaper announced that Trice, "the fast and crafty colored boy, is the most outstanding."[19] Following his inaugural game against Simpson College (Indianola, Iowa), the campus press declared that he was "by far the most outstanding performer and gave evidence of being one of the best tackles in the Missouri valley this year."[20] Teammate Harry

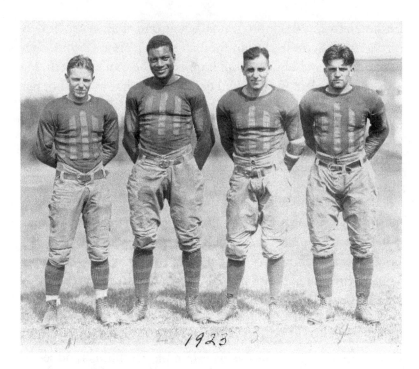

3. Iowa State University teammates Johnny Behm, Jack Trice, M. Behm, and William Nave, 1923. Jack Trice Collection, Special Collections and University Archives, Iowa State University Library, Ames.

Schmidt felt that Trice would have "certainly made All-Conference his sophomore year, because he was really tremendous. I think he would have made All-American. . . . He would have made all the teams that would recognize a Negro at that time."[21] Schmidt's brief statement provides three important commentaries: it recognizes Trice's abilities, it indicates that Trice's potential was snuffed out too soon, and it alludes to the exclusionary practice of omitting deserving black athletes from prestigious lists and awards.[22] Over the years each aspect played a pivotal role in the legend of Jack Trice.

But a series of events that took place in and around the University of Minnesota contest of October 6, 1923, truly set this legend in motion. Leading up to the game, the press speculated that the Gophers, outweighing the Cyclones by an average of fifteen pounds per man, would be the dominant team.[23] Minnesota boasted sev-

eral all-conference veterans, and many football experts considered it the best team in the Midwest. As Trice and his teammates
took the Minnesota field, it did not take long for them to bear the
brunt of the Gophers' force.

In one of the first plays of the game, Trice injured his shoulder but continued to play. At halftime, with the score tied at 7–7,
Coach Willaman supposedly asked, "How are you, Jack?" Trice
supposedly answered, "I'm okay, but my shoulder hurts a little." His
shoulder, doctors later determined, would have certainly caused
him pain; however, this conversation between coach and player
did not come out until fifty-three years after Trice's death. The
press relayed no such account in 1923. The apocryphal exchange
suggests that journalists took poetic license in retelling events,
inventing dialogue to undergird the athlete's resolve, and therefore played pivotal roles in emplotting the legend of Jack Trice.[24]

Equally if not more important to the emplotment were journalists' interpretations of the events that caused Trice's death. Perhaps all one can say with any degree of certainty is that a play at
the beginning of the third quarter found Trice on his back, and
several opponents trampled his supine body. Teammates helped
Trice from the field, and medical personnel took him to a local
hospital. Without his defensive prowess, Iowa State lost to Minnesota 20–17. Meanwhile, doctors determined that Trice's injuries
were not serious and deemed him fit to travel back to ISU. Lying
on a makeshift straw mattress aboard a railroad car, he made the
nearly 250-mile return trip in terrible pain. He arrived in Ames
on Sunday morning, and team officials immediately rushed him
to the Iowa State College Hospital.

Initially doctors thought that Trice's condition was improving,
but his breathing became shallow and irregular. They detected
severe abdominal distress and discovered that his sore shoulder
was a broken collarbone, an injury sustained at the start of the
game. Physicians at the Minnesota hospital had failed to diagnose
either problem. The following day the hospital staff summoned
an internal specialist from nearby Des Moines who pronounced
Trice's abdomen and intestines so severely damaged and his con-

dition so precarious that the athlete could not withstand surgery. Years later Cora Mae Trice recalled the moment of her husband's death: "When I saw him I said, 'Hello Darling.' He looked at me, but never spoke. I remember hearing the campanile chime 3 o'clock. That was October 8, 1923, and he was gone."[25]

Remembering Jack Trice

Iowa State administrators canceled afternoon classes the following day so that the community could pay its respects to Jack Trice. Acting as pallbearers, his teammates carried his casket to the memorial service, held in the center of campus (fig. 4). Before an estimated three thousand to four thousand mourners, Iowa State's president Raymond Pearson read what journalists alternately called "Jack Trice's Creed" and his "last letter" (fig. 5).[26] It was, as the story goes, a note Trice wrote to himself the night before the Minnesota game. Hospital employees apparently found it in the breast pocket of his coat just hours before the service. The words scrawled across a sheet of Curtis Hotel stationery have become the cornerstone of the legend of Jack Trice, for they depict a man who saw his performance on the field as larger and more significant than a game and indicate his determination to prove his personal worth, as well as that of his entire race. He wrote:

To whom it may concern,

My thoughts just before the first real college game of my life. The honor of my race, family, and self is at stake. Everyone is expecting me to do big things. I will! My whole body and soul are to be thrown recklessly about on the field tomorrow. Every time the ball is snapped, I will be trying to do more than my part. On all defensive plays I must break thru the opponents' line and stop the play in their territory. Beware of mass interference—fight low with your eyes open and toward the play. Roll-block the interference. Watch out for cross bucks and reverse end runs. Be on your toes every minute if you expect to make good.

(meeting) 7:45 Jack

4. Jack Trice's memorial service, October 9, 1923. Jack Trice Collection, Special
Collections and University Archives, Iowa State University Library, Ames.

This "creed worthy of general emulation" clearly struck a chord
with those who attended the memorial service.[27] Students there
announced their plan for "a fund to express in a material way the
sympathy of the college" and ultimately collected $2,259 to help
ease the Trice family's financial burdens.[28] The impressive sum
covered funeral expenses, reconciled the mortgage his mother had
placed on her home to assist with her son's tuition, and provided
her and Cora Mae each with $580.[29] Soon thereafter officials pre-
served Trice's letter in the university's archives.

Reactions to Trice's death were not confined within the city limits of Ames, as he was reportedly "mourned by millions of football fans of both races throughout the country."[30] Newspaper and
magazine tributes began to roll off the presses, lauding the val-
iant hero and lamenting his mortality. One elegy, first published
in a Minnesota newspaper and, later, in Iowa State's student paper
and its yearbook, *The Bomb*, seemed especially poignant. No one

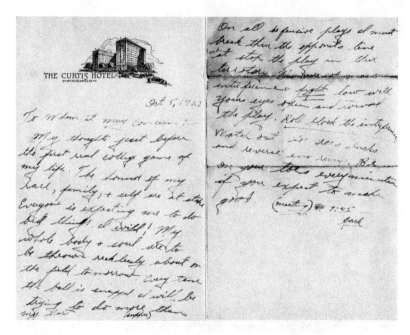

5. Jack Trice's "last letter." Jack Trice Collection, Special Collections and University Archives, Iowa State University Library, Ames.

has been able to identify the author (listed only as C. A. W.), a point consistently made in the legend of Trice to highlight both the anonymity and the universality of the message.[31]

TRICE

Tribute to him who in the first fair flush
Of glory won upon the fatal field
Fell hurt before the fierce contested rush
And joy of worthy battle; fell to yield—
Not to the charging line that swept along;
In body stricken; but with changeless mind
That gained respect of friend and foe in throng
Who witness it; and in the groups aligned.
A heart, that with a loyal aim beat fast
For that to which his fealty was pledged;
The honor of the deed was first; he last
As in the plunging mass that form was wedged.

Tribute to him; for a worthy foe
The steel of character is just as pure,
Build on such precepts as we failed to know—
The bedrock of true manhood full as sure
Honor to him, as true modern knight
Who, striving, fell before the shock of fight,
Nor knew the shock alone; for either side
Bows saddened head for him who fighting died.

C.A.W.[32]

The characterization is complete: Trice's loyalty, honor, and "steel of character" cast him as a "true modern knight" and reveal the 1923 penchant for emplotting a romantic narrative about "football's fallen hero," the "victor on the fatal field."[33]

While the majority of these sentiments identified Trice as "Negro," they otherwise ignored the issue of race. In a rare instance, though, a writer for the *Minnesota Alumni Weekly* opined that because Trice was "conscious of the noticeable racial incongruity of his situation," his performance on the football field was both an athletic and a political act. "Not daunted by the immensity of the racial vortex into which he had thrown himself, he saw the injustice of that supremacy and sought to prove its fallacy. He knew that if anything is to be accomplished for the Negro race it must be done through the achievement of individuals. It would take the resounding character of a few to show the sort of a race."[34] Trice "was only a negro [*sic*] boy in an agricultural college," the *Seattle Post-Intelligencer* professed, but "he left a message that will not be forgotten while determination endures."[35] These types of tributes paint Trice as a champion who fought boldly against tremendous obstacles, including his racial "otherness," until overwhelmed by the enormity of his opposition.

The issue of race also surfaced, albeit briefly, in attempts to sort out the cause of Trice's fatal injuries. In 1923 the general consensus seemed to be that he mis-executed a roll block. Indeed, in his note before the Minnesota game he reminded himself to "Roll-block the interference" and underlined the phrase for emphasis.

William Thompson, a member of the ISU football coaching staff in 1923, described the maneuver as "a dangerous block to use. . . . You had to roll under the backfield and that had a devastating effect on the runner, you see. It trips him right at the ankles."[36] Thompson explained that instead of correctly ending on all fours, Trice wound up on his back, which left him susceptible to the pounding cleats of Minnesota's backfield. Other eyewitness accounts support his report. Minnesota's dean L. D. Coffman wrote to Iowa State president Pearson to explain that "the play in which he was injured took place directly in front of me . . . it seemed to me that he threw himself in front of the play on the opposite side of the line. There was no piling up."[37] In other words, the Gophers inflicted no intentional or unnecessary roughness on Trice.

The majority of the press corps deemed Trice's death an "accident."[38] But in response to an Associated Press dispatch from Ames stating he "died from injuries received when most of the Minnesota line piled on top of him in off tackle play," John L. Griffith, commissioner of the Intercollegiate Conference of Faculty Representatives (also the Western Conference or the Big 10), to which Minnesota belonged, inquired if ISU officials would like to investigate whether "unfair play" was involved.[39] Iowa State's dean S. W. Beyer replied that he did not believe there had been any misconduct, writing, "Inasmuch as Mr. Trice was a colored man it is easy for people to assume that his opponents must have deliberately attempted to injure him. In my experience where colored boys had participated in athletic contests I have seen very little to indicate that their white opponents had any disposition to foul them."[40]

Serious injury was commonplace in football. In 1923 alone, eighteen athletes died as a result of gridiron incidents.[41] Although Beyer refers to speculation that white opponents targeted African American athletes for especially injurious hits, officials quickly dismissed the possibility. In fact, there is little evidence from the 1920s to suggest racially motivated violence on college gridirons. This does not mean that it did not happen—only that few dared to address it in a public forum. The black press had not yet begun to comment on the issue or on other injustices black athletes encountered at PWCUS, and it would be decades before the white press did the same.

In a rare example, author William Henry Harrison touched on racially incommensurate attacks in his 1921 *Colored Girls and Boys' Inspiring United States History*. In a poem that served as an epigraph to his chapter "In Athletics," Harrison praised the black athlete's ability to withstand his "cave men" opponents:

> When a white star fames in football fray,
> Three rivals at most against him play;
> And he gets the cheers of every fan
> For they feel for him no racial ban;
> But when Colored star in white games set
> Eleven "cave men" play him "to get";
> And when thro it all they can't him "can"
> He sure must be what is called "SOME MAN."[42]

In a decidedly less critical commentary, Elmer Mitchell—a coach, a writer, and the "father of intramurals"—also gives some evidence of the practice in his 1922 article "Racial Traits in Athletics."[43] He begins by writing that in sports the "negro [*sic*] mingles easily with white participants, accepting an inferior status and being content with it." Even when Mitchell witnessed "college players play pranks upon a colored team mate . . . the spirit of reception was a good spirited one." This "same spirit," he continued, "enables the player of this race to meet intentional rough play and jibes of his opponents with a grin."[44] Acknowledging that there was "intentional rough play," Mitchell does not connect it to racism, but that is hardly surprising considering his demeaning characterization of black athletes. This type of mentality may further explain why so few athletes of Trice's generation spoke out against mistreatment. To do so was to fly in the face of cultural expectations, a dangerous proposition for people of color.

Any consideration of the role that race played in Trice's injuries was short lived. So was the public bereavement over his death. On November 26, 1923, a plea appeared in the *Iowa State Student*:

Tributes were paid to Jack Trice by men in all parts of the country. . . . But we cannot allow men in other schools to be the authors of the finest appreciations of his life. The crowning tribute must come from the minds and hearts of this college, where his heroic life was uncovered by Death. . . . Some tribute, some tangible thing, must be set up to the memory of Jack Trice. Then all who come into the influence of this memorial will experience the steadfastness of purpose which was Jack's. What form this tribute may best take cannot yet be known, but the thought and comment of a student body can determine it.[45]

The words seem prophetic today, but in 1923 the "tangible thing" to remember Jack Trice came from the hands of a football teammate, who cast in bronze a passage of Trice's last letter. In a small ceremony an assemblage of students and staff hung the plaque in the southwest corner of the Old State Gymnasium (fig. 6). Sixty years later a *Newsweek* article recapped the story of Jack Trice and the modest memorial: "They meant well, all of them, and gradually they forgot."[46]

In 1957 Tom Emmerson, a student who would go on to become an ISU professor of journalism and mass communication, as well as a driving force in the Jack Trice Stadium campaign, came across the plaque. At the time Emmerson had never heard of Trice, so he turned to Harry Schmidt, the school's intramural director and a former teammate of Trice's, who recounted the basic story. Emmerson fleshed out the details from the university archives and composed "Jack Trice: Victor on the Fatal Field" for the campus magazine. "There was no reaction after I wrote it," he recalled. "Nothing happened."[47]

Campus Unrest at Iowa State University in the 1970s

It may have been that the timing of Emmerson's story was off by about decade, at least when it came to prompting any type of collective action. In contrast to 1957, the late 1960s and early 1970s were times of heightened political awareness, especially on college and university campuses across the United States. Students

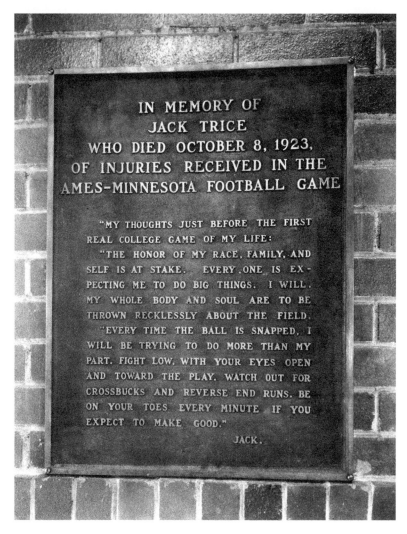

IN MEMORY OF
JACK TRICE
WHO DIED OCTOBER 8, 1923,
OF INJURIES RECEIVED IN THE
AMES-MINNESOTA FOOTBALL GAME

"MY THOUGHTS JUST BEFORE THE FIRST
REAL COLLEGE GAME OF MY LIFE:
"THE HONOR OF MY RACE, FAMILY, AND
SELF IS AT STAKE. EVERY ONE IS EX-
PECTING ME TO DO BIG THINGS. I WILL.
MY WHOLE BODY AND SOUL ARE TO BE
THROWN RECKLESSLY ABOUT THE FIELD.
"EVERY TIME THE BALL IS SNAPPED, I
WILL BE TRYING TO DO MORE THAN MY
PART. FIGHT LOW, WITH YOUR EYES OPEN
AND TOWARD THE PLAY. WATCH OUT FOR
CROSSBUCKS AND REVERSE END RUNS. BE
ON YOUR TOES EVERY MINUTE IF YOU
EXPECT TO MAKE GOOD."

JACK.

6. Jack Trice memorial plaque. Jack Trice Collection, Special Collections and University Archives, Iowa State University Library, Ames.

participated in protests, black voter registration drives, and Freedom Rides. Black students, bolstered by the civil rights movement and the "ideology of Black Power," especially engaged in campus demonstrations. A 1969 study found that although African Americans accounted for just 6 percent of the total college student population, they were involved in 51 percent of campus protests.[48] These students, the researchers concluded, fought to "alleviate their alienation, facilitate their resiliency, increase their retention, enhance their own chances of school success, and make education more relevant to the Black experience."[49]

The activist spirit accelerated into a period of campus unrest as young people became passionate in their efforts to combat racism, sexism, economic poverty, and environmental corruption and to advocate for students' rights. Perhaps no issue was more radically charged than that of the Vietnam War, and students demonstrated against the conflict on more than half of all college campuses, including Iowa State's.[50] Although the ISU yearbook characterized the school's undergraduates as typically "conservative and apathetic," thousands signed petitions and gathered for various sit-ins, teach-ins, marches, rallies, and protests.[51] They disrupted the drills of the Reserve Officers' Training Corps, blocked the entrance of the Selective Service Office, and gathered to stop traffic on the city's main thoroughfare. Approximately a hundred ISU students and faculty members briefly prevented the departure of a bus filled with military draftees headed for their preinduction physicals. While the protesters did not resort to violence, police and university officers responded with tear gas, fines, and arrests.[52]

Antiwar sentiments intersected with feelings of disenfranchisement and distrust of authority, intensified by the implication of President Richard Nixon and other high-ranking officials in the Watergate scandal. During an antiwar demonstration in 1970, members of the U.S. National Guard shot and killed four students at Ohio's Kent State University. Months later state and local police fired on a group of students, killing two, at Jackson State College, a historically black institution in Mississippi. The Black Student Organization (BSO) of ISU paid tribute to the Jackson State casualties by organizing a 350-person march to a memorial service on center campus, where they demanded that the flag be flown at half-mast.[53]

The BSO was then relatively new on the Iowa State campus, and while membership was low, the group's presence spoke to the need for solidarity in turbulent times. Former affiliates remembered that the 1968 assassination of Martin Luther King Jr. "was the catalyst that got us all focusing on the same thing—that African Americans needed an identifiable presence on this campus."[54] Among other accomplishments, the BSO helped establish Iowa State's Black Cultural Center and pushed for the dedication of George Washington Carver Hall. The group also expressed dissatisfaction with the school's failure to recruit black students, and members voiced their discontent with the "rampant discrimination and extreme difficulties" they encountered on campus and in surrounding Ames.[55] In response President W. Robert Parks introduced a number of initiatives to increase diversity. Few were successful.[56] "We should do the best we can to recruit minority students," he commented, "but there's a limit here. We're in competition with other states, but we just don't have many blacks in Iowa."[57]

Racial tensions reached a crisis point when a series of incidents converged in the early 1970s. The first involved an altercation at a local tavern between black students and white members of the school's wrestling team. Police charged two wrestlers with fighting and Roosevelt Roby, an African American, with assault and battery.[58] Following Roby's arrest the president of the BSO issued a statement, declaring that group members would "tolerate no further attacks by whites" and that "if any black man, black woman, or black child is harassed in any way by a white person there is going to be war up here. I mean W-A-R war." Black students, editorially backed by the *Iowa State Daily*, claimed racial discrimination and protested on Roby's behalf.[59]

The Roby affair took a frightening turn when the judge assigned to the case found a crudely made bomb in his garage. Although no evidence connected anyone to the device, the judge was certain that "the blacks are behind this. . . . I feel it was the militants and I don't know of any professed white militants around."[60] In a letter to the *Daily*, Ray Greene, a black assistant football coach, chided the judge, writing, "It would seem that a man of his stature and influence would be a bit more careful than to throw out some of the clichés which have become popular since Black people began to assert themselves in the quest for equality and justice in this country."[61] Less than a month later, a bomb exploded in Ames's City Hall, which housed the judge's office. While there were no fatalities, it was the single most destructive terrorist act in the city's history, injuring thirteen people and causing extensive damage to the building and at least a dozen downtown businesses. Again many residents speculated that black activists were behind the explosion, though the crime remains unsolved.

Another racially charged flashpoint ignited when more than two dozen black students demanded to speak with President Parks and Wilbur Layton, vice president for student affairs, about the continued discrimination they faced at Iowa State. There were rumors that the students had guns, but the only weapon that materialized during the confrontation was a galvanized pipe, with which someone struck Layton in the head. As one protester told a reporter, "If it comes down to a Kent State, we are prepared."[62] Layton left to receive medical attention (including six stitches) but quickly returned to talk with the students.

The ensuing meeting was tense, but there was no further violence. Dissidents voiced their demands for larger minority student enrollment, the right to speak to the university's president directly when problems arose, and the establishment of a fund to help finance the education of black athletes who had completed their varsity eligibility but not their undergraduate degrees. They also charged Ames residents, the police department, and Iowa State students and faulty with prejudice and harassment. It is unclear what long-term effects the meeting had. At the very least, Layton remarked, school officials got the message that "Ames is not a very comfortable place for Blacks to live."[63]

All told, as Iowa State professor William Kunerth recalls, the "late sixties and early seventies were kind of a nutty, violent time. There was a lot of upset, a lot of strange things had happened." These sentiments, he reasoned, "may have set the stage for organized activism" to remember Jack Trice.[64]

A Forgotten Story Remembered

In 1973 Alan Beals, a counselor for the ISU Athletic Department, came across Trice's "fading" memorial plaque, by then covered in rust, dust, and bird droppings.[65] He collaborated on an article for the *Iowa State Daily* titled "Trice: A Forgotten Story Remembered," recounting the man's brief career at the school and commemorating the fiftieth anniversary of his death.[66] Beals shared his excitement over the Trice material with his friend Iowa State professor Charles Sohn, who recognized it as the ideal project for his freshman English class. The students, according to Sohn, "were immediately motivated to go to libraries, to set up local interviews, and to track down any of Jack's acquaintances and relatives still alive more than forty years after the drama."[67]

Energized by what they learned, the students set out to determine a means to honor the fallen athlete. At the time Iowa State was in the process of constructing a new seven-million-dollar football stadium, scheduled for completion in 1975. Administrators had yet to determine a name for the facility. Sohn recalled that one student voiced what the entire class was thinking: "They should call it Jack Trice Stadium." He remembered that "one of the black males [in the class] immediately responded that there was no way the establishment would honor some poor dead black kid like that. . . . I think it was that same day that we voted to become the Jack Trice Memorial Stadium Committee, and the decades-long campaign was launched."[68]

Whereas students of the 1920s romanticized Trice's death, half a century later they reframed him as a victim of racial violence. The real travesty, they argued, was that the school failed to recognize him in a prominent way. He had not been liberated by death, as his peers once envisaged; instead, his legacy mired in the muck of disregard and disrespect. Commemorating Trice would, in part, redress the school's racist heritage.

The Jack Trice Memorial Stadium Committee engaged in several activities to draw attention to its cause. Members circulated pamphlets to educate the community about Trice and urged people to sign petitions supporting the stadium's proposed title. They held design contests for T-shirts and stationery letterhead, and they distributed buttons bearing the messages "We'll Carry the Torch of Jack Trice" and "Meet Me at the Jack Trice Stadium."[69] The editorial staff of the *Iowa State Daily* unanimously backed the name and exhorted administrators to "do the right thing." The paper also sponsored a "Creative Trice Banner Designing Contest" that would air during a 1975 nationally televised football game. "Lots of big signs," the editors argued, "can make viewers aware of what students have decided to call the stadium."[70] The Government of the Student Body (GSB) assisted the cause by endorsing resolutions and petitions to name the stadium after Trice.[71]

From the beginning there were definitive lines between student and administrative interests. When the naming issue first surfaced, observers acknowledged that those in charge would have to "decide between a dedicated football player who gave his life playing . . . and a dedicated alum or friend who gave his money for the stadium for other players to play in."[72] Professor Sohn felt that the "only noticeable reluctance to support the name 'Jack Trice Stadium'" came from university officials.[73] Among them was Gary Mulhall, director of field activities for the ISU Foundation (the group that solicited funds to pay the stadium's construction costs), who remarked that a "number of people involved in the building of the stadium . . . have definite sentiments against naming the stadium after Jack Trice."[74]

Consequently Iowa State's director of athletics Lou McCullough told a local radio host that there was a "good possibility" the facility would be named after its largest donor.[75] Students, however, cast nearly two thousand votes in the 1975 GSB elections to designate it the Jack Trice Memorial Stadium, a three-to-one choice over any other option.[76] That same year a poll found that more than 70 percent of ISU students supported naming the stadium for Trice. Fourteen percent opposed it for a variety of reasons; one student called it an act of "racial appeasement."[77]

An editorial in the *Iowa State Daily* suggested that in the midst of the campaign to remember Trice, the importance of his legacy had been forgotten. "Instead," the commentary read, "he stands for a controversy that has pitted students against decision makers; another in a long list of causes to be grasped for the simple reason of disagreeing with the administration."[78] President Parks likewise took issue with the divisiveness, remarking, "It has been made to appear as some sort of combination of all the world against the students."[79]

Hoping to reconcile the dispute, Parks formed a fourteen-person committee made up of students, faculty, staff, and alumni to propose a name for the newly completed stadium.[80] Members voted 11–3 in favor of the generic "Cyclone Stadium." The only dissenting ballots came from the committee's three students, who endorsed naming it for Trice.[81] Parks accepted the majority decision, but students urged him to reconsider. Their rhetoric often pitted monetary donations against mortal contributions by asking, "Who paid the most?" (fig. 7) and "Jack Trice gave all he had; can anyone give more?"[82]

A contemporary controversy over renaming the University of Iowa's football stadium provides an interesting point of comparison. Nile Kinnick, who was white, was the school's only Heisman Trophy winner, a member of Phi Beta Kappa honor society, a campus leader, and an All-American on the Hawkeyes famed 1939 "Ironmen" team. Just a few years later he died in a training flight while serving as a naval pilot during World War II, and students subsequently pushed university officials to rededicate the stadium in his name.

The only resistance came from Kinnick's father, who felt it inappropriate to single out his son when so many other students had lost their lives during the war. The issue lay dormant for the next twenty-five years, but Gus Schrader, a longtime *Cedar Rapids (IA) Gazette* sports editor, revived the initiative in the early 1970s. The Hawkeyes were then in a slump and had failed to tally a winning season in the past decade. Schrader thought that a Kinnick crusade might reinvigorate the flagging team. University of Iowa president Willard Boyd agreed but thought Duke Slater, the former African American football great who went on to a dis-

Who Paid the Most?

7. "Who Paid the Most?" Jack Trice Collection, Special Collections and University Archives, Iowa State University Library, Ames.

tinguished legal career, also deserved recognition. A lifelong supporter of the university, Slater died in 1969, after which ensued a spate of memorial efforts. President Boyd hoped to contribute to the trend and presented the option of "Kinnick-Slater Stadium" to the campus planning committee.[83]

Schrader was outraged and suggested Boyd's proposal was little more than racial conciliation. The president had "compromised to include a black man for fear of offending a segment of Iowa fans, administrators, and athletes," the journalist fumed.[84] Boyd stood firm in his convictions. Only when Iowa State representative Ivor Stanley suggested naming the stadium for Kinnick and another campus building for Slater did the process move forward. In 1972 university administrators dedicated Kinnick Stadium and Slater Residence Hall, a dormitory near the stadium. The first campus building named after an African American, Slater Hall was something of a cruel irony; for during Slater's time at Iowa, racial

RESURRECTING JACK TRICE

segregation denied him the opportunity to live in on-campus dormitories. Slater Hall suggests a brand of early twentieth-century racial tolerance that had been entirely fabricated in the 1970s, making it decidedly different than the situation at Iowa State, where students pushed for Jack Trice Stadium as a form of reconciliation for past racial wrongs.

The Campaign for Jack Trice Stadium

Central to Iowa State students' efforts was their insistence that Trice's death had been brought about by racially motivated violence. Officials dismissed that possibility in 1923, but more than half a century later, interpreters of Trice's legacy argued to the contrary. "Opinion was, and is, divided as to whether the Gophers were targeting the black player or simply playing power football," wrote one journalist. "Decades later, many automatically assume the former."[85] In the 1970s and 1980s editorials in the student newspaper charged that Minnesota "trampled" Trice "after the play was obviously over."[86]

Other newspapers published similar accusations. The *Ames Daily Times*, for instance, interviewed the former business manager for the Iowa State Athletic Department who recalled that Minnesota "ganged up" on Trice because he was black. "I was sure that was their purpose, to get him out of the game," he told reporters.[87] *Des Moines Register* columnist Donald Kaul intensified the charges on several occasions, writing that Trice had been "stomped to death" and had died on the "field of battle, so to speak, a martyr to the bigotry of his time."[88] Fellow *Register* reporter Chuck Offenburger opined that Trice was "a great black player of another era—an era when blacks were often beaten to death, as Trice essentially was, because of skin color."[89] More writers have since fanned the flames to claim that Trice was "deliberately injured" to become "an unnecessary victim of the racial hatred of that day."[90]

The stadium campaign significantly racialized additional episodes in Trice's life. Without question, Trice experienced much discrimination in his short life, though specific inequities are matters of contention. Some observers mistakenly recorded that Minnesota "was his first and only game," thereby heightening the drama of his death.[91] Others erroneously claimed that Cyclone officials capitulated to the racist demands of the University of Nebraska and Washington University in St. Louis and withdrew Trice from those competitions.[92] Southern institutions commonly made such requests to avoid interracial competitions; yet at the time of Trice's death the Iowa State football team had competed in only two games—the first against Simpson College and the second against Minnesota—and Trice had played in both.[93]

Among those who misremembered these episodes were two men affiliated with the 1923 Iowa State squad. Teammate Harry Schmidt recounted an incident when athletic officials withheld Trice from the Washington University game, explaining, "Missouri, at that time, would not play against a Negro."[94] Coach William Thompson remembered that Trice was not allowed to travel to Nebraska. In the same interview, however, Thompson also conceded that "nobody knew that this was going to amount to anything, you know, and so we just hunt back for the impressions that we have."[95] His commentary speaks to the ways in which personal and collective memories can change over time.

Another discrepancy in the legend of Jack Trice concerns where and with whom he lodged the night before the 1923 Minnesota game. Several stories published in the 1970s and 1980s claimed that he stayed in the same Minneapolis hotel as his teammates, who successfully lobbied to allow Trice to eat with them in the otherwise segregated dining room.[96] Years later, Robert Fisher, Trice's teammate, told a different story: "When we went to Minneapolis, I noticed [Trice] wasn't in our hotel. I asked somebody about it and they said that hotel did not allow blacks and that he was staying at the Curtis Hotel."[97]

It is entirely possible an area hotel had turned away Trice. Just four years later, when Henry Graham, a black player on the University of Michigan's tennis team, arrived in Minneapolis for a match against the University of Minnesota, "the captain of the team was told by the night clerk that Negroes could not stay in the hotel."[98] The captain chose not to "fight the color question," explaining, "I'm from Iowa and I don't know too much about colored people."[99] Despite antidiscrimination laws, several Minnesota hotels denied residence to African Americans in the first decades of the twentieth century.[100]

Although where Trice actually stayed that night is an important detail, memories of his trip, regardless of their historical accuracy, illuminate political appropriations of the past. On the one hand, asserting that his teammates fought to gain Trice entrance to the restaurant casts ISU in a favorable light, furthering the position that the school has a long history of racial activism. On the other hand, segregating Trice in a different hotel is merely one plot point in an extended narrative of racial discrimination. Although one cannot know for certain if he stayed alone or with the rest of the Cyclone team, his "last letter," written on Curtis Hotel stationary, offers a clue.

Assigning racism to these elements—that Trice suffered fatal injuries, that he was withheld from competition, and that he was not allowed to stay in the same hotel with his team—whether correct or incorrect, all add up to a cohesive story of a life riddled with obstacles and injustice. Every attempt to describe historical events, notes Hayden White, relies on narratives that "display the coherence, integrity, fullness, and closure of an image of life that is and can only be imaginary."[101] It would be wrong to speculate that individuals strategically altered the details in the legend of Jack Trice to fit their own agendas. Rather, one should consider that history and memory both rely on comprehensive, consistent narrativization in order for people to make sense of the past within their present circumstances. When it came to students in the 1970s, they specifically crafted a "narrative of victimization" to shore up their cause. Little had changed since the time of Trice's death, they insisted. The opposition to naming the stadium in his honor stemmed from that same racism writ anew.[102]

Despite these types of charges, state and university officials continued to use Jack Trice as a symbol of historically consistent practices of racial equality, not only at ISU, but also in the state of Iowa. When asked his opinion on naming the stadium for Trice,

Iowa governor Robert Ray told reporters that the Trice story is "a good indication that Iowa a long time ago believed there are equal rights for people and that people ought to be able to play football regardless of their color."[103] Governor Ray's statement obscures significant facets of Iowa's athletic history. Most important, perhaps, was that after 1927, when Holloway Smith played on the Cyclone football team, ISU did not have another black athlete—in any sport—for more than two decades.

In 1928 Iowa State joined the Big 6 Conference. The other members—the University of Nebraska, University of Kansas, University of Missouri, University of Oklahoma, and Kansas State University—were larger state schools from southern or border states that insisted upon segregated sport.[104] Conference officials denied they banned black athletes and deflected responsibility onto state mandates. As Walter Kraft, chairman of the University of Oklahoma's Athletic Council, explained, the "states themselves enforce segregation laws. It is something that is out of the hands of the school officials."[105] Yet the stipulation that black athletes could not play in states that upheld de jure segregation was actually buried in the conference bylaws, effectively perpetuating the Big 6's color line into the 1950s (by then the Big 7).[106] Governor Ray's comment on the spirit of inclusiveness in Iowa football history is not necessarily deceitful, but it is selective.

Half a Loaf

Taking the final step needed for approval, President Parks accepted his committee's recommendation and proposed the name Cyclone Stadium to the Iowa State Board of Regents. In a complicated resolution, though, the board voted to defer naming the stadium because ISU was not its official owner. Instead, the board maintained that the title belonged to the ISU Foundation. Only when the university repaid the foundation and took ownership of the stadium would it be appropriate to settle on a name. Professor Kunerth, then faculty adviser to the *Iowa State Daily*, felt that the delay "was ridiculous. In fact, you know, quite often you name a stadium in order to get money. . . . It didn't make any sense at all.

Here they've got this legend laid out in front of them and it was perfectly fine and logical and they just hemmed and hawed and stalled."[107] Tom Emmerson agreed: "In all probability that was just another ploy. They could have named it, in my opinion, anytime they wanted to."[108] At least one student thought that, in stalling, administrators hoped "students will forget."[109]

But students did not forget, and the crusade for Jack Trice Stadium remained strong into the next decade. For the 1980 Iowa State–Oklahoma football game, the Jack Trice Memorial Foundation rented a plane trailing a banner that read "Welcome to Jack Trice Stadium" to fly over the stadium.[110] Later that year the GSB bought advertising time on local radio stations and urged listeners to write letters of support for the cause.[111] In 1981 students returned from summer break to find that proponents had procured a billboard, located on the city's busiest thoroughfare, announcing, "Welcome to Ames. Home of Jack Trice Memorial Stadium."[112]

Before the 1983 Iowa State–University of Kansas game, committee members collected more than a thousand signatures in support of naming the stadium for Trice. They also distributed armbands that approximately three hundred to four hundred students and alumni wore in a demonstration of solidarity.[113] The date of the ISU-Kansas game was particularly important to the stadium cause as it marked the sixtieth anniversary of Trice's death. Yet the ISU Athletic Department declined requests to dedicate the game to Trice or to recognize him with a five-minute halftime ceremony. Athletic Director Max Urick explained the he did not "think it is appropriate for the athletic department to get involved in the stadium-naming process."[114] As a compromise students asked that Trice's name be announced at halftime; the Athletic Department denied this appeal as well. As concession administrators demonstrated that they had "some understanding of what Trice meant to the University" by observing a moment of silence in the third quarter.[115]

Finally in 1984 ISU secured ownership of the stadium and struck a compromise: Jack Trice Field at Cyclone Stadium. At the dedication ceremony *Register* columnist Donald Kaul lamented, "You can't always win the good fight." But, he added, Cyclone Stadium–Jack Trice Field was not a total loss; it would go down in the record books as a "tie."[116] The decision received national media attention, and in an article for *Newsweek*, renowned sociologist and racial activist Harry Edwards commented, "Jack Trice gets half a loaf. I'm surprised."[117]

To assuage students' disappointment and "as an opportunity to say we recognize and honor this man that died because of racism," the GSB erected a statue of Trice.[118] Student fees funded the project entirely, and it demonstrated, as one journalist assessed, that students had "more institutional memory" than their administrators did.[119] They commissioned artist Chris Bennett, who took careful pains to emphasize Trice's role as a student first and athlete second (fig. 8). Cast in bronze and reading his final letter, Trice stands dressed in "collegiate wear" rather than his football uniform. On the bench where he rests his right foot are two books that "emphasize the importance of academics above all else," as described in Iowa State's "Art on Campus Information." The cover of the closed book is titled *Animal Husbandry, Iowa State College* by C. Sohn, referencing Trice's intended program of study and the professor who initiated the stadium drive; the other book lies "open as if he has been interrupted from his studies." A pair of cleats sit on the nearby ground as a reminder of his final game.[120]

Unveiled in 1988 on ISU's central campus, the statue weighs more than a thousand pounds and stands 6 feet 6 inches tall, literally "making Jack Trice larger than life."[121] More than five hundred people gathered for the dedication ceremony, including Rev. Chester Trice Jr., a cousin and boyhood admirer of Jack's, who marveled at the "tremendous 15-year relay race" that brought about the event. "The baton has passed from student to student," he told those assembled, "from class to class, and without dropping it once."[122] Doug Jeske, a student involved with the project, remarked that "this reminds us that we can never become complacent when it comes to racism."[123] *Jet* magazine applauded the statue with a cover story titled "White University Rights 65-Year Wrong Done to Black Athlete."[124]

8. Jack Trice statue. Jack Trice Collection, Special Collections and University
Archives, Iowa State University Library, Ames.

Jet, like those involved in the commemorative efforts of the 1970s and 1980s, framed the legend of Jack Trice in black and white. This approach was a significant departure from the 1923 version, which concluded that "the defeat of Jack Trice was a triumph. For death always loses when a hero dies."[125] Fifty years later Iowa State University students re-emplotted the story from romance to racialized tragedy and, in the process, found little to celebrate. Trice was not a hero but a victim; his death was not a triumph but a shameful event evinced by a racist society, and administrative opposition to commemorate him with a prominent site on campus only appended the narrative of victimization. In the end the Cyclone Stadium–Jack Trice Field resolution brought what students felt was a "disappointing" conclusion but a conclusion nonetheless.[126]

2

Iowa State University's Commemorative Balancing Act

Jack Trice Stadium and Carrie Chapman Catt Hall, 1995-97

Observers believed that the 1984 Cyclone Stadium–Jack Trice Field compromise was the "closing chapter in the Jack Trice story."[1] They were wrong. In 1997 Iowa State officials dedicated Jack Trice Stadium, making it the only NCAA Division I football facility then named for an African American athlete. The occasion, remarked journalist Bob Dolgan, showed that Trice "still lives in memory at Iowa State University."[2]

Historian Patrick Geary argues that all memory is political because it is "memory *for* something." Yet the stadium decision that remembers Trice was especially politicized. It happened during a time when the university came under intense racial scrutiny, typified by the 1995 dedication of Carrie Chapman Catt Hall. Catt was an ISU alumna and an important figure in feminist history. But over the course of her campaign for women's rights, she expressed a number of racist, classist, and xenophobic remarks that many members of the ISU community felt tainted her legacy and reflected poorly on the institution. At the very least, they reasoned, Catt's comments should have ruled out the possibility of a Catt Hall.

As a form of memory, then, the names that institutions affix to their various structures and spaces always carry political import. "Place names," maintain historians Katherine Hodgkin and Susannah Radstone, "are one way of insisting on the reality of a particular version of the past, and also (therefore) of the present."[3] By memorializing Trice, Iowa State University asserted its identity as a racially inclusive institution at a moment that threatened to brand the school deficient when it came to minority students and affairs. This could not have happened without the racialization of Trice's legacy that the students set in motion in the 1970s. Two decades later ISU administrators joined in the process and, in dedicating Jack Trice Stadium, rewrote the school's "official memory," affirming its historic commitment to racial equality despite protests to the contrary.[4]

Political Football

During Iowa State's 1996 Government of the Student Body elections, presidential candidate Adam Gold revived the Trice Stadium cause as part of his campaign platform. He went on to win and, making good on his promise, pursued the Trice issue once in office. He presented his case to the GSB, where constituents unanimously approved changing the name of the stadium. Gold then arranged to have the Jack Trice statue moved from central campus to the entrance of the school's football complex. His reasoning, he later disclosed, was "if we don't get the name of the stadium changed, we can at least get a memorial for [Trice], and we can feel like there's a sense of accomplishment. . . . That turned out to be the first block that fell that got the whole thing done."[5]

Student monies financed the statue in 1984. Twelve years later university administrators not only agreed to relocate and renovate the monument but also paid most of the associated costs. This was an encouraging sign to those who supported the Trice Stadium drive, especially after so much administrative foot-dragging in the 1970s and 1980s. Additional blocks began to fall with surprising swiftness and efficiency. The ISU Advisory Committee on the Naming of Buildings and Streets recommended "Jack Trice Stadium" to Iowa State president Martin Jischke, who passed along the decision to the Iowa State Board of Regents. "Universities have precious few opportunities to recognize heroic qualities," Jischke told reporters. "This is one of those opportunities."[6]

On February 19, 1997, the Board of Regents approved the name change by a 7–2 vote, marking the final phase in the lengthy bat-

tle for Jack Trice Stadium. Assistant Dean of Students Terri Houston called the move "an excellent recruitment tool for all students
because the university has supported a student movement. This
shows that the university listens to the students."[7] It was an aston-
ishing stab at revisionist history, for, as detailed in chapter 1, student requests had fallen on deaf administrative ears for more
than two decades.

So why did the process take so long? It had been seventy-four
years since Trice's death and twenty-four years since students initiated their campaign. Perhaps a better question is, why, at this particular moment, did officials finally acquiesce? Sociologist Barry
Schwartz maintains that although "the object of commemoration
is usually found in the past, the issue which motivates its selection
and shaping is always found among the concerns of the present."[8]
In the case of Jack Trice Stadium, it is important to recognize that
the decision took place during what Adam Gold called "a very
intense time at Iowa State in terms of race issues."[9]

Epitomizing this intensity was the 1995 dedication of Catt Hall.
Catt graduated from Iowa State in 1880 as the valedictorian and
only woman in her class. She went on to become a leading activist in the fight for women's rights, especially women's suffrage.
Among her many accomplishments, Catt served as the founder
and president of the National American Woman Suffrage Association, as a leader in an international alliance of suffrage groups,
and as an originator (with Jane Addams and others) of the League
of Women Voters and the Women's Peace Party.[10]

With Catt, as they had with Trice, members of the ISU community sought to pluck a former student from obscurity and celebrate her contributions to the advancement of oppressed groups.
Both undertakings consisted of passionate, grassroots efforts. The
campaign to commemorate Catt began in 1983 at the behest of
ISU archivist Laura Kline. Six years later Kline, working with the
Ames chapter of the League of Women Voters, formally peti-
tioned ISU to rename the Old Botany building after Catt.[11] By
1990 the request had passed through the proper channels, and in
1992 the Iowa State Board of Regents approved Carrie Chapman

Catt Hall without much debate. Board members had little indication that the suffragist's legacy would soon become a political football on campus.

Letting the Catt out of the Bag

On September 29, 1995, *UHURU!*, the newsletter of Iowa State's Black Student Alliance, published "The Catt Is out of the Bag: Was She Racist?"[12] The essay documented Catt's use of racist, nativist, and classist rhetoric in her efforts to win rights for women. The subsequent September 29th Movement, so named for the article's publication date, adopted what its associates described as the twin tasks of reversing the Catt Hall decision and promoting civil rights at ISU. Identified in the press as a group of "black students," movement members made it clear that theirs was not exclusively a black organization but rather inclusive of all students willing to work for social change.[13] Together they sought to "eliminate racism, classism, xenophobia, sexism and homophobia on the campus of Iowa State University, recognizing that changing the name of Carrie Chapman Catt Hall must be the first step in that direction."[14]

Affiliates of the September 29th Movement poured through Catt's speeches and writings, finding instances in which she denigrated blacks and Mexicans, recommended barring uneducated immigrants from the ballot box, and blasted policies that gave the vote to "brutal, treacherous, murderous Indians" but not to white women.[15] Perhaps the most damning citation came from Catt's 1917 *Woman Suffrage by Federal Constitutional Amendment*, in which she argued, "White supremacy will be strengthened not weakened by woman's suffrage."[16] Catt's supporters insisted the students had taken the line "totally out of context."[17] Others maintained that the line was commonplace in early 1900s political discourse. Still others adopted a moderate position, reasoning that "while Catt held terrible views, she also did some good, particularly for women," and that "sometimes good people can do bad things."[18]

Catt's advocates also pointed out that the suffragist endorsed racial equality throughout her career. She spoke at African Amer-

COMMEMORATIVE BALANCING ACT

ican churches and clubs, defended slandered black soldiers during World War II, and supported establishing the League of Nations and the United Nations.[19] The fact remains, however, that in spite of her good works, she did express several reprehensible sentiments. As her biographer Robert Fowler explains, "Though her views require careful treatment, no gloss can be given to her routine discussion of blacks in generic and highly unflattering terms."[20] Members of the September 29th Movement refused to accept the excuse that Catt's racist language was politically expedient. Remarked one student, "I would say if she were still alive, what did you do after 1920 to guarantee that women of color could vote? She didn't do anything."[21]

It is clear that objections to Catt Hall, which movement leader Milton McGriff referred to as "a burning cross" on campus, represented larger issues.[22] "Catt Hall has always been about more than a politically racist woman's name on a building," McGriff railed. "It's about a pattern of behavior at ISU that says people of color don't count."[23] President Jischke's adviser on ethnic diversity concurred, asserting that Catt's "politically racist comments" made minority students "question their true acceptance on this campus." Changing the building's name, he continued, "would show that the university is committed to confronting its own racism."[24]

Of the 24,000 undergraduate students who attended Iowa State in 1996, just 661 were black. These students, studies found, were less likely to graduate and more likely to drop out than their white counterparts were.[25] Moreover, African Americans reported that their lives at ISU were "rife with instances of racism," the aggregate of which were feelings of frustration, depression, alienation, and isolation. "Iowa State is racism," asserted one undergraduate. "[I deal with] institutionalized racism definitely . . . that's almost daily."[26] With alarming regularity, students of color reported both overt and subtle varieties of abuse. They also lacked authority figures to whom they could turn. African Americans made up fewer than 2 percent of the faculty and fewer than 1 percent of tenured professors at ISU.[27] It was even worse at the administrative level. As one student articulated, "Blacks don't want to stay in Iowa because they don't think that they can get a fair chance to succeed. . . . You aren't going to see any Black on the Board of Regents."[28]

These criticisms joined with a number of divisive incidents that preceded the Catt Hall controversy. Although Iowa State historian Charles M. Dobbs contends that the episodes were "unrelated," they coalesced to support charges of the university's failings when it came to racial equality.[29] In 1992, for instance, an ISU student posted Nazi propaganda on the door of his dormitory room. The school's solution was to forbid all students from displaying anything outside their rooms, but it did little to address the root of the problem. Around the same time, a black graduate student noticed a cafeteria worker with a KKK (Ku Klux Klan) tattoo on one arm and a swastika branded on the other. In spite of vocal protests against the employee, administrators permitted him to keep his job. The following year a black student declared a jihad against a white history professor, charging that her views were racist and inaccurate.[30] In 1994 the GSB president vetoed funding for a Mr. and Ms. Black ISU pageant. There were threats that the GSB's minority senate seat would be abolished, concerns that the Black Cultural Center lacked adequate funding, and accusations that administrators ignored racial grievances. "If you're constantly having to fight for rights you think you should have," one African American student insisted, "then that's not a nurturing environment."[31] In light of these and other issues, including the dedication of Catt Hall, Derrick Rollins, the school's director of minority student affairs, called the racial climate on campus a "sinking ship."[32] President Jischke objected and countered that relocating the Jack Trice statue from center campus to the football stadium demonstrated the school's commitment to diversity.[33]

A Nation of Divisions

The divisiveness between black and white students at Iowa State was indicative of larger cultural patterns, and the controversies over Catt Hall and the dedication of Jack Trice Stadium happened amid a number of racially polarizing issues in the United States.[34] Thurgood Marshall, who provided legal counsel to the NAACP in such landmark cases as *Brown v. Board of Education* before becoming the first African American Supreme Court justice (1967–91), articulated this fracture as he accepted the National Constitution Center's Medal of Liberty on July 4, 1992: "I wish I could say that this nation had traveled far along the road to social justice and that liberty and equality were just around the bend," he told the crowd at Philadelphia's Independence Hall. "But as I look around, I see not a nation of unity, but of division: Afro and White, indigenous and immigrant, rich and poor, educated and illiterate."[35]

There had been, of course, significant progress since the era of Jim Crow racism. By the 1990s the demographics of the country (and certainly college sports) had shifted. People of color earned status in the areas of politics, education, and economics. The country saw the ascendancy of a sizable black middle class, and the number of interracial marriages and multiracial births continued to rise. President Bill Clinton took office in 1993 and assembled the most racially diverse cabinet in American history. In 1997 he kicked off his "One America in the 21st Century: The President's Initiative on Race," designed to create "a diverse, democratic community in which we respect, even celebrate our difference, while embracing the shared values that unite us."[36] Themes of reconciliation, understanding, and "racial harmony" dominated the president's initiative.[37]

Still racial disparities remained in terms of income, education, health, and de facto segregation. Throughout the 1990s federal and state governments ramped up their penalties for racially motivated crimes; yet the need for stricter punishments indicated the persistence of these offenses. Plaintiffs waged a number of high-profile legal battles involving voting rights, racial profiling, and discrimination levied at major corporations such as Coca-Cola, Avis, Nationwide Insurance, Denny's, Disney, and Texaco. Although several of the court's decisions favored people of color, the frequency with which these cases materialized indicated that the country had not progressed as many Americans believed.

Some glaring examples underscored a perception gap between white and black citizens on social, political, and legal issues. Foremost among them was the 1991 incident in which white patrolmen with the Los Angeles Police Department beat black motorist Rodney King. Caught on video, "the King tape clearly showed a helpless man being brutally clubbed by police officers, a kind of naked aggression that conjured up images of Selma and Birmingham," assesses film theorist Mike Mashon.[38] The officers' subsequent exoneration set off a series of civil disturbances in Los Angeles. It was one of the costliest urban protests in American history, resulting in fifty-five deaths, two thousand injuries, the damage or destruction of 1,100 buildings, and more than $1 billion in property damage.[39] Many citizens, and especially black citizens, saw the officers' acquittal, determined by a jury without African American representation, as another indication of racial bias within the legal system. Critics pointed to some jarring statistics to substantiate the claim: 6.8 percent of all black adult males were incarcerated in 1994, compared to just 1 percent of adult white males; at a time when blacks made up about 13 percent of the total U.S. population, they were 42 percent of the 3,600 inmates on death row.[40]

Attorneys defending former football great O. J. Simpson built their case around allegations of racism in law enforcement and the justice system. In his 1995 criminal trial, a jury found Simpson, an African American, not guilty of murdering his ex-wife Nicole Brown Simpson and her friend Ron Goldman, both of whom were white. Public reactions appeared stratified along racial lines. A *USA Today* poll determined that 49 percent of white Americans disagreed with the decision while only 10 percent of African Americans believed it unjust.[41] "After three decades of 'integration,'" wrote journalist David R. Carlin Jr., "we saw the depressing truth: we were still two nations."[42] Whether the racial divide was as clear-cut as it seemed, the popular media tended to frame reactions to the Simpson case in a particular way. "Black Americans were reported to have responded to the verdict with unmitigated glee whereas white Americans were said to be at once incredulous, outraged, and demoralized," contends communications scholar Lauren R. Tucker. Thus, "race and the tenuous nature of U.S. race relations became the lens through which all the other issues were viewed."[43]

High-profile topics continued to draw attention to the black-white breach in 1990s America. There were debates about affirmative action programs and welfare reform. Minister Louis Farrakhan, leader of the Nation of Islam, led the Million Man March on Washington DC in 1995 to raise black unity, pride, and empowerment while simultaneously espousing ideologies of racial divisiveness and anti-Semitism. Nationwide disputes raged over whether it was appropriate to teach Ebonics, or black vernacular English, in public schools.[44] Commemorative issues related to the Civil War and icons associated with the Confederate States of America and "Southern pride" (especially the Confederate battle flag) provoked additional antagonism.[45] "Perhaps above all," assessed New York Times journalist Kevin Sack, "the disputes over symbols illustrate how difficult it is for many blacks and many whites to relate to one another."[46]

Then there was the controversial book The Bell Curve: Intelligence and Class Structure in American Life, in which scholars Richard J. Herrnstein and Charles Murray attributed racial differences in intelligence scores to genetics.[47] The proposition generated considerable media attention, addressed on talk shows and in popular publications and even making the covers of Time, Newsweek, and National Review. It was no coincidence, assert critical race scholars Hernán Vera, Joe R. Feagin, and Andrew Gordon, that "this ideological book appeared at a time when congressional actions were increasingly focused on restricting immigration, cutting back affirmative action programs, and eviscerating many welfare programs, an agenda made clear in the Republican Party's 'Contract with America' that emerged after the 1994 elections."[48] In the same way it was also no coincidence that racial divisiveness characterized the disputes over whether and how to honor Jack Trice and Carrie Chapman Catt at Iowa State University.

Change the Name of Catt Hall

Members of the September 29th Movement remained committed to their agenda, the centerpiece of which was changing the name of Catt Hall (the group apparently "tried to stay out of the Trice stadium crusade").[49] They circulated petitions and fliers, held candlelight vigils and marches, organized an impressive letter-writing campaign, and sold T-shirts emblazoned with "Change the name of Catt Hall." They also adopted tactics with strong ties to the civil rights movement, often referencing Rosa Parks and Martin Luther King Jr. in their efforts. They adopted King's four-step program for civil disobedience, outlined in his "Letter from Birmingham Jail," and used teach-in and sit-in techniques taken from 1960s student protests. One member of the movement waged a hunger strike, intending to continue until administrators met several requests, including reopening the naming process of Catt Hall. The strike ended after six days when the student was hospitalized.[50]

In November 1996 the September 29th Movement convened a "town meeting" on renaming Catt Hall. Staged in the lobby of Beardshear Hall, the school's main administrative building, four individuals addressed a crowd that consisted of about two hundred members of the ISU community. In planning the event, however, group members failed to follow university protocol, which required they secure permission for all public events held on school property. Administrators tried to break up the rally, arguing, "We have certain places on campus for students to do their First Amendment thing." Campus police apprehended several attendees.[51] "It was a farce," recalled William Kunerth, then a faculty adviser to the *Iowa State Daily*. "It was very selective in who they arrested. There were faculty people there and they didn't arrest any faculty people. Who they arrested were the ringleaders"—namely, members of the September 29th Movement.[52]

The accused appeared in a closed meeting with the Office of Judicial Affairs. Administrators handed out written reprimands to fifteen students, a sanction that carried no punishment but remained on their permanent records. The following spring another five students, all affiliates of the movement, received the same punishment. Administrators dealt an additional three movement members the more serious verdict of conduct probation, which banned them from holding leadership positions in university organizations and from serving on university committees. A number of

COMMEMORATIVE BALANCING ACT

the school's faculty and staff objected and circulated a petition to "demonstrate [their] extreme discomfort at this harsh sanction against mature, heartfelt expression of ideas on this campus."[53] At least 185 signatories denounced university officials for violating the students' right to assemble and their freedom of expression. The students, through their attorneys, filed appeals with the All-University Judiciary Board, which later reduced the penalties but only after a series of controversial closed-door meetings and a somewhat loose adherence to judicial processes. In the end the affair did little to inspire student confidence in the school's administrative ranks.

Time for Closure

The September 29th Movement was not alone in its fight to change the name of Catt Hall. At least fifteen chapters of the NAACP from across the United States championed the cause, and they helped change the opinions of several one-time Catt supporters. Nowhere was this more conspicuous than in the controversy involving the Plaza of Heroines. For a hundred dollars, donors could purchase a brick in the plaza (located at the south entrance of Catt Hall) to be engraved with an honoree's name. It was a way to raise money for the building's renovations, and the engraved bricks would serve "as a testament to the women whose lives inspired many others with their leadership and service," as explained in the plaza's informational brochure.[54]

After the movement publicized Catt's contentious comments, several individuals requested the removal of their bricks.[55] One woman, who received hers as a gift from her sons, fumed that the "product sold to my children was a fraudulent product."[56] Several women glued black cloths over their names in protest. "I don't feel [the brick] is an honor any longer," explained a graduate student who had purchased one for her mother. "It's been disrespected by Catt's comments and the reaction of the university."[57] On approximately "60 or 70" occasions, the school newspaper reported, "someone" (it was never revealed who) peeled off the cloths; each time either the women or members of the September 29th Movement replaced them.[58] The women asked the school to investigate and threatened to permanently deface the bricks, even though the act carried charges of criminal mischief. Officials removed those belonging to the complainants later that year.[59]

The Government of Student Body also got involved in the debate and voted to ask the Iowa State Board of Regents to change the name of Catt Hall. The GSB president, however, vetoed the request, calling the resolution "a sham, a crock and an embarrassment."[60] It seemed as if President Jischke agreed, though he used less inflammatory rhetoric. Jischke explained that based on his examination of Catt's legacy, he believed "her motives were honorable, she was not a racist and her accomplishments are worthy of recognition."[61]

By 1998 and nearly three years after the September 29th Movement initiated its battle against Catt Hall, most Iowa State students had grown apathetic to the cause. Only the sheer will and staying power of the original agitators kept the fight alive. They continued to ask for face-to-face meetings with President Jischke; he denied them. When they turned up at his office and refused to leave, campus security arrested them. The students' persistence paid off, though. They finally had their summit with the president and, eventually, presented their case to the Iowa State Board of Regents. Cause leader Milton McGriff told officials there that Catt Hall "'represents an attitude that manifests itself in all areas of Iowa State,' including the lack of an Asian-American studies program, a low graduation rate for African-American students and low overall minority enrollment." The board recognized that the "climate of diversity" on campus should be a central concern, but it backed Jischke's decision to let the name of building stand.[62]

Once again the GSB weighed in and, in a 26–1 vote, passed a "Time for Closure" resolution. Representatives did not endorse a particular position; rather, they moved to bring an end to the ongoing debate.[63] In other words, the issue was dead. The September 29th Movement apparently dissolved soon afterward. The final act came with the formation of the Committee for the Review of the Catt Controversy, whose members apparently represented "a cross section of the university community."[64] School officials charged the committee with recommending whether the university should take any action to resolve the affair. The group could not reach a consensus, but their ambivalent report nevertheless lowered the curtain on the Catt Hall drama.[65] To this date Catt Hall houses the administrative offices of the College of Liberal Arts and Sciences, of which the Department of African American Studies is a part.[66]

Jack Trice in the New Millennium

In all the uproar over Catt Hall, it may have been easy to lose track of the Jack Trice Stadium issue, but administrative tactics fixed it in the foreground. Students had been working to honor Trice in this way since the early 1970s, yet they were only successful during the time of protest against Catt Hall. It therefore seems as if naming the stadium for Jack Trice was a conciliatory gesture designed to placate those offended by the memorial for the venerated suffragist. Iowa State's collective identity as a place of racial acceptance was sustained by a type of commemorative balancing act: the decision to designate Catt Hall tipped the scales dangerously close to supporting claims that the school was deficient when it came to issues of race, but administrators restored equilibrium by honoring Jack Trice, the first African American student-athlete at the institution. Each memorial counterbalances the other when it comes to the history of race relations at Iowa State University. Like the 1984 Cyclone Stadium–Jack Trice Field decision, the school seemed satisfied to register another "tie" in its record books.[67]

At the 1997 stadium dedication ceremony, President Jischke maintained that Trice's "story is an important part of Iowa State's history and deserves prominent recognition."[68] Trice spent a little more than one year at the university and competed in only two varsity football games, Jischke explained; so the stadium celebrates the fallen athlete not for what he did but for his "immeasurable" contributions to ISU's "history and to its character." In the seventy-four years since his death, Trice had come to "symbolize many ideals that are important to Iowa State University—

the ideals of devotion to team, giving one's all, and the land-grant ideals of inclusiveness, access, and making the most of an opportunity."[69] Repeatedly referencing Iowa State's "history," Jischke scripted a narrative of continuity between Trice's character and that of the university to establish an official memory, one concretized in the stadium's name.

The commemorative cheer failed to convince all members of the Iowa State collective. Writing for the *Iowa State Daily*, one student expressed her cynicism: "'Jack Trice Stadium' gives everyone a warm fuzzy [feeling]. Minority students get to immortalize a hero, the administration gets to toss a bone to its critics, and the GSB gets to appear as though it has actually done something under Adam Gold's leadership."[70] Another student called the rededication a "ploy to make the university look good. . . . I think this should have happened 22 years ago. If [Trice] had not been African American, it would have happened shortly after he died."[71] Ironically one could argue that if Trice had not been African American, renaming the stadium for him might never have happened at all.

Administrators objected to speculation that the renaming was a strategic maneuver as opposed to their acquiescence to student requests or an abiding desire to honor Trice. "The name change recommendation was based on its own merits," protested university spokesman John Anderson. "It's an idea that's been around a long time."[72] Indeed, the idea had been around for some time— nearly a quarter of a century—but it was only in the face of allegations of racism and insensitivity that those efforts finally came to fruition.

Memories of Jack Trice keep emerging in new and unexpected ways. In 2009 Iowa State commissioned sculptor Ed Dwight to create a multi-panel installation on the outer wall of the Jack Trice Club (a premium seating area) on the east concourse of Jack Trice Stadium (fig. 9). A four-panel layout represents "key moments in the Trice saga," beginning with his journey from Cleveland's East Technical High School to Iowa State University (fig. 10). The second plate includes a 1923 team photograph and a copy of Trice's last letter (fig. 11). The third duplicates the photograph from his

9. Jack Trice memorial, *I Will: Jack Trice Legacy*. Photograph by Paul D. Hefty.

memorial service on campus and the subsequent commemorative plaque (fig. 12). The fourth and final panel depicts "Student Action," paying tribute to those who toiled so long to have the stadium named for Jack Trice (fig. 13). At the center of it all is a bas-relief of Trice in his football uniform. The title above the panels reads *I Will*, referencing Trice's famous letter; below is the subtitle *Jack Trice Legacy*. Read from left to right, the display is meant to convey what Dwight calls a "transcendence story."[73] It offers both edification and inspiration, etching the Trice legend's most poignant moments onto the structure that now bears his name.

Four years after officials unveiled Dwight's work, a number of individuals set out to determine what number Jack Trice wore for Iowa State (he played at a time when jersey numbers were neither prominent nor important). What inspired their investigation is unclear, but they concluded that Trice had been assigned number 37.[74] Professor Tom Emmerson, who since 1957 played an important role in remembering Trice, approached Iowa State athletic director Jamie Pollard about retiring number 37 from use. Pollard dismissed the proposal, admonishing that "we have honored Jack Trice by naming the entire football stadium after him . . . have dedicated two statues of Jack Trice in and around the stadium and have named the premium seating area on the

10. Jack Trice memorial, panel 1. Photograph by Paul D. Hefty.

11. Jack Trice memorial, panel 2. Photograph by Paul D. Hefty.

12. Jack Trice memorial, panel 3. Photograph by Paul D. Hefty.

13. Jack Trice memorial, panel 4. Photograph by Paul D. Hefty.

west side of the stadium after him. In addition, the entire premium seating area is branded after his legacy including retelling his life story on a mural outside the club area where all fans can see it during games."[75]

It is true that Trice's legacy features prominently on the Iowa State campus, but Pollard's enough-is-enough response is curious, particularly because less than a month later, Iowa State football initiated a new marketing campaign dedicated to "preserving our history, honoring our past." This effort included an announcement that the team would wear throwback jerseys for its 2013 game against its intrastate rival, the University of Iowa. It was not just that the uniforms were reminiscent of what the Cyclones wore some ninety years earlier. Instead, coaches and players understood that the ensemble recalled the "Jack Trice Era," was a "tribute to Jack Trice," a chance to "give back to Jack Trice who meant a lot to this program."[76] The general sentiment was that the jerseys honored Trice specifically rather than the program's past in general. Athletic officials also revamped a stadium tunnel to feature a graphic of Trice, along with lines from his "last letter."

Head football coach Paul Rhoads approved of the initiatives, remarking that the "legend of Jack Trice is a critical piece of Iowa State football history. . . . His profound impact on our program resonates with our players today. This is a fitting tribute."[77] Iowa State's Marketing Department then produced a local commercial that featured an actor in the role of Trice. Although "never mentioned," reported the *Des Moines Register*, the fabled athlete's "name was . . . creatively implied. The article continued, "The quick-hitting, 30-second commercial begins with a football player walking down a darkened path toward the football field. The video board shows highlights of past games, watched by the player who now is standing at midfield. . . . The commercial ends with the player walking off the field, nodding his head in approval." The spot, the *Register* explained, "is meant to spur fans into purchasing tickets."[78] The legend of Jack Trice continues, incorporated, perhaps exploited, by these latest promotional campaigns.

Since his death in 1923, Trice has become a floating signifier, a

COMMEMORATIVE BALANCING ACT

symbol of various political choreographies that have little to do with the actuality of his short life. At assorted moments in history, Trice has been a romantic figure, eulogized as a "victor on the fatal field"; a tragic victim of past racial violence and renewed racist disregard; a rallying point against administrative insensitivity to ISU student matters and, more specifically, to the concerns of students of color; a token used to diffuse the volatility evinced by the commemoration of Carrie Chapman Catt; a site at which to establish the school's ostensibly long-standing commitment to diversity and to reassert that identity in the twenty-first century; and a commodity in a marketing strategy used to sell that identity to the public.[79] Trice is no longer a casualty of bigotry, as he seemed in the 1970s, 1980s, and even into the 1990s. He has once again become, as he was in 1923, "football's fallen hero" but in a way that honors Iowa State more than the man himself.[80]

Even so, the multiple expressions of Trice iconography do important pedagogical work. Like other forms of public history, the stadium's name, artwork, and promotional materials secure Trice in public culture. They educate onlookers and inspire them to learn more. In his 2009 bestselling *The Girls from Ames*, for example, Jeffrey Zaslow recounts the real-life story of adult women who, at a young age, forged the bonds of friendship in the midwestern town. For one of the women, Jack Trice Stadium represents "a victory of sorts that young people in Ames, boys and girls, are now taught the details of Trice's life, and that on football Saturdays, tens of thousands of people pass that fifteen-foot-tall statue bearing his likeness."[81] Sculptor Ed Dwight believes that upon viewing his *I Will* installation at the stadium, people will "walk away and go to the Internet and find out more about the guy on the basis of what they see here—kids, especially, and the black players."[82]

In their critical investigation of college sport, C. Richard King and Charles Frueling Springwood likewise assert, "What sets apart the selection of Trice is that it underscores not simply the historical struggles endured by black athletes but foregrounds the asymmetrical, painful, and even tragic race relations structuring college athletics during the interwar period. In pairing glory with tragedy, it demands that race not be forgotten. Consequently, Jack Trice Stadium does something extremely rare in college sports spectacles. It reminds fans, students, alumnus, and players of the centrality of race."[83]

My appraisal is not quite as sanguine (though a more complete study on the subject would examine the ways audiences interact with the commemorations of Trice). I remain hopeful, but I worry that rather than reminding the public about the "centrality of race," Jack Trice Stadium will instead be made evidence of a post-racial society—that memorializing the long-ago death of a black athlete will encourage those who encounter his legacy to think of racism as something that happened in the past, as something from "back then" instead of an enduring social problem. Such a prominent form of public remembrance, paradoxically, may authorize forgetting. Celebrating his memory as a significant, conspicuous part of the school's identity and imagined community may congratulate both Iowa State University and American society for its racial progress, for having evolved to the point that Jack Trice is now a major figurehead in college athletics, while distancing abiding social issues from consideration and response.

I suppose that, after all, remembering Jack Trice is better than forgetting him. An academic memory study endeavors to explain *why* Iowa State remembered him at a particular moment in time. But is that important to the public? Or is it enough that the final decision anchors his name in its collective consciousness?

This brings up a host of other questions, not least of which is, how many deserving individuals remain buried beneath the rubble of historical disregard? When it comes to college football, the University of Iowa's Ozzie Simmons is just one among thousands, but it is not historical lethargy that keeps him and, especially, the injuries he sustained in 1934 relatively unknown. Rather, omitting his story from that of the traditional narrative of the Floyd of Rosedale trophy was an active, concerted effort to distance his injuries from cultural memory. While the Jack Trice Stadium decision relied on the racialization of the legend of Jack Trice, the Floyd of Rosedale trophy effectively de-racialized its inciting incident.

3

Ozzie Simmons, Floyd of Rosedale, and a Tale of Two Governors

From a field of competition that includes the Broomhead, the Telephone, Gertie the Goose, and the Shot Glass, the *Los Angles Times* selected Floyd of Rosedale as the number 1 "favorite weird rivalry prize" in college football.[1] Since 1936 the University of Iowa and the University of Minnesota have vied annually for the twenty-one-inch-long, fifteen-inch-high bronze sculpture of a hog (fig. 14). Those curious about the trophy's beginnings typically find stories similar to the following from the official website of the Iowa Hawkeyes: "A bet in 1935 between Minnesota Governor Floyd B. Olson and Iowa Governor Clyde Herring gave birth to Floyd of Rosedale. Tensions between the two state universities had been running high and a wager was made in an effort to relieve the situation."[2]

This much is true, but too often left out of Floyd's origin story are the reasons *why* tensions ran so high between the two states and their flagship institutions. Only recently have fuller, more critical accounts recognized the significance of Iowa great Ozzie Simmons and the injuries he sustained in the 1934 Minnesota contest. These attempts to write Simmons back into the trophy's narrative suggest that what seems to be merely a "weird rivalry prize," set in place by the ostensible jocularity of two midwestern politicians, obscures a racialized incident in college football history. Rather than facilitating memories of Simmons, Floyd of Rosedale was designed to make people forget.[3]

Football scholar Michael Oriard writes that Ozzie Simmons "was the quintessential black football player of the 1930s: immensely talented and hugely celebrated initially in both the mainstream and

14. Floyd of Rosedale trophy. University of Iowa Photographic Services, Iowa City.

the black press, but confronted by constant racial obstacles that ultimately blighted his once-glorious career."[4] The 1930s was a contra-
dictory time for black athletes. Some pundits believed the decade
was the "golden era of athletic achievement" for African Americans.[5] Black boxing champions, such as Henry Armstrong, John
Henry Lewis, and the incomparable Joe Louis, proved their met-
tle against white opponents. Eddie Tolan, John Woodruff, Mack
Robinson, and, of course, Jesse Owens became (if only temporar-
ily) American heroes on Olympic tracks.[6] "In fact," notes sport historian David Wiggins, "few periods have witnessed such a large
influx of well-known and talented black athletes."[7] The number
of black athletes at predominantly white colleges and universities
also increased during this time, and their presence heightened
"sensitivities to racial wrongs," according to Arthur Ashe.[8] In the
process, argues historian Patrick B. Miller, African Americans'
sporting exploits "subverted some dominant racial stereotypes"
and "did indeed become part of a larger civil rights strategy."[9]

A TALE OF TWO GOVERNORS

Yet despite the rising tide of notable black athletes, "the exclusion of African Americans in American sports actually increased in the 1930s," contends historian Charles H. Martin.[10] This included more benchings, brought about, in part, by the growing importance of intersectional football contests. Between 1932 and 1937 at least seven major teams, including Iowa and Minnesota, sidelined their black players against schools from southern or border states.[11] Upon hanging up their college cleats, the slighted athletes found few opportunities to further their gridiron careers. In 1933 the National Football League initiated its "gentlemen's agreement," a tacit accord among owners not to sign black players that remained in place for the next thirteen years.

While a number of black athletes found short-lived glory on college fields, their academic and social lives often suffered. Approximately 1,500 black students attended predominately white institutions in the 1920s and 1930s; most of them were "essentially pariahs" on campus, maintains historian Raymond Wolters.[12] "Those were bad years," Ozzie Simmons reminisced about his time in intercollegiate sport. "We all recognize those were not good years for us. We didn't have more than six or seven blacks playing major college football."[13] In fact, in 1936, Simmons's senior year, journalists identified eleven black players on "otherwise white teams": Ozzie and Don Simmons, Homer Harris, Wilbur "Windy" Wallace, and Richard Dobson at the University of Iowa; Dwight Reed and Horace Bell at the University of Minnesota; Bernard Jefferson and Clarence Hinton at Northwestern University; London "Brutus" Gant at the University of Cincinnati; and Frank "Doc" Kelker at Western Reserve University in Cleveland. University of Wisconsin coach Harry Stuldreher, failing to field an African American gridder, nonetheless complimented "the race for its activity of late in the 1936 Olympics."[14]

Following Jesse Owens's four gold medals in the 1936 Games, along with a slew of outstanding performances from other tracksters of color, the German newspaper *Der Angriff* ("The Attack," the organ of the Nazi Party founded by Minister of Propaganda

Joseph Goebbels), chided, "If the American team had not had their black auxiliary tribes, the result would have been sad."[15] Americans bristled at the term "auxiliary," which suggested they had appropriated talent from outside the citizenry to win athletic battles. But as the magazine *The Crisis* (published by the NAACP) gauged, there was "something a little pathetic and yet quite logical in the cry." When Uncle Sam "gets in a pinch, he reaches down and uses his colored citizens-in-name-only. . . . In the hour of crisis they become American citizens, 'our fighters,' 'our athletes.'"[16] There was an unfortunate ring of truth to the "auxiliary" charge, for even as African Americans helped advance the country, including its sports, they were denied access to many of the rights and privileges associated with being an American.

Outside of sport African Americans living in the 1930s found themselves especially disadvantaged by the economic Great Depression. The fiscal crisis also exacerbated tensions between racial groups, with an upsurge in white-on-black violence. Historian Walter T. Howard notes, for example, that in the 1930s, lynchings were "a routine, everyday sort of villainy that were . . . almost always inflicted on Black, rather than White, people."[17] In 1935 alone *The Crisis* chronicled around twenty such atrocities. At the same time a proposed federal antilynching bill evoked nationwide debate, drawing in nearly every American political figure.[18] With the benefit of hindsight, it is difficult to view racialized gridiron violence as distinct from the larger patterns of contemporary violence against African Americans.

Even so, wrote Ashe, "in the midst of the Depression, the athletic exploits of blacks were touted as a viable way out of a dreary future."[19] At least it was apparent in the black press, where Ozzie Simmons's star shone especially bright. He became a point of pride for African Americans, many of whom made pilgrimages to Iowa City to see the "Wizard of Oz" work his magic.[20] Yet the constant racial obstacles Simmons faced throughout his career took their toll on this exceptional athlete and contributed, at least in part, to creating the Floyd of Rosedale trophy.

A TALE OF TWO GOVERNORS

The Wizard of Oz Comes to Iowa

Born in Gainesville, Texas, in 1915, Ozzie Simmons moved with his family to Fort Worth, about sixty-five miles to the south. There he and his older brother Don attended Terrell High School, where they both excelled athletically. Ozzie Simmons won eleven varsity letters in football, basketball, baseball, and track and field. A state champion in the 110-yard dash, he was also a three-time all-state halfback and a member of the segregated Texas state championship football team his senior year.[21]

The brothers entertained relatively few options upon graduating high school. Institutional segregation denied them the opportunity to attend white colleges and universities in the South, and northern pwcus did not typically recruit black athletes, especially from so far away. Had Ozzie Simmons stayed in Texas, speculated the *Pittsburgh Courier* in 1936, "he might still have been a mechanic's flunkie in a pair of greasy overalls. He would have been thrown for heavy losses before he got started down the glamorous highway which leads toward greatness in football's glittering hall of fame" (fig. 15).[22] Instead, the Simmons brothers, virtually unknown outside their home state, made their way north.

How the two decided on the University of Iowa, like many of the details about Ozzie Simmons's life, is a matter of conjecture. As the *Chicago Defender*'s Al Monroe described in 1934, "I have before me no less than ten papers dealing with Simmons' escapades in the Big Ten and no fewer than eight attempt to explain how the famous ball-player man came to be on Iowa's team."[23] Most accounts agreed that the men traveled north by freight train. Although a fairly common mode of transport, particularly at the height of the Depression, this detail adds a folkloric dimension to their arrival story.

A mysterious white stranger offers another point of intrigue. Some storytellers claimed an unidentified man saw the Simmonses play football in Texas and suggested they go to the University of Iowa; others maintained this man contacted an Iowa alumnus, who, in turn, wrote to the brothers and urged them

15. Ozzie Simmons in Hawkeyes uniform, University of Iowa Football, 1933–36. Frederick W. Kent Photographic Collection, University of Iowa Libraries, Iowa City.

to attend his alma mater.[24] An alternative version held that a white man may have enticed the two to head for the Hawkeye State with railroad tickets and a "box of food large enough to keep Oze and brother Don from worrying about wolves until the practice season was well under way."[25] These stories, regardless their origin or veracity, invoke an impression of paternalism,

A TALE OF TWO GOVERNORS

suggesting the brothers owed their athletic careers to an anonymous white benefactor.

In a 1934 interview Ozzie Simmons did not mention any such individual when recounting his reasons for selecting Iowa. Instead, he told a reporter from the *Daily Iowan*, the University of Iowa's student newspaper, that he had "heard that Ossie Solem was a swell coach and a great guy to work under." Simmons continued that he and his brother boarded a boxcar in Fort Worth and arrived at the school five days later.[26] More than fifty years after making that trip, he offered a slight variation: "The crux of the whole thing was we knew that Duke Slater had played there and Iowa had a history of being fair with blacks. That was enough. Most universities you could not get into. Today they won't let you out of the state if you are a good ballplayer, but back then it was almost impossible to go to school."[27]

Among these pioneering players were Archie Alexander, who joined the Hawkeyes in 1909, and Frederick Wayman "Duke" Slater, a three-time All–Big 10 Conference selection and a two-time All-American tackle who played for Iowa from 1918 to 1921. Slater would later be one of the few African Americans to play professional football before the league unofficially banned interracial competition. Over time he also served as an important mentor to Ozzie Simmons in a number of different capacities.[28]

After the Simmons brothers detrained in Iowa City, they sought out Iowa's coach Solem. The *Daily Iowan* imagined a version of this initial meeting. "We's de Simmon boys from Texas," said Don in the scene. "Mah brother here is a halfback and he's de best halfback in de land." To which Ozzie added, "Yahsah, I'se kinda tricky."[29] Newsreel footage demonstrates that Simmons did not speak this way; the *Daily Iowan* erroneously reduced their dialogue to a demeaning "Sambo" dialect. This shameful and unfortunately widespread practice played out in the 1930s on popular radio programs such as *Amos 'n Andy* and the *Jack Benny Show*, in movies staring "Stepin Fetchit" (played by Lincoln Theodore Perry), in Octavus Roy Cohen's *Saturday Evening Post* stories about Florian Slappey, and in the blackface performances of Al Jolson—all of which, according to historian Joseph Boskin, were done "in the Sambo vein."[30] The racist tradition served an ideological mission in sport as well. "Casting black football players as Sambo," argues Oriard, "reaffirmed the white superiority, as blacks were making slow inroads in the sport where American masculinity was most conspicuously on display."[31]

The introduction of the Simmons brothers to Solem likely bore little resemblance to the *Daily Iowan*'s imaginings, but the coach apparently consented to let them try out for the team. Dick Bolin, a teammate who witnessed their debut, later recalled how Ozzie Simmons dazzled those in attendance: "His first day out for practice he was playing safety, handling punt returns. Every time he caught a punt he would run it in for a touchdown—he would just snake through everybody—he had three touchdowns that day. The last time he scored, he sort of knelt down in the end zone for a minute and then he fell over."[32] According to Bolin, Simmons's teammates learned that he had nothing to eat during his trip from Texas, which caused him to faint during that first practice. Bolin remembers that from that point on, Simmons received regular meals: "I wasn't sure who started feeding him then, it was kept a secret, but I would imagine that it was Smith's café. I'd say Smith [a white, Iowa City business owner] started feeding him so that he wouldn't have to go hungry anymore."[33]

Simmons's hunger contradicts the story that a white benefactor supplied the brothers with food for their northern migration, but it is important to consider the ends that these competing narratives serve. The apocryphal recollections of Simmons's journey and arrival to Iowa allude to his financial deficiencies and lack of resources. Moreover, they imply that he owed his prospects, perhaps even his very survival, to the kindness and generosity of white strangers.

Ozzie Simmons's talents continued to impress peers, coaches, and journalists throughout his freshman year. Eligible to join the varsity squad as a sophomore in 1934, both the black and "mainstream" presses heralded his arrival. The *Daily Iowan* exhorted readers to "strike up the band for here comes two boys from Texas," and fans hoped that the brothers might reinvigorate the football program, which had been in a slump for several years.[34] A good deal of the Hawkeyes' difficulties had to do with the team's 1929 suspension from the Big 10 Conference for numerous recruiting violations and illegal payments to players. The conference representative from Minnesota, James Page, supported the decision, and his involvement may have contributed to the burgeoning animosity between the two schools.[35] Iowa's suspension lasted only one month, but the scandal devastated the team. Combined with the Depression, which hit the agricultural state hard, it was a tough time to be a Hawkeye. Solem took on a daunting task when he became coach in 1932, and the windfall of the Simmons brothers provided a boost he and the football program so desperately needed.[36]

The black press particularly rejoiced in the impending career of the Simmonses, for black athletes, especially those who played for predominately white institutions, served as powerful symbols of muscular assimilation. Simultaneously the *Chicago Defender* criticized college football's practice of omitting deserving African Americans from its All-Star teams, wondering "what will [the Big 10 Conference] do about the two brothers, C.Z. and Fred Simmons at Iowa, should either or both of them come through as predicted?"[37] Though the *Defender* got their names wrong, it proved prescient on two accounts: Ozzie Simmons did "come through" to become one of the top players in college football, and despite his talents, he would be left off nearly every one of the sport's top All-Star lists.

The Hawkeyes opened the 1934 season with a 34–0 rout over the University of South Dakota. Although Ozzie Simmons played well, it was his second varsity contest that served as his true coming-out party. His performance that day was nothing short of brilliant in the Hawkeyes' 20–7 victory over the Northwestern University Wildcats. Simmons returned a kickoff for a touchdown, rushed for 166 yards in twenty-four carries, and added 124 more yards on seven punt returns (fig. 16). When he left the game in the fourth quarter, opposing fans rose to their feet in a standing ovation. Northwestern coach Dick Hanley commented that Ozzie Simmons had "the most nearly perfect change of pace I ever saw. I played against Fritz Pollard and he stood out as my all-time ball carrier—until Saturday." Hanley continued, "Compared to Simmons, Fritz was just a real good halfback."[38] To another reporter the opposing coach remarked, "I have seen and played against a lot of great backs, but Simmons is 'tops'—absolutely the best I have ever seen." As he concluded the interview, Hanley enthused, "And boy, wouldn't I like to be there when Iowa and Minnesota come together!"[39]

The 1934 Iowa-Minnesota Contest

On October 26, 1934, the Iowa Hawkeyes met the Minnesota Golden Gophers in Iowa City for the anticipated showdown between two prominent Big 10 members. Minnesota was a formidable opponent. The Gophers, led by Coach Bernie Bierman, were in the middle of a three-year undefeated streak. In 1934 Minnesota would go on to win both the conference and the national championships. They repeated these triumphs in 1935 and 1936, leading many of Bierman's contemporaries to believe that this particular Gopher squad was the best team in the history of college football.[40]

Iowa, in contrast, flagged after its first two contests of the season, losing miserably to Iowa State 20–7 and then to Nebraska 31–6. Many wondered what happened to the Hawkeyes and its star running back, stirring up rumors that Simmons had either "gone yellow" or had grown a "big head" from all the praise.[41] Whether these charges had any merit, they conformed to the era's racial stereotypes. In his 1922 "Racial Traits in Athletics," for instance, Elmer Mitchell wrote that black stars on white teams were quick to assume "an air of bravado" and that "the negro [sic] is 'yellow,' that he is good only to a certain point and fails in crisis."[42] Teammates were said to be "jealous" of Simmons's success and the amount of attention he received. On the contrary, the *Defender* described Simmons as "very reticent, almost apologetic about his success and abashed by the blaze of publicity."[43] The competing versions of Simmons's personality—his humility in the black press and arrogance in the white—spoke to the racialized agendas of the publications and their readerships.

16. Ozzie Simmons running with football, University of Iowa Football, ca. 1935.
Frederick W. Kent Photographic Collection, University of Iowa Libraries, Iowa City.

As journalists assessed Simmons's character, the Minnesota team
took special care in preparing for him on the field. The Hawkeye
standout was "a triple threat," excelling offensively, defensively,
and on special teams.[44] Bierman devoted a special practice to strategies designed to stop the "unusually elusive running back" and

changed the team's kicking game in order to keep the ball out of Simmons's hands.[45]

In Iowa City fans readied for the "gridiron Goliaths from the Northland."[46] Covering the game for the *Chicago Daily Tribune*, journalist Edward Burns described their efforts: "Bells are resounding throughout the charmin' municipality and huge portraits of Coach Ossie Solem adorn store fronts."[47] Expecting above-capacity attendance, the Athletic Department added temporary seating at the stadium. The day before the contest, more than 3,500 students stormed Iowa's practice field. Led by a fifty-piece band, they presented Coach Solem with a thirty-foot petition signed by two thousand people pledging their loyalty to the team.[48]

The fans' support failed to lift their local squad. The Minnesota Gophers soundly beat the Iowa Hawkeyes 48–12, during which the record crowd of more than fifty-two thousand spectators witnessed little locomotion from the "Ebony Express." Recapped one *Chicago Tribune* reporter, "Those who had come in the hope that Oze Simmons would give them a few thrills, such as he had against Northwestern three weeks ago, were disappointed, because the young Texas Negro was not in the game long."[49] Although nearly seventy-five newspapers sent sportswriters to the contest, the journalists provided limited commentary and no consensus as to what happened. Was the injured Simmons knocked unconscious two times or three? Did the devastating hits happen when he was on offense, on defense, or "during an exchange of punts"? Who was to blame, and did race play a role?[50] The only point the commentariat seemed to agree upon was that at the end of the second quarter, Simmons left the field and did not return.

Three articles from regional papers illustrate the competing ways that writers interpreted what happened. The first was a somewhat surprising assessment from the *Chicago Defender*, the most influential weekly black newspaper of its day.[51] Discussing "the Negro Press" in 1939, sociologist Frederick G. Detweiler wrote that "any news that touches racial issues is played up."[52] The *Defender*, like other black newspapers, regularly addressed racism in U.S. sport and society and often levied charges of discrimination. In this instance, though, columnist David Kellum argued that the violence against Simmons was not racially motivated: "It just happens that he was the best man on Iowa's team and it is the policy of the Gophers to get the best man." Kellum reminded readers that a decade earlier, Harold "Red" Grange, the University of Illinois's white football idol, "was forced to leave the gridiron at Minnesota on stretchers during a game with the Gophers."[53] It was, in a sense, a compliment to Simmons that Minnesota would target him in this way.

A conflicting opinion appeared in the *Cedar Rapids (IA) Gazette*, a daily newspaper published approximately thirty miles north of Iowa City. The *Gazette* carried a regular sports column by a writer identified as "Earl." Following the Iowa-Minnesota contest, Earl accused the Minnesota players of racism, stating, "It is only being candid to say that [Simmons's] color would cause the players of opposing teams to bear down on him harder than on his white teammates. That the Gophers did this very thing was obvious."[54] Rather than Grange, Earl likened Simmons's injuries to those of Jack Trice, locating the two men within the same violent, racialized tradition.

The *Minneapolis Journal*'s regular sports columnist, Jack Quinlan, offered a distinctly different account. In a fictitious interview Quinlan drew on the debasing "Sambo" stereotype to make Simmons take the blame for his injuries.

> "But," confesses Oze, "whose fault was 'at but mine?" . . . Experts in Iowa yesterday went over the whole messy mistake with Mister Simmons and finally got it all straightened out to their satisfaction. Oze, it seems now, tried to pass [Minnesota's Sheldon] Beise on the right and this is contrary to the traffic laws of Iowa. "But," declares Oze, "I went 'honk honk' twice and I thought that Misto Beise would stay right where he was at in the middle of the field. But he pulled over to my side and that's whar my front bumper mixed up with something hard."[55]

Here, Simmons becomes a buffoonish, simpleminded character who does not and cannot understand the rules that govern modern society. Quinlan represents the athlete as one who confuses traffic laws for on-field behavior, putting him at fault for his injuries because he does not know how to conduct himself on the field and, simultaneously, not at fault because he is incapable of understanding what he is supposed to do. Other players are not a hazard to Simmons; he is a hazard to himself.

This type of bigotry seemed to be a regular part of Quinlan's repertoire. In a front-page column, the editor of the *St. Paul (MN) Recorder*, a black weekly newspaper, condemned the columnist for his use of the term "darky" when referring to Joe Louis, noting that it was "not the first time that Quinlan has taken opportunity through his column to show how small is his regard for Negroes."[56] Minnesotans, like Iowans, believed that their state's history had long confirmed the ideals of racial equality. That the University of Minnesota boasted prominent black football players, such as two-time All-America second-team selection Robert Marshall (1905 and 1906), offered verification.[57] Still the legacies of both states are also riddled with policies and incidents of racial discrimination, and the publication of racist propaganda in the *Minneapolis Journal*, just as in the *Daily Iowan*, perpetuated damaging stereotypes.

After the initial reports there was little follow-up on the nature of Simmons's injuries, which were apparently severe enough to prevent him from starting in the next game against Indiana University. His "stiff neck and bruises," one journalist speculated, may have been the cause.[58] Coach Solem later explained that in the Minnesota game, Simmons received "a blow over the kidneys and another in the neck" that compounded the trauma he had sustained in earlier contests. But there was almost no direct, sustained, or extensive commentary devoted to Simmons's 1934 injuries, making it all the more curious that those same injuries should incite such uproar the following year.

A Tale of Two Governors

Minnesota ended its 1934 season with an 8-0 record and its first national championship. Iowa did not fare nearly so well, finishing

2-5-1 overall and in ninth place among the Big 10 teams. In spite of this record, fans looked forward to the 1935 matchup between the conference rivals. They included a significant number of African American spectators, who traveled to Iowa City to witness the exploits of Simmons, as well as those of Dwight Reed, a black standout on the Gopher squad. As a result, the *Defender* observed, the "university town's Race population of nine families was augmented . . . to nearly 350 as football fans from many parts of the country motored here for the Hawkeye homecoming struggle with the University of Minnesota."[59]

As before the press declared that Simmons was "the man Minnesota must watch."[60] Even a beer advertisement in the *Minneapolis Tribune* told readers, "The double war-cry in front of thousands of radios will be 'hold that guy Simmons' and 'how about another glass of Gluek's.'"[61] The odds of Minnesota beating the Iowa team in 1935 were fixed at three to one. Undaunted, Iowa governor Clyde Herring expressed his utmost confidence in the Hawkeyes, telling reporters, "The University of Iowa football team will defeat the University of Minnesota. Those Minnesotans will find 10 other top-notch players besides Ozzie Simmons against them this year. Moreover, if the officials stand for any rough tactics like Minnesota used last year, I'm sure the crowd won't."[62] It marked the first time an official publicly addressed Simmons's injuries. When asked if he thought that Minnesota had unfairly converged on Simmons, Herring replied, "Yes I do. I saw the game myself and I saw that boy come off the field with tears streaming down his face. I think Minnesota players were pretty hard on him."[63]

Neither Herring's prediction of an Iowa victory nor his attention to the violence against Simmons drew the most media attention; rather, it was his warning that Hawkeye fans would attack the Gophers should the team resort to any "rough tactics." The popular press grabbed ahold of the comment, imagining what might happen. The *Chicago Defender*, for example, speculated: "Spectators at the game, who are expected to number more than 52,000, may be treated to the sight of white people defending a member of the race with fists and clubs, it was said. Outsiders contend that

Simmons was 'ganged' in the Minnesota game last year, causing the flashy ball carrier to leave the game after the first period."[64]

Hostilities mounted quickly. Reacting to Governor Herring's comment, Minnesota's coach Bierman told the *Minneapolis Tribune*, "I will instruct my boys to go out and play their usual game. If the spectators get tough with them, it will probably be the last game between Minnesota and Iowa as long as I am coach."[65] The situation further escalated when Bierman refused to hold a pregame practice in Davenport, Iowa, opting instead for the border town of Rock Island, Illinois, where state and city police officers and a detachment of fire fighters guarded the team. The coach demanded further police protection during his team's arrival in Iowa City.

At that point Minnesota's governor Floyd B. Olson, a man with a history of diffusing potentially volatile situations, intervened.[66] In a telegram to Iowa's governor Herring, Olson proposed a way to deflect attention from Simmons and the brewing conflict and, instead, focus it on the good-humored relationship between two politicians:

> Dear Clyde, Minnesota folks excited over your statement about the Iowa crowd lynching the Minnesota football team. I have assured them that you are a law-abiding gentleman and are only trying to get our goat. The Minnesota team will tackle clean, but, oh! how hard, Clyde. If you seriously think Iowa has any chance to win, I will bet you a Minnesota prize hog against an Iowa prize hog that Minnesota wins today. The loser must deliver the hog in person to the winner. Accept my bet thru a reporter. You are getting odds because Minnesota raises better hogs than Iowa. My best personal regards and condolences. Floyd B. Olson Governor of Minnesota.[67]

Olson's seemingly offhanded reference to "lynching" elicited no commentary, despite concerted and racialized attention directed toward the crime in the mid-1930s.[68] Governor Herring offered a concise retort through the press: "It's a bet."[69]

As the final seconds of the 1935 Iowa-Minnesota contest ticked away, it was clear that the wager had effectively quelled the simmering antagonism. By all accounts the game was a hard-fought, fair competition that resulted in a 13–6 Minnesota victory. More important the game concluded without incident. The Gophers treated Simmons neither gingerly nor with excessive roughness, and fans made no motions to riot. The *Minneapolis Tribune* related that "all of the furore that was created in advance of the game remarking what might happen in the event of the Iowa rooters thinking the Gophers were unnecessarily rough with Simmons, faded away in the misty air that hung over Iowa's stadium Saturday."[70] It seemed as though the anger over Simmons's injuries faded as well. Political intervention not only calmed interstate anxieties, it also glossed over and de-racialized any controversy concerning Simmons's place on the gridiron.

Governor Herring got on with the prosaic matter of settling the bet, assuring the *Minneapolis Journal* that as soon as he could "find an old razorback in the state of Iowa that's about the same quality as your Minnesota hogs, [I] am going to bring it up and stand over your Governor and make him eat it."[71] Herring's recompense was no run-of-the-mill swine. Named in honor of Governor Floyd B. Olson and selected from the Rosedale farm outside Fort Dodge, Iowa, Floyd of Rosedale was something of porcine royalty, as the progeny of a four-time grand champion and the brother of Blue Boy, which had appeared in the 1933 movie *State Fair* with Will Rogers (fig. 17).

Governor Herring and Floyd of Rosedale traveled to Minneapolis to meet with Governor Olson, and subsequent play between the two politicians continued to distance Simmons from public consciousness (figs. 18 and 19). Newspapers recounted slapstick renditions of Governor Herring's personal delivery of Floyd of Rosedale to the Minnesota State capitol. Upon release in Olson's office, the hog promptly ran amok. "Governor Olson tackled him and caught him near the tail. Governor Herring, who herded pigs back in 1907, was more deft and grabbed an ear," detailed the *Minneapolis Journal*.[72] The *New York Times* included the incident in a column on "Laughter and Reform" and declared, "There is noth-

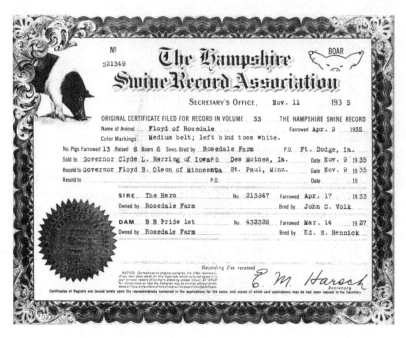

Nº 321349

The Hampshire Swine Record Association

BOAR

SECRETARY'S OFFICE, Nov. 11 193 5

ORIGINAL CERTIFICATE FILED FOR RECORD IN VOLUME 33 THE HAMPSHIRE SWINE RECORD

Name of Animal Floyd of Rosedale Farrowed Apr. 9 1935

Color Markings Medium belt; left hind toes white.

No. Pigs Farrowed 13 Raised 8 Boars 6 Sows Bred by Rosedale Farm P.O. Ft. Dodge, Ia.

Sold to Governor Clyde L. Herring of Iowa P.O. Des Moines, Ia. Date Nov. 9 19 35

Resold to Governor Floyd B. Olson of Minnesota St. Paul, Minn. Date Nov. 9 19 35

Resold to P.O. Date 19

SIRE The Hero No. 213347 Farrowed Apr. 17 19 33
Owned by Rosedale Farm Bred by John C. Volk

DAM B B Pride 1st No. 432336 Farrowed Mar. 14 19 27
Owned by Rosedale Farm Bred by Ed. S. Rennick

Recording Fee received

E. M. Harsch
Secretary

NOTICE: Corrections on original pedigree are often necessary. If any have been made on this Certificate which does not agree with your private record of animal's breeding please return AT ONCE for corrections so that the Pedigree may be printed without error. Make all future transfers of this animal on the back of this Certificate.

Certificates of Registry are issued solely upon the representations contained in the applications for the same, and copies of which said applications may be had upon request to the Secretary.

17. The Hampshire Swine Record Association certificate. Clyde Herring Papers, University of Iowa Libraries, Iowa City.

ing in nature which demands that a tribune of the people shall abstain from laughter."[73]

Herring and Olson did their best to make sure the laughter continued. In the official ceremony marking the transfer of Floyd of Rosedale's ownership, Herring told Olson, "Down through the years you are going to notice a continued improvement in Minnesota hogs as the blood of Floyd of Rosedale spreads through your pig colony." Governor Olson replied, "In consideration of Iowa's extreme thoughtfulness, we will pledge you that Minnesota football teams will continue to teach Iowa football teams how to play a great game of football."[74] Their exchanges helped set the seal on a performance that pushed Simmons and his injuries into the recesses of cultural memory. Society focused its attention on Floyd of Rosedale, the comic prize in a wager between the two governors, and effectively forgot Ozzie Simmons in the process.

In a November 12, 1935, telegram to Herring, Olson proposed

18. Governor Clyde Herring of Iowa delivers Floyd of Rosedale to Governor Floyd
B. Olson, 1935. Minnesota Historical Society, St. Paul.

that the wager become an annual tradition. Getting in another
dig, the Minnesota politician teased that the "hog would die of old
age before you got possession of him again."[75] Olson ensured the
swine's mortality by commissioning a local artist to craft a bronze
likeness of Floyd of Rosedale, producing the statue for which the
two football teams continue to vie each year.[76] Governor Herring
hoped that the tradition would "link the two states in friendship,"
demonstrating, as historian Michael Kammen argues, that "there
is a powerful tendency in the United States to depoliticize traditions for the sake of 'reconciliation.'"[77]

Beyond the Cheers

Amid all the hog hoopla, the 1935 football season marched on.
Minnesota continued its gridiron dominance, again compiling an
undefeated record to earn its second consecutive national championship. Iowa improved to 4-2-2. Many suspected the Hawkeyes

19. Governor Floyd B. Olson with Governor Clyde Herring of Iowa and the original Floyd of Rosedale. Minnesota Historical Society, St. Paul.

might have done better if Simmons had had more support. Since his inaugural varsity season, there had been murmurs that Simmons's "own teammates failed to block or to interfere or to produce the holes through which he might have sped," as the *Chicago Tribune* professed.[78] This practice had at least two consequences: it kept Simmons from gaining yardage, and it left him susceptible to opponents' hits.[79] After watching the 1935 Iowa-Northwestern game, the *Chicago Defender*'s Al Monroe dubbed Simmons the "lad who ran alone," explaining that "something like twelve attempts to negotiate distance were made by Oze Simmons Saturday and only once was he aided on his runs."[80] Simmons, the *Philadelphia Tribune* concurred, was "unable to do his stuff because his teammates will not block. The school paper, the *Daily Iowan*, made mention of the defect when it published a picture of four Illinois men about to get Oze and over the picture said 'where are the blockers?'"[81]

A TALE OF TWO GOVERNORS

These types of accusations surfaced with enough regularity that Hawkeye captain Dick Crayne addressed them in a radio interview, declaring, "Nobody has been or will be laying down in blocking or tackling."[82] Coach Solem, too, took umbrage with the charge, asserting that there was "no truth to the reports" and that "he could not figure out how such a libel got started." He did concede, however, that there was "no use kidding any one—a Negro player, even when opponents play cleanly, always gets plenty of bumps and particularly when he is a star ball carrier."[83]

Years later Solem expressed a different take on the team's failure to block for Simmons. "He was one of the two or three greatest backs I've ever coached and the best halfback I have ever seen," the coach began. "He had only one weakness. Sometimes he would think a little faster than his interference and get away from his blockers and get himself into trouble."[84] Solem managed to blame Simmons for running without interference while seeming to pay him a compliment, and once again, Simmons's talent became an excuse for what might be construed as racist practices.

All the same Simmons amassed impressive statistics his junior year, achieving the best rushing statistics of his career with 592 total yards in ninety-eight attempts for an average of 6 yards per carry.[85] And though he might have clashed with his coach and teammates, he remained a fan favorite. In a statewide poll, Iowans voted Simmons the top amateur athlete of 1935, indicating that his "popularity with Iowa grid fans is tremendous."[86] The Urban League Community Center in Omaha, Nebraska, likewise honored him at its first Annual Athlete Award banquet.[87]

Simmons's senior year proved his toughest to withstand. The Hawkeyes chalked up a second-rate record of 3-4-1, with all of their wins coming in nonconference competition. Despite the team's weaknesses, many speculated that Simmons would finally get his due, even if his teammates failed him. Former Hawkeye and All-American Dick Crayne, who went on to a stint with the National Football League's Brooklyn Dodgers, professed, "If the All America selectors give Ozzie Simmons credit for his brilliant past performances as they should, Oz should make a berth on the first team!" He continued, "Ozzie is the greatest and most elusive backfield man in college football today. . . . He is the most deceptive ball-carrier I ever saw. And he's also deadly on the defense. . . . When Oz gets any kind of support from a line, well, you just can't stop him."[88] The black press also continued its admiration of the "Texas Tornado." The *Philadelphia Tribune*, for example, effused that Simmons "runs as if he were lathered in grease and has the mechanical perfection of a Rolls Royce motor. A flip of the hip and he slides past tacklers like water through a sieve. . . . Blocking or no blocking, Oze is a terror on returning punts."[89]

For the third and final time, Simmons took the field against the Golden Gophers. It was Minnesota's homecoming, and the game program, titled "Hog-Tie the Hawkeyes," affirmed the Floyd of Rosedale tradition (fig. 20). The cover depicts a Gopher player riding astride the porcine prize as he lassoes a hapless Hawkeye. It forecast the game's outcome. Before a crowd of sixty-three thousand people, the Gophers crushed the Hawkeyes 52–0, and for the third and final time, the Iowa-Minnesota game brought trouble for Simmons.

Coach Solem evidently blamed Simmons for the team's poor showing. According to the *Chicago Tribune*, the coach criticized the athlete after the team reviewed the game film. "Solem is said to have called attention to a defensive mistake Simmons made, permitting one of Minnesota's touchdowns. Simmons evinced keen resentment at the criticism. 'Okay, okay, I lost the game 52 to 0,' he replied. A further attempt to explain some of his shortcomings as revealed in the picture resulted in Solem telling him to 'shut up,' Simmons claims, and he was ordered from the dressing room."[90] Simmons did not show up for training the next day. "I'm through with football," he told reporters. "I am not going back. I have taken too much abuse this season because of Iowa's failures."[91] Teammates pleaded with their star to return to practice. He assented, but when Solem drew him aside and demanded an apology, Simmons refused, and the coach banished him from the field.

The idea of finishing the season's final two games without their

20. Cover, Iowa vs. Minnesota, Gopher Goal Post Official Program, November 7, 1936. University of Minnesota Archives, University of Minnesota–Twin Cities.

best player concerned university officials. Late that night Professor Clarence M. Updegraff, Iowa Athletic Board chairman, convened a meeting between the embattled coach and athlete. The summit apparently worked, and Simmons rejoined the squad. He finished his Hawkeye career with a beautiful 72-yard touchdown run against Temple University, where he repeatedly "brought the crowd to its feet by his startling changes of pace as he carried the ball through the befuddled . . . defense."[92]

What should one make of the discord between Simmons and Solem? The coach was under a great deal of pressure. He failed to produce a winning season during his tenure at Iowa, and alumni repeatedly called for his resignation. The high-profile blowup with Simmons did not help his standing. But their relationship had been rocky from the start, and Simmons's widow, Eutopia Morsell-Simmons, attributed it to Solem's racial biases.[93] Simmons looked into transferring to Northwestern University at the end of his sophomore year, seemingly dissatisfied with the situation at Iowa. Over the course of the next two years, the recurring commentary on the athlete's discontent and the contentious relationship with his coach indicates that something must have been amiss.

Commenting on the skirmish in 1936 the *Philadelphia Tribune* made clear that "Solem is not charged with being prejudiced against colored boys."[94] The *New York Amsterdam News* likewise related that "whatever the trouble at Iowa is, race has nothing to do with it. Critics believe it is purely a question of personality, and not of color."[95] The fact remains, however, that during his time at Iowa, Solem acquiesced to George Washington University's request and benched two black Hawkeyes—Wilbur Wallace and Voris Dickerson. The *Defender* declared it "as rank an injustice as was ever dealt a college football player and a slur the Race fans will not soon forget."[96] It was a lamentably common practice, but some coaches, university administrators, and athletic programs still remonstrated. Solem was not among them, and he continued to bench African American players after leaving Iowa. In his subsequent position at Syracuse University, the coach withheld Wilmeth Sidat-Singh from the 1937 game against the University of Maryland at the Terrapins' request.

When Homer Harris, an African American lineman, edged out Simmons by just one vote as the Hawkeyes' Most Valuable Player of 1936, journalists speculated "that Simmons' tiff with Coach Ossie Solem and resentment against his obtaining the lion's share of Hawkeye publicity robbed him of the award as most valuable player in this, his senior year."[97] Whereas the selection of Harris may indicate that Simmons's loss was not due to racial discrimination, it was nevertheless part of a larger pattern of slights against the great Texan. Just one year earlier Simmons seemed the "only logical choice" when it came time to select captains. Instead, the team voted to "abandon the election of a permanent captain" and in its place would "have a captain appointed for each game."[98] African Americans almost never found themselves elected to such positions; yet the following year, the Hawkeyes promoted Harris to captain for the 1937 season, "thus spiking rumors," according to the *Amsterdam News*, that Simmons "was denied the post . . . because he was a Negro."[99]

Some observers chalked up the lack of recognition to Simmons's personality. Stories circulated that all the attention he received after the 1934 Northwestern game had gone to his head, for he had been immediately "swamped . . . with back-slappers, autograph seekers, newspaper men, and photographers."[100] Whether justified or not, he gained a reputation for having a difficult personality. While such behavior from a white star might have been tolerated, Simmons had been cast as an "uppity" black player—an unforgivable offense at the time.

Simmons also found himself snubbed by the men who put together the mythical lists of All-Americans.[101] Fritz Pollard, a former All-American halfback from Brown University, felt that Simmons should have been a "sure-fire" choice for the prestigious honor, yet voters left him off the official All-America Team. In an article for the *Amsterdam News*, Pollard wrote, "What excuse the critics offer for not having placed Oze Simmons on the All-American team, the author does not know."[102] The *Philadelphia Tribune* hazarded a guess: "Simmons is a brown boy. That means, just as it has in the selection of All-American teams each fall, he will be passed over by most white voters."[103] There were grounds for this indictment. Between 1924 and 1937, black football players did not rank on All-America first teams despite the era's increase in outstanding black athletes participating in white college sports.[104]

The black press kept up with Simmons after he turned in his

Hawkeye uniform. He and his brother Don made their 1936 debut with the American Giants, a semiprofessional football team in Chicago, while Ozzie completed his studies at Iowa and organized a pro basketball team to help pay his remaining tuition. He wanted to sign with a major league football team, explaining, "I understand Negroes may be barred . . . and that I may not get a contract, but I sure hope I do."[105] While there may have been "some talk that he might join either the Detroit Lions or the Chicago Cardinals," it was clear that NFL owners joined Major League Baseball in instituting a "gentlemen's agreement" not to sign black players.[106] With the country at the depths of the Depression, NFL attendance slumped, and a number of teams folded. To employ black men to play the game, at a time when so many white men were out of work, would have grated the sensibilities of white fans.

The fact of the matter is that Simmons and his black contemporaries, including Jerome "Brud" Holland of Cornell, Northwestern's Bernard Jefferson, Syracuse University's Sidat-Singh, Minnesota's Horace Bell, and Willis Ward from Michigan, represented some of the best gridiron talent of the mid-1930s. For the NFL to disregard these men was a clear indication of the league's de facto segregation. "If Simmons could not get a contract or even a tryout with an NFL team," asks Duke Slater biographer Neil Rozendaal, "then what black player could?"[107]

Denied opportunity, acknowledgment, and respect, Simmons remains "largely forgotten today," observes historian John M. Carroll.[108] Following the 1936 season at Iowa, Simmons predicted his fate: "Football's a racket. I play it because I love it. I know I'll be forgotten in two or three years."[109] Floyd of Rosedale, widely considered "the famous wager of Iowa and Minnesota governors," did little to prevent it from happening.[110]

Ozzie Simmons went on to stints with several semipro and minor league teams, including the St. Louis Gunners of the Midwest Football League. While playing with the Patterson Panthers in New Jersey (1937–39), a member of the minor league American Association with NFL ties, he was reportedly the only "Race player on the team."[111]

The year 1938 brought an unprecedented opportunity for black footballers to test themselves against some of the best white professional players in the nation. The Chicago Bears, the NFL's defending Western Division champions, agreed to an exhibition game against a team of African American "All-Stars." Former collegiate standouts from historically black and predominantly white universities assembled what the black press proclaimed to be "the greatest sepia team that ever stepped out on a football field." With the matchup, many hoped "to draw some definite conclusions as to the comparative ability" of black and white footballers.[112] After all, black journalists noted, African Americans had already proven themselves in several sports.

> Joe Louis has won the world heavyweight championship, John Henry Lewis is the world light heavyweight champion, Henry Armstrong holds the word featherweight and the world welterweight crowns. We hold any number of national junior and national senior A.A.U. [Amateur Athletic Union] track and field championships. We hold several Olympic titles and now the Tuskegee girls team is National Women's A.A.U. champs. In baseball we can hold our own against any team providing we can pick a team of stars so now bring on the football and we'll show the folks we "have something here."[113]

Unfortunately the game turned out to be, as William G. Nunn of the *Pittsburgh Courier* described it, "the most disappointing sports spectacle of the decade . . . it was a tragedy which converted itself into comedy in the closing moments of the fray. . . . It was actually pitiful."[114] The black all-stars were ill prepared and poorly organized. The Bears, meanwhile, had already completed their grueling preseason training and had several regular-season games under their belts. The solid trouncing at 51–0 did little to support the call for integration. Instead, it served as confirmation to those who suspected that African Americans lacked the talent and discipline to play in the big leagues.[115]

Simmons eventually settled in Chicago, briefly joining in 1940 the all-black Chicago Panthers that Duke Slater coached. Simmons served in the U.S. Navy during the Second World War and went on to a thirty-eight-year career as an educator in Chicago's public school system. In 2001 at age eighty-seven he died of complications from Alzheimer's and Parkinson's diseases. His family buried him in his Hawkeye letterman's jacket.

Sociologist Bridget Fowler characterizes obituaries as "a major form of collective memory within modernity."[116] In registering the death of Ozzie Simmons, a number of popular outlets, including the *Chicago Tribune, Jet*, the *Village Voice*, and ESPN, listed his achievements alongside the insults he endured as a black athlete competing in discriminatory times. Several obituaries also mentioned Simmons's connection to Floyd of Rosedale, including the following from the Associated Press: "While playing at Iowa, Simmons' presence as a black player started the tradition of awarding a prize to the winner of the Iowa-Minnesota matchup. State governors first offered the prize in 1935 to smooth tensions that developed because of Simmons' presence on the team. The award started out as a living pig and is now a bronze trophy."[117] The eulogies are not necessarily "counter-memories," for Simmons's 1934 injuries and any assignment of blame are conspicuously absent.[118] They do, however, demonstrate a critical edge to the otherwise celebratory convention.

There were precursors to the posthumous associations between Simmons and the trophy. Among the first was a 1989 *Iowa City Press-Citizen* piece titled "The Man behind Floyd of Rosedale," in which journalist Matt Trowbridge asserted that Floyd of Rosedale "is known throughout Iowa—and Ozzie Simmons is forgotten."[119] Sixteen years later a Minnesota Public Radio story "The Origin of Floyd of Rosedale" recounted, "Few people know [the trophy] had its origins in a 1934 game with racial overtones."[120] The *New York Times* reached a broader audience in 2010 with "Trophy Tells a Tale of Rivalry and Race."[121] Yet the trophy only tells this particular tale if commentators give it voice. These efforts indicate that memories of Simmons, and especially his role in the creation of Floyd of Rosedale, are not part of a past confined to oblivion.

Despite all the obstacles Ozzie Simmons faced, his widow asserts that he was "never once bitter." Eutopia Morsell-Simmons felt certain that the Gophers brutalized her husband in the 1934 game because of the color of his skin, yet as of 2003, she had no knowledge of the connection between those injuries and the Floyd of Rosedale trophy.[122] She was not alone. In 1935 the governors' wager did important cultural work that allowed the public to overlook Simmons's injuries, as well as larger racial problems. Sixteen years later, though, Pulitzer Prize–winning photographs of the "Johnny Bright incident" made it impossible to look the other way.

4

Photographic Memory and
the Johnny Bright Incident of 1951

Shortly after the Baltimore Colts selected Penn State running back Lenny Moore in the first round of the 1955 NFL draft, they nearly lost their top prospect. As Moore reminisced in his autobiography, "I almost never made it. The experience of a little-known black pioneer named Johnny Bright tempted me to shun the NFL altogether and head for Canada."[1] Ultimately Moore did sign with the Colts and went on to a Hall of Fame career, though not without significant reservations.

Had Moore gone through with his northern migration to the Canadian Football League (CFL), he would have found himself shoulder to shoulder with Bright, who, in a move that confounded many Americans, had turned down an offer to play for the Philadelphia Eagles in 1952 and instead signed with the Calgary Stampeders. Two years later Bright joined the Edmonton Eskimos for an illustrious tenure that included three consecutive Grey Cup championships, multiple record-setting performances, several All-Star selections, and the Schenley Award for the CFL's Most Outstanding Player. By spurning the NFL, Bright, according to Moore, "made an impression on many prominent black athletes from all sports."[2]

The injuries Bright sustained as a standout at Drake University further impressed upon the era's black athletes. Those same injuries also swayed Bright's decision to decline the Eagles' offer. In 1951 Bright and his teammates played Oklahoma Agricultural and Mechanical College (A&M, now Oklahoma State University). During the game, Aggie tackle Wilbanks Smith knocked Bright senseless on three different occasions, landing a blow that shattered Bright's jaw and cut short his illustrious collegiate career.

The episode differed from those involving Jack Trice and Ozzie Simmons in at least three significant ways: temporally, geographically, and evidentially. First, Bright played college football in the wake of World War II, a time of heighted attention to issues of racial inequality. Second, national publications disseminated photographs of the incident such that the violent episode resonated with those outside of Drake University's imagined community. Third, the images, which went on to win the Pulitzer Prize for photography, offered proof that a white athlete deliberately injured a black athlete in a college football game. "Without those pictures," one journalist profoundly observed, "there wouldn't have been a 'Johnny Bright incident.'"[3]

Don Ultang, one of the two prize-winning photographers who captured the infamous moments of impact, later remarked that with the images the "reality of racial bias on the college playing field was forced into the American consciousness."[4] However, a close reading of contemporary reactions to the photos suggest that racial bias was not the most immediate frame most people used to make sense of the "slugging of Johnny Bright."[5] Rather, racialized memory has evolved over time. It was only during the turn of the twentieth-first century that critics issued strong rebukes against what they understood to be a vicious act of racism.

Sport in a Changing Society

That Bright even had the opportunity to play in the National Football League demonstrates some of the societal changes of the post–World War II era. Racial lines, which previously excluded Ozzie Simmons and countless others from the ranks of professional sport, became more porous. Professional football reintegrated in 1946 after a thirteen-year drought, when the Cleveland Browns of the All-America Football Conference signed Bill Willis and Marion Motley and the NFL's Los Angeles Rams signed Kenny Washington and Woody Strode.[6] The following year Jackie Robinson made his Major League Baseball (MLB) debut with the Brooklyn

Dodgers. Other African Americans, including Roy Campanella and Don Newcombe, also of the Dodgers, and Larry Doby of the Cleveland Indians, followed Robinson in short succession.

Before long, many athletic organizations began to ease, if not completely abolish, their segregationist policies. In college sports northern football teams increasingly refused to kowtow to "gentlemen's agreements," and southern schools were less inclined to demand them, effectively desegregating many southern stadiums and postseason bowl games.[7] Barriers against black athletes in other sports started to fall as well. In 1945, for example, the University of Iowa's Dick Culberson desegregated Big 10 basketball; eleven years later Iowa State's John Crawford became the first African American basketball player in the Big 7 Conference. And Johnny Bright desegregated the sport in 1949 both at Drake and in the Missouri Valley Conference (MVC). In fact, between 1948 and 1958, the number of black basketball players at predominantly white institutions grew 34 percent.[8]

By the mid-1940s college basketball and football were among the preeminent pastimes in American culture. The G.I. Bill and other initiatives increased the number of African American athletes at PWCUS, and that coincided with the rising prominence of intercollegiate athletics and the importance of intersectional competition for national prestige.[9] The growing emphasis on big-time college sport led schools to make use of the best talent, regardless of race, but this philosophy also engendered a number of scandals involving bribery, gambling, recruiting abuses, and player subsidies. Among those accused of these crimes, determined historian Donald Spivey, was "a disproportionately high percentage of black athletes."[10]

These and other examples of advancement, determent, and even regression characterized the "romantic era" of desegregation, for in spite of significant and hypervisible symbols of sport's racial progress, limits and even outright resistance to integration remained.[11] In the late 1940s and 1950s, for example, a number of southern politicians either proposed or passed statewide legislation to ban interracial competition. MLB's Boston Red Sox failed to sign a black athlete until 1959. That same year the Professional Golfers'

Association rescinded its de jure "Caucasian only" clause, but white members made it apparent that blacks were not welcome. The NFL's Washington Redskins waited until the draft of 1962 to sign a black player, capitulating only under pressure from the John F. Kennedy administration. At the collegiate level, southern athletic conferences refused to dismantle their racial ramparts until well into the 1960s. Member schools, including Louisiana State University, the University of Georgia, and the University of Mississippi, did not integrate their major sports teams until the early 1970s.[12]

At mid-century the United States was on the cusp of great change. The era marked a number of important milestones in civil rights campaigns, yet much of the country remained lodged in residual and long-standing racist thinking and policies. In this context Johnny Bright lived and played out his collegiate career at Drake University. It was also the context he sought to escape by moving to Canada. And, at least today, it is the context that people use to make sense of the Johnny Bright incident.

Bright Star Rising

Like Jack Trice and Ozzie Simmons, Bright was not originally from Iowa. And, as with the other two men, limited opportunities and providence guided his journey to the Hawkeye State. In the mid-1940s Bright may have been Indiana's best all-around high school athlete. At Fort Wayne's predominantly white Central High School, he led his basketball team to a pair of Final Four appearances at the state tournament. In track and field he won as many as five events in a single meet, earning enough points on his own to secure the team's victory. He also boxed and was an outstanding softball pitcher. In football a teammate described Bright as "a man playing boys [sic] games," and Bright guided his squad to a city title in 1945.[13] Yet despite Bright's extraordinary talents, Indiana schools did not recruit him. Purdue never contacted him. Neither did Notre Dame, which did not field its first black football player until 1953. And Clyde Smith, Indiana University's football coach, reportedly commented that he "already had enough black running backs."[14]

So with few options Bright accepted an offer to attend Drake University in Des Moines, Iowa. Established in 1881 by members of the Disciple Church, founders declared Drake "opened to all without distinction of sex, religion, or race."[15] By the 1890s its enrollment "included a few blacks" though, as with other Iowa colleges and universities, these students were "tokens"—few in number, socially isolated, and often alienated from their white peers.[16]

In his official history of Drake, Orin L. Dahl perpetuates Iowa's racially progressive sporting narrative, writing that the "university pioneered participation by black athletes. Instead of being excluded, they were encouraged to participate." He continues, "Sadly, black players often had to sit out games when the Bulldogs traveled south and faced segregated opponents," as if to suggest that Drake officials had no choice in the matter.[17] Dahl failed to note additional indications of the school's racial problems. In 1947, for example, Owen Miller, an African American student-athlete who excelled in the classroom as well as on the gridiron and track, quit Drake and returned home to Chicago. The *Chicago Defender* reported that "university officials were completely indifferent to his request for room accommodations and that he was not allowed café service on or near the campus." His high school football coach "expressed disappointment and chagrin that a student of Miller's caliber, both in scholarship and athletics, should have been so 'pushed around' on the Drake campus."[18]

Jim Ford, an African American student-athlete who shared an apartment with Johnny Bright, also encountered difficulties during his time at Drake. Years after he left the school, Ford recalled that there "was a distinct line between us and the rest of the student body. . . . Because of [Bright's] athletic skills, he could run around in the white community. But he realized he was not accepted."[19] Although athletics afforded black students some notoriety on campus, they remained separate and unequal from their white peers in many respects.

Bright entered Drake in 1948 on a full athletic scholarship. Half of the grant was in exchange for his basketball talents; the track team covered the rest. "The understanding," Bright explained,

21. Johnny Bright, Drake University, ca. 1950. Archives at Cowles Library, Drake University, Des Moines, Iowa.

"was that I was being recruited mainly for those two sports. I said I'd come, providing I could also try out for the football team."[20] It was a lucky break for head football coach Warren Gaer. "I coached football for 24 years," he later remarked, "and [Bright] was the best I ever had."[21] Others shared Gaer's opinion. In 1969 Drake University named Johnny Bright its "greatest player of the century" (fig. 21).[22]

In his 1949 sophomore year, Bright earned a varsity letter in basketball. He also lettered in track and field as a standout pole-vaulter and high jumper. But he soon quit those sports to concentrate on football.

It was initially uncertain what role Bright might play on the gridiron. As a sophomore he did not start his first varsity game. When Coach Gaer sent him in for the first-string tailback, Bright carried the ball for 3 yards. After that play any ambiguity about Bright's place on the team quickly vanished. He scored two touchdowns, passed for a third, and finished the game with 250 yards of total offense. From that point he took the lead in the Bulldogs' single-wing offense, and Gaer developed a spread formation he called B-U-R-P (Bright, run or pass), to take advantage of his star's multiple talents. Bright became the first sophomore to win the national total offense title, running and passing for 975 yards each to finish with a total of 1,950 yards (figs. 22 and 23).[23]

As a junior in 1950 Bright again topped the nation in total offense with 2,400 yards, breaking an eight-year-old NCAA record. Even more remarkable was that while Frankie Sinkwich of the University of Georgia set the old record playing in eleven games, Bright did it in nine. With 1,232 yards rushing and 1,168 yards passing, Bright had his hand in more touchdowns than any other player in the history of the game. His average of 266.7 yards per game exceeded the total game offensive yardage of 39 of the 119 major college teams, yet he only earned second-team All-American honors.[24]

By the end of his collegiate reign, Bright had set twenty athletic records at Drake. He amassed 5,903 yards in total offense, establishing a national career record that stood for thirteen years. He tallied forty total career touchdowns and passed for another twenty-four. He became the first player in history to gain more than 1,000 yards passing and more than 1,000 yards rushing in the same season. He was, without question, exceptional.

Again poised to capture the national offensive title his senior year, Bright also became a candidate for college football's most prestigious award, the Heisman Trophy. He was apparently popular with his teammates too, for they elected him co-captain (with

22. Johnny Bright passing. Archives at Cowles Library, Drake University, Des Moines, Iowa.

Bob Binette) in 1951, making him the first player of his race to hold the distinction at Drake. In the third game of the season, Bright broke the national career total yardage record. He kept increasing that total in successive games, scoring multiple touchdowns in each contest. By the time the Bulldogs traveled south to play Oklahoma A&M, they had complied a 5-0 record and a No. 1 ranking in the MVC.

It was Bright's second time playing in Stillwater. Two years ear-

23. Johnny Bright running. Archives at Cowles Library, Drake University, Des Moines, Iowa.

lier Aggie coach Jim Lookabaugh, according to the *Des Moines Register*, told his team that as "the first Negro ever to play at A&M" Bright "should be treated fairly."[25] There were no reports to the contrary. When Bright exited the 1949 game, Oklahoma fans "gave him a full ovation," and following Drake's 28–0 loss, opposing players "shook his hand" in a gesture of sportsmanship and respect.[26] Drake's Athletic Council commended the opposing school, writing, "Especially do we appreciate the fine manner in which Mr. John Bright, our Negro halfback, was treated—both on the field and off."[27] The next year the heavily favored Aggies traveled north to Des Moines, playing the Bulldogs to a 14–14 tie. Again there was no reported trouble between the two teams.

But it was under different circumstances that Bright ran onto the Aggies' Lewis Field on the afternoon of October 20, 1951. Ray Eiland, an African American who had traveled to A&M with Drake's track team several months earlier, warned Bright that "it might be a little hazardous. . . . It was a horrible time for us." Eiland explained, "We were an integrated team in a segregated conference."[28] Additional episodes foretold trouble ahead. During Bright's previous trip to Stillwater, he became the Guthrie Hotel's first black patron. In his second visit, however, the same hotel denied him accommodation.

Contemporary events, including mounting pressures to desegregate southern colleges and universities, may have exacerbated racial tensions in the interim. Territorial legislation passed in 1897 mandated racial separation in Oklahoma's public schools, and a 1908 law decreed it "unlawful for any person, corporation, or association of persons to maintain or operate any college, school, or institution of this state where persons of both the white and colored races are received as pupils for instruction."[29] This law restricted black college students to Langston's Colored Agricultural and Normal School, Oklahoma's only all-black institution (there were forty-three for whites), but it did not offer graduate, professional, or specialized programs.[30]

In the late 1940s and 1950s, with help from activist organizations, African American students Ada Lois Sipuel and George W. McLaurin challenged Oklahoma University's policies.[31] Nancy Randolph Davis did the same at Oklahoma A&M in 1949, and two years later more than 350 black students enrolled at the Stillwater institution for advanced study, though the registrar restricted their admission to summer sessions.[32] Thus the months preceding the 1951 football season presaged the first inklings of integration at A&M, a proposition that did not sit well with hoary segregationists.

The Stillwater air was also thick with the school's athletic ambitions. At the time Oklahoma A&M was part of the Missouri Valley Conference, but administrators had designs on joining the larger, more prestigious Missouri Valley Intercollegiate Athletic Association, or Big 7, which included Oklahoma University, Iowa State University, Kansas State University, and the Universities of Kansas, Nebraska, Missouri, and Colorado. Previously known as the Big 6, established in a 1928 split from the MVC, all the schools except for Colorado banned black athletes until 1949.[33]

A&M invested heavily in its football program as a means to gain entrée into the Big 7. The school hired a new coach with deep southern roots, Jennings Bryan Whitworth, who took the helm after the 1949 season. Whitworth demanded hard-nosed play from his team, and in the weeks leading up to the 1951 Drake game, the word around town was that he had instructed the Aggies to "get" Bright. Whether it was the Drake standout's race or his talents (or a combination of the two) that incited Whitworth's alleged charge, a strong anti-Bright sentiment pervaded the contest.

The Oklahoma press added to this as local journalists warned that Bright was a "marked man."[34] The *Stillwater News Press* positioned him as the "No.1 target" of A&M's hunting party, writing that Coach Whitworth had declared "open season" on Bright and that the Aggies would "try and corral the Negro comet."[35] A subsequent piece augured that Bright would "be a 'wanted man' all afternoon as the Aggie deputies try to throw him into the 'cooler.'"[36] Naysayers might chalk up the rhetoric to colorful journalistic fancies, but to represent Bright as either fugitive or prey played on terrifying traditions in the history of U.S. race relations.[37]

The Slugging of Johnny Bright

News of the hostility directed toward Bright reached the office of the *Des Moines Register*, which carried one of the most acclaimed sports sections in the country. Editors changed their usual protocol and sent a photography crew to the contest, for although the paper extensively covered Drake's home contests, they rarely dispatched personnel to away games. In this case, however, the possibility that something sinister might happen coalesced with Bright's renown, Drake's success, and the racial tensions between the all-white southern Aggies and the integrated northern Bulldogs to heighten the impending drama. Photographers John Robinson and Don Ultang had it all in mind as they traveled to Stillwater and told each other, "We'll try to keep an eye on Bright."[38]

The two men set up their equipment in the upper deck of the Aggies' press box. Shooting "machine gun photos," Robinson used a Bell and Howell Eyemo movie camera he had altered to take still photographs at four frames per second. Ultang employed a large, single-exposure camera that produced "howitzer photos." The two styles complimented one another. Ultang's photographs could be enlarged to show a single critical moment, but unlike Robinson's, Ultang's camera could not shoot more than one image of the same play.

The two men could only stay at the game for fifteen minutes. A Sunday morning deadline required their quick return to the *Register*'s darkroom. As Ultang remembered, "If all this had happened in the second quarter we wouldn't have been there."[39] As it turned out, just seven minutes would have sufficed. That was all it took for the Aggies to dispense with Bright, who sustained his initial injury in the Bulldog's first offensive play. Ultang remembered the moment: "When the play developed, the first play from the line of scrimmage . . . I thought it was the most dramatic moment I'd seen so far, so I took a photograph. Up in the far corner of the photograph would be Bright, but I wouldn't be concentrating on him at that point. Robinson had followed it the same way. When we got through . . . we looked down there and here's Bright on the ground. Cold. Knocked out cold. Now we started saying, 'What happened?' We couldn't say what happened."[40] With their lenses trained on the progress of the ball, the two photographers failed to notice Bright, who, at that point, was not involved in the play.

Competition stopped for two minutes while trainers attended to the injured player. It seemed that Bright was able to shake off pain and stupor, for on the next play he threw a 61-yard touchdown pass. Drake quickly regained control of the ball. As Ultang described, "I now see a halfback coming the same way. I take [the photograph] the same way and Bright is knocked out cold again. Now we knew there was something going on that we were not seeing."[41] Moments later Bright again lay unconscious on the ground. Once more, miraculously, he stayed in the game after coming to. He carried the ball on the next play, only to be taken down by several Aggies. When trainers came onto the field this time, it marked the end of the contest for Johnny Bright. He had participated in only nine plays. The Aggies went on to victory, beating the "Brightless" Bulldogs 27–14.[42]

Amazingly none of the four officials whistled foul in any of the assaults on Bright and later reported that they had witnessed no unusual roughness.[43] This raised a number of suspicions. The Drake staff had been wary of the officiating even before the start of the match, noting that the referees hailed from Kansas, Texas, and Oklahoma. To assign men "entirely from this section of the country for this particular game was unwise," protested Drake administrators.[44] Their concerns likely stemmed from both the interracial and intersectional dimensions of the contest. Drake coaches had requested that the referees keep watch on their star player, and following Bright's second injury, Gaer specifically asked for extra vigilance, but to no avail.[45] It was a spectacular failure that the referees did not keep an eye on Bright, but it may have been that they, as with most of the coaches, teammates, opponents, and the more than twelve thousand spectators who filled the stands, had been focused on the movement of the football. Consequently they did not see the Aggies' Wilbanks Smith repeatedly strike Bright in the face, for on these occasions Bright was approximately 10 to 12 yards away from the ball and direct play.

Initially newspapers reported that "A&M defenders caught Bright in a high-low tackle" or that "Herbert Cook, 195-pound center and right line backer, barreled into Bright with his head down. The best opinion was that his helmet smashed Bright's jaw."[46] Even Maury White, a Des Moines Register sportswriter in attendance, relayed that Bright had "collided violently with an Aggie defensive player."[47] Only later, in the Register's darkrooms, did both the film and an understanding develop.

One of the "charms of photography," explained Henry Fox Talbot, an originator of the documentary form, is "that the operator himself [sic] discovers on examination, perhaps long afterward, that he [sic] has depicted many things he [sic] had no notion of at the time." Elements missed by the naked eye are "unconsciously recorded" and only revealed upon examining the film.[48] Such was the case for Don Ultang, who recalled the instant he understood what he had captured: "I can remember going through these holders, bringing [the images] up against the light. . . . I said, 'There! He's got his elbow in his jaw!' That's the first time anyone knew anything." The single-frame photographs showed the impact of Smith's forearm against Bright's face. Robinson, in a different darkroom, found that he had "a sequence which showed the left tackle coming around, avoiding everyone else. . . . So," Ultang remembers, "we had it nailed once we got it all put together."[49]

Robinson's sequence depicts Drake's first offensive play of the game: Bright takes the snap, hands off to fullback Gene Macomber, and rolls away. He stands flat-footed, with his hands at his sides, and watches Macomber, now several yards down field. Bright appears unaware of Smith accelerating toward him. In Robinson's final frame, Smith, fist cocked, leaves his feet and strikes Bright in the face. The blow ultimately rang the death knell for Bright's collegiate career. "I knew [my jaw] was broken the first play," he commented after the game. "I felt it bust."[50]

Game film shows Smith administering similar blows with either his fist or forearm on at least two other occasions; each time Bright is no less than 5 yards behind the line of scrimmage and clearly uninvolved in the play.[51] In his final seconds of the game, Bright keeps the ball on a sweep to the right. He is tackled hard, and several Oklahoma players pile on top of him. "Bright's down, finished for the entire ball game," read the *Register*'s caption.[52]

With similar captions, the use of surrounding text, and other "acts upon photographs," the editors directed readers' attention to Smith's egregious acts.[53] On Robinson's sequence, the *Register* staff circled Bright and labeled where he and Smith were in relation to Macomber and the ball, cropping the final three frames

24. Six-photograph sequence of Johnny Bright incident, 1951.
Des Moines Register, Des Moines, Iowa.

to center on Smith's shiver to Bright's jaw (fig. 24). Editors spliced Ultang's larger photographs into a split scene. The top, labeled "John Bright's First Play," illustrates the distance between the direct play and Smith's attack. The bottom image, "And Here's His Last," depicts Bright, reeling from another hit, and his distance from Jim Pilkington, the ball carrier (fig. 25). Although photographs are always open to interpretation, as A&M would later argue, it is difficult to dispute Smith's intentionality. His singular focus is on Bright. His trajectory pays no heed to the position of the ball. According to game reports, he did not exhibit similar behavior once Bright left the game.[54]

The *Register* devoted the entire front page of its sports section to the photographs. Major newspapers throughout the country quickly reprinted them, as did the magazines *Time* and *Life*, which called the play "the year's most glaring example of dirty football."[55] Photography historian Marianne Fulton characterizes *Life* as a "sort of national newspaper" and writes that the "distri-

25. "John Bright's First Play . . . and Here's His Last," 1951.
Des Moines Register, Des Moines, Iowa.

bution and publication of pictures make visible the unseen, the unknown and the forgotten."[56] It was certainly the case with the Johnny Bright incident. Without visibility—from the photos and their widespread distribution—reactions to Bright's injuries, as with those incurred by Simmons, Trice, and countless others, would have been, at best, fleeting.

Official Reactions

Armed with the photographic evidence, Drake officials decided to "give Oklahoma A&M a chance to clean its own house if it sincerely decided to do so."[57] There was no indication that A&M's administrators had any such designs, though Coach Whitworth wrote formal apologies to Coach Gaer and to Bright, swearing that he had not coached his team to "slug" anyone.[58] The hits were "illegal but unintentional," Whitworth explained, and Smith "just lost his head for a few minutes." The defensive tackle had "always been a little bit timid and bashful. I'm ashamed that it happened and so is Wil. I don't think there's any finer boy anywhere than Smith."[59] The Aggie coach elected not to punish Smith. A&M athletic director Henry Iba concurred, stipulating he would not pursue the matter unless Drake submitted a formal protest to conference officials.[60] With that statement, the *Stillwater News Press* reported, the "slugging of . . . Johnny Bright appeared to be closed at Oklahoma A&M."[61] Des Moines residents, however, were reportedly "boiling mad."[62]

Members of Drake's Athletic Council were among those who had reached their boiling points. Meeting on October 23, they determined that they would not dispute the outcome of the contest or seek any type of compensation, but they decided something must be done for the good of the game, the conference, and college sports. The councilmen voted unanimously to protest "the unsportsmanlike conduct and unnecessarily rough play on the part of the Oklahoma A&M football team," specifically citing the violation of "the Conference regulations, explicitly condemning unsportsmanlike conduct and rough tactics," and highlighting the "negligent officiating." They requested that the Missouri Valley Conference conduct an "immediate investigation of all the circumstances surrounding the game" and made clear that they did not "enter a formal protest *until we were forced by A&M to do so.*"[63]

In response the MVC convened a special committee made up of representatives from Wichita State University, the University of Houston, Bradley University, and the University of Tulsa. On the morning of Sunday, October 28, Drake's coach Gaer, athletic director Jack McClelland, and faculty representative Frank Gardner made their way to Kansas City, Missouri, to present their case. Joining them were A&M's coach Whitworth, athletic director Iba, and dean C. H. McElroy, chairman of the school's Athletic Council.

Drake went to great lengths to prepare its case, putting together a seventeen-page "Preliminary Statement" that included signed statements from spectators, members of the coaching staff, and players who either witnessed the rough play or heard rumors about the Aggies' intent to "get" Bright. Several Bulldog team-mates alleged they overheard Oklahomans gambling on what the Aggies would do to Johnny Bright. One player testified that he was "offered a chance to pick up a bet that John would not make 100 yards during the first half." Another reported hearing simi-lar talk at a Stillwater barbershop, where patrons bet that Bright would not finish the game.[64] Yet another met an A&M coed who told him that Coach Whitworth had instructed his players "to get Bright if you have to kill him."[65] Subsequent investigations uncov-ered similar claims about Whitworth's role in the slugging, but he vehemently denied all charges.[66]

Drake representatives presented this information, along with photographs and the game film, to the special committee. A&M officials asked for more time to review the case and determine what, if any, action they might take. To the consternation of the Drake men, the committee granted A&M another six days to deliberate.

After nearly three weeks A&M envoys reaffirmed that they would take no punitive action against anyone connected to the school. Drake officials found the response "wholly unsatisfactory."[67] A&M declared that Drake's case was weak, based on little more than statements "adduced from idle conversations overheard in rest-rooms and barbershops." No one, including the coaches or the four referees in charge of the game, actually saw any wrongdo-ing. As for the photographs, "either through want of skill on the part of the photographer, or inadequate instruments, or materi-als, or through intention and skillful manipulation, or through the accidental factors and distortions inherent in the art," they alleged "that photographs may not only be inaccurate but dan-gerously misleading." As such, the council members "firmly and categorically deny and reject the wholly unfounded accusations made against our team and the gentlemen who serve us as coaches in our athletic program," and with that declaration, they consid-ered the matter closed.[68]

Any retribution would have to come from the conference. While the MVC's guidelines prohibited unsportsmanlike conduct, they specified no penalties for such offenses. The presidents and faculty representatives of all the conference schools met, deciding that they had no power to reprimand an individual player. They did, however, have the authority to reprimand a school, but in this case they would not. Dr. Henry Harmon, Drake's president, remarked that he was "bitterly disappointed" with the decision.[69]

The minutes of Drake's Athletic Council meetings emphasize that officials did not want to leave the conference. Multiple council members went on record to stipulate that withdrawal was a last-ditch effort and that they preferred to work within the organization as much as possible. Conference secession was precarious, and among the many risks Drake faced was that the remaining member institutions might retaliate and cancel all future competitions with the disaffiliated school.

Drake executives made little mention of race in their proceedings, except to argue that leaving the conference might ultimately improve relations by limiting contact between black and white student-athletes. Because of Drake's insistence on allowing black athletes on its teams, one member remarked, the school had already alienated itself from most MVC schools. Another member questioned whether Drake should continue to subject its black athletes to the discrimination they invariably faced when playing against southern opponents. President Harmon approached the subject from a slightly different angle, suggesting that withdrawing from the conference would afford its southern members an opportunity to "re-introduce the ban on negro [sic] athletes" so that "they could have a Conference that practices segregation."[70] Looking back, present-day observers tend to read Drake's decision to withdraw as a protest against racism and a statement about the demands for equality of all U.S. citizens, but Harmon's statement undercuts this virtuous characterization. Instead, he seemed willing to allow segregation to stand.

In a press release Drake University announced its decision to withdraw from the Missouri Valley Conference, ending its forty-three-year affiliation.[71] Administrators immediately dropped all scheduled contests with A&M in every sport. In a show of solidarity, Bradley University likewise withdrew from the MVC, explaining that it was the "morally right" thing to do.[72] Drake received additional encouragement from football great Red Grange, who publicly complimented the school.[73] The *Chicago Defender* named Drake to its 1951 Honor Roll of Democracy, and the Des Moines Jewish War Veterans of the United States of America post awarded President Harmon its annual Americanism award.

Drake's secession from the MVC barely raised a proverbial eyebrow on the A&M campus. General opinion seemed to be that "Drake has chosen a comparatively small incident and magnified it to ridiculous proportions."[74] Over the years, this interpretation has filtered into A&M's official memory. In his *Oklahoma State University since 1890*, Philip Reed Rulon writes that the *Des Moines Register* "reported the story in sensational fashion and published photographs and comments that created a national incident."[75] In *A History of Equal Opportunity at Oklahoma State University*, Pauline W. Kopecky similarly assesses that Drake and its supporters had "sensationalized" the affair.[76] Only in recent history have officials from Oklahoma State (previously Oklahoma A&M) tempered this understanding to recognize the magnitude of the Johnny Bright incident.

Making Sense of the Incident

As the two schools and their affiliates debated conference protocol, the general public went about making sense of what happened to Bright. Groups and individuals used several contemporaneous issues to frame the controversy. Rarely, remarked the *New York Times*, had "a football incident taken on such widespread proportions."[77] Most immediate, it seemed, were matters related to college football and college sport more generally. Quite a few football brutalities occurred during the 1951 season, and they became emblematic of the overall lack of sportsmanship in postwar sport. *Time*, for instance, reported that

> the Bright incident pointed up a rash of win-at-any-cost football that seemed to be breaking out all over the country.

During a rough & tumble first half in Berkeley, Calif., the University of Southern California laid for California's star fullback Johnny Olszewski (pronounced O'Shevsky), sent him to the sidelines with a wrenched knee. After an even rougher game between Marquette and Tulsa, Marquette Coach Lisle Blackbourn complained that Tulsa players were guilty of "flagrantly illegal tactics." Tulsa Coach Buddy Brothers denied the charges, called them "unfair, unsportsmanlike, and onesided." The name-calling finally stopped when the two schools found one answer to the question of dirty football: they canceled the 1952 game.[78]

Two weeks after the Drake-A&M contest, Princeton quarterback Dick Kazmaier, who in 1951 would go on to win the national offensive title and the Heisman Trophy over Bright, found himself in a similar situation when Dartmouth players battered the star in his final collegiate contest. Kazmaier suffered a broken nose and concussion in what commentators referred to as a "dirty" and "illegal" play, and Princeton teammates reported their opponents had been "out to get" him from the start.[79] These particular episodes involved attacks on white players, complicating the charges of racism against Wilbanks Smith for his assaults on Johnny Bright.

The media drew attention to football-related violence as part of its larger critique of sport. In the late 1940s corruption was something of an open secret in intercollegiate athletics. Football and, increasingly, men's basketball were wildly popular, and there were reports of players receiving illegal subsidies and other improper benefits, of illegal recruiting, and of academic dishonesty. The overemphasis on college sports, the exploitation of student-athletes, and a win-at-all-costs mentality ran rampant, setting the stage for a number of high-profile scandals in the months leading up to the 1951 Drake-A&M contest.

It began when an investigation uncovered a massive point-shaving scandal involving members of the Manhattan College basketball team. Shortly thereafter authorities found similar violations at the City College of New York (winner of the 1950 NCAA and National Invitation Tournament basketball championships),

Long Island University, the University of Toledo, Bradley University (which may have contributed to the school's decision to follow Drake's lead out of the MVC), and the esteemed University of Kentucky, which canceled its entire 1952–53 basketball season as a result. In 1951, according to scholar Murray Sperber, "law officials claimed a total of seven crooked teams, thirty-two dishonest players, and eighty-six fixed games." It was likely just the tip of the iceberg, for, as Sperber qualifies, "official statistics were kept artificially low because many DAS [district attorneys] in college towns and in some cities were unwilling to investigate and/or prosecute local sports heroes and damage their schools' reputations."[80]

Later that year West Point expelled 90 of its 2,500 cadets in a disgrace that "made even the college basketball gambling scandals pale in comparison."[81] Of those dismissed for cheating on exams, and thereby violating the Military Academy's sacrosanct honor code, were thirty-seven members of the football team and a number of their tutors. All together the offenses generated both outrage and disillusionment with college sport.

These concerns were, apparently, foremost on Americans' minds when they read reports of the 1951 Drake-A&M football game. By consulting the popular media, scholars can approximate the dominant narratives of historical events, but what "this perspective often produces," cautions Jeffrey Hill, "is a neglect of how the newspaper was *read* and of what, historically, was important in the text for the reader." Those who study the past often lack the sources to get at contemporary readers' interpretations, "but if such evidence exists," Hill continues, "it is a stroke of good fortune."[82] Providentially what remains in this case is a collection of letters that people wrote following the Johnny Bright incident.[83] Specifically Oklahoma A&M archived 137 letters, addressed primarily to the school, the football coach, and the school's president, that provide material with which to consider how the public understood the event or, more accurately, the photographs of the event.

Based on the media's coverage of Bright's injuries, it is unsurprising that most correspondents related Smith's actions to the general perversion of sportsmanship and fair play in sport. Based on my crude coding system, at least 93 percent (128 of 137) of all letters mentioned unsportsmanlike conduct, dirty or foul play, disgust or contempt for Smith (who was repeatedly called cowardly), his coach, and the school that refused to enact any type of punishment. The photos were "virtually unquestionable evidence of currently low tactics that some colleges employ in order to win," castigated one man.[84]

Some critics offered racial commentary but only as a way to express just how disgusted they were by the actions of Smith and Oklahoma A&M. One writer rebuked the attack "even though the recipient was a negro [sic]." Another described himself as "a staunch died-in-the-wool Southerner who believes strongly in segregation," yet the photos captured "the sorriest brand of football, the saddest sportsmanship" that he had ever seen.[85] Still another asserted that he was "born and raised in Texas and no nigger lover," but he could not abide the shameless attack on Bright.[86]

The second theme that emerged in this epistolary collection had to do with U.S. involvement in international politics. About 20 percent of the letters included commentary on the ways the assault undercut the nation's democratic principles: "One of the reasons for fighting Germany was to put an end to racial discrimination," reproved one writer.[87] Still others were troubled by what the photographs might do to America's reputation during the Cold War with the Soviet Union and the hot war in Korea. They worried the pictures would be "good grist for the Communist propaganda mills" and would justify "Russia and the Asiatic countries in pointing the finger of scorn at our country."[88]

Several critics offered veiled references to the issue of race, but strong racial rebukes appeared in just 10 percent of the letters. "I protest this incident," one man wrote, "because it was obviously based on race prejudice."[89] Some made their accusations specific to the state: "Oklahoma's attitude on color has long been a disgrace to the decent parts of America."[90] Others broadened their condemnation: "This southern white student is the product of the mental attitudes of all the whites of the South."[91]

That racism figured so infrequently in these letters is somewhat consistent with the media coverage, for only the contemporary black press offered consistently scathing, race-based indictments, finding it "regrettable that racism continues to confuse young men in college."[92] As the *Chicago Defender* saw it: "We know and every other American who is familiar with racism knows why Johnny Bright was attacked. The boys who have been brought up on white supremacy propaganda simply cannot stand to see their illusions threatened. The Negro quarterback struck fear into them, fear that this presumably 'inferior' should make monkeys out of them. Too many whites are afraid that in a true test of individual merit, their racist convictions will be shattered."[93] This stands in stark contrast to earlier reports of the attacks on Trice and Simmons. The post–World War II era, the burgeoning civil rights movement, the incontrovertible photographic evidence, and its sweeping publicity emboldened activists in their condemnation of racial violence and deep-rooted bigotry.

Johnny Bright after the Johnny Bright Incident

As the drama unfurled there were still three games left in Bright's senior season. He missed the following matchup against Iowa State, but with his jaw wired shut, he returned to the gridiron two weeks after the A&M contest. He was ten pounds lighter, courtesy of his liquid diet, which necessitated the removal of one of his teeth so that he could eat through a straw. Outfitted in a helmet equipped with a special facemask and periodically taking oxygen on the sidelines, he rushed for more than 200 yards and accounted for three touchdowns in Drake's victory over the previously unbeaten Great Lakes Naval Training Station. But during the course of the game he reinjured his jaw, causing him to miss the Bulldog's final contest against the University of Wichita. Wichita team members presented the sidelined star with a trophy that honored him as their "most respected competitor."[94] In spite of missing two complete games and the majority of the Oklahoma A&M contest, Bright still earned 70 percent of Drake's total yardage and scored 70 percent of the Bulldogs' points during the 1951 season.

Bright's broken jaw probably cost him an unprecedented third national title for total offense. Following the Oklahoma A&M contest, he led the nation, and at the end of the season, his average of 6.75 yards gained per effort ranked highest among those who handled two hundred or more plays during the season. He also might have been the first African American to win the Heisman Trophy, but instead he finished fifth in the voting.[95] "He would have been in New York [as a finalist for the Heisman]; I'm sure of that," commented Bill Coldiron, a sophomore on the 1951 Bulldog squad. "I don't know whether he would have won it or not, but he would have been called up there. If he wouldn't have been hurt, we probably wouldn't have lost those two ballgames. That would have helped too."[96] That Bright was only selected for the All-America second team, for the second year in a row, added further insult to injury.

Johnny Bright entered the 1952 NFL draft with a long list of impressive credentials (and a few glaring slights), but it was uncertain when, or even if, a professional team might choose him.[97] The league had only reintegrated six years earlier, and the first black draftee to play in the NFL, Penn State's Wally Triplett, joined the Detroit Lions in the nineteenth round of the 1949 draft.[98] Three years later six NFL teams WERE still without African American athletes on their rosters. "It's known," reported the *Pittsburgh Courier*, "that quite a few of the pro clubs are eager to land the highly heralded blacks."[99] Among them were the Philadelphia Eagles. Jim Gallagher, the Eagles' public relations executive, remembered that "Jim Trimble was our coach then and he had seen Bright when he coached at Wichita. He said he would make a great choice."[100] Taking Trimble's advice, the Eagles made Bright their first selection in the 1952 draft, putting him as the fifth choice overall. Bright ranked ahead of a number of that year's most renowned players, including future Hall of Famers Frank Gifford and Hugh McElhenny.

But Bright declined the Eagles' contract. Instead, he accepted an offer from the Canadian Football League, becoming the first top-round draft pick to "head north," in a major coup for the organization that had aspirations of competing with the NFL. Explaining his decision, Bright remarked that the terms of his CFL contract "were just too fabulous to turn down. I have worked for four years to get in a position to help my mother and dad. I just couldn't let the offer go."[101] There was some speculation that a paltry offer from the Eagles may have contributed to his decision.[102]

Bright enjoyed a storied career in the CFL. He led the Western Conference in rushing and was a six-time all-conference selection. The league's top rusher for three consecutive years, he guided his team to Grey Cup championships in 1954, 1955, and 1956. Elected to the CFL All-Star team several times over, he earned the Schenley Award as Canada's most valuable professional football player in 1959. By the time he retired in 1964, Bright had rushed for 10,909 yards, a league record that, to this day, only two players have surpassed. He still holds the records for most career playoff touchdowns, for the most yards rushed in a Grey Cup game, and for playing in 197 consecutive games.

Bright became a Canadian citizen in 1962, once remarking, "I never get in any problems up here because of my race."[103] Bob Dean, a kicker for the Edmonton Eskimos and Bright's longtime friend, said that black players who came from the United States around the same time appreciated living in Canada because they felt they were treated with more respect.[104] Yet sport studies scholars John Valentine and Simon Darnell qualify that "black players were more acceptable in football in Canada not because of antiracist policies or thinking, but because football in Canada did not carry the same cultural importance as it did in the United States."[105] In all the CFL was not free from racial prejudice but was "more tolerant of blacks than its American competitor," and many top African American players went north during this time.[106] In addition the Canadian league often paid higher salaries than the NFL and demanded less rigorous practice schedules, which allowed athletes time to pursue other vocations.

Bright went on to a career in education, first as a teacher, then as principal of D. S. Mackenzie Junior High School in Edmonton. He also coached football and basketball. He died in 1983 at the age of fifty-three, when he suffered a heart attack during surgery for an old knee injury. Edmonton subsequently dedicated a municipal football stadium in his honor, and the *Edmonton Journal* annually presents its Johnny Bright Award to high school athletes committed to academics, athletics, and their community. Few of Bright's fellow Canadians knew about the events that convinced him to leave the United States. "He wouldn't mention it at all," Bob Dean said.[107] Wilbanks Smith also reportedly refuses to discuss the game, except only to say that "race had nothing to do with what happened that day."[108]

Contrary to Smith's denial, many observers have become increasingly bold in their racialized assessments. In 1985, for instance, the *New York Times* called it "one of the ugliest racial incidents in college sports history."[109] It was a far cry from the newspaper's earlier reportage that simply cited an "illegal forearm" as the cause of Bright's injuries.[110] The *New York Post* similarly characterized Smith's actions as "genuine racism" and "the football equivalent of a lynching."[111] In 1951 Bright's teammates supported him wholeheartedly and were indignant about the Aggies' behavior, but no one mentioned race. Sixty years later, though, Jim Ford, who had been a Drake student-athlete with Bright, remarked that he had "always read it as a racial incident."[112]

The last half century has changed the tenor of cultural memory. This is not to say that groups and individuals have misremembered the event over time, but they have significantly and publicly racialized their memories of the Johnny Bright incident, assigning racism as the root cause of what happened that day on the Aggies' Lewis Field. What was once perceived as evidence of dirty tactics and corruption in college athletics now represents the bigotry of an ostensibly bygone era.

Bright also became more vocal about race throughout his life. After retiring from the CFL, he explained the real reason he turned down the chance to play in the NFL: "I would have been [the Eagles'] first Negro player. . . . There was a tremendous influx of Southern players into the NFL at that time, and I didn't know what kind of treatment I could expect."[113] In 1980 he spoke to a reporter about the notorious Oklahoma A&M game, recalling, "I heard rumors that there was a $500 bounty for me, and I got a broken jaw in the game. It was racially oriented."[114] In another interview that same year, he asserted that there was "no way it *couldn't* have been racially motivated."[115]

When it comes to Bright (and others), though, racialized memory might not be the foundation for later outspokenness. Without a doubt, it was dangerous for Bright to charge racism in the 1950s. Certainly it was the case for black athletes throughout much of the twentieth century. Lenny Moore, who in 1955 nearly followed Bright's lead to the CFL, commented on the scare tactics and the ever-present threat of violence that exercised powerful forms of social control over African Americans. "Society had trained us not to make a fuss. . . . It was the classic, 'Will he lynch me?' syndrome that controlled the slaves, through fear. As fellow slaves watched their family members being whipped, beaten, hanged, or burned to death, there were few among them who would speak out. In the America of the fifties, there were enough newspaper pictures of violent acts against blacks that this type of fear still reigned. It was suicidal to protest such acts; far better to remove oneself from the environment that condoned overt racism."[116] The violent acts of the 1950s went far beyond the confines of the gridiron. Although no one publicly connected Smith's attack (why not refer to it as the "Wilbanks Smith incident"?) with episodes of lynching, racial profiling, unjust incarcerations, and corporal punishment, rape, brutality, and other acts of terrorism that whites performed against blacks, the link may not have been lost on contemporary audiences.

Perhaps this ever-present threat of violence is why Bright moved to Canada. Perhaps it is why so few racial indictments appeared in 1951. Perhaps under different geographical and historical circumstances, it became a bit safer for Bright and others to express how they really felt. Whatever the case, memories of the "slugging of Johnny Bright" have grown increasingly racialized. Indeed, by the time Drake University dedicated Johnny Bright Field in 2006, not even Oklahoma A&M could resist the process.

PHOTOGRAPHIC MEMORY

Afterword

Coming to Terms with the Past

"Dear Dr. Maxwell," wrote President David Schmidly of Oklahoma State University (formerly Oklahoma A&M), "I welcomed our phone conversation this week and was pleased to discuss the 1951 Johnny Bright incident." In a letter dated September 28, 2005, Schmidly began his response to Drake's president, answering Maxwell's request to bring "formal closure" to the episode before the dedication of Johnny Bright Field at the Des Moines, Iowa, institution. Schmidly continued:

> The incident was an ugly mark on Oklahoma State University and college football and we regret the harm it caused Johnny Bright, your university, and many others. OSU and those involved later apologized, but a great damage was done.
>
> OSU moved beyond the episode and I am pleased to say created a legacy of respect and fairness. We also have a proud legacy of success by countless African-American athletes.[1]

Schmidly's allusion to Oklahoma State's racial progress is important. He suggests that the university underwent more than a name change; it also left behind its segregationist past to become a place of equality where "countless African-American athletes" have experienced success. Even more, Schmidly insinuates that racism lay at the core of what happened to Bright in 1951, marking a significant departure from Oklahoma A&M's decades-old position, in which officials denied any wrongdoing, racially motivated or otherwise. Indeed, the slugging of Johnny Bright has been so thoroughly racialized in the past half century that it would have been foolhardy for Schmidly to suggest otherwise.

At least one journalist puzzled over the osu president's act of contrition. "These institutional apologies can be strange," mused Berry Tramel of the *Oklahoman*. "Schmidly apologized for something he had nothing to do with, apologized for an institution that not only has changed its name, but its attitudes. osu was the first Big Eight school to hire a black man as head basketball coach, Leonard Hamilton in 1986. Nine years later, osu was the first to do the same in football, Bob Simmons in 1995."[2] Tramel, like Schmidly, offers examples of racial progress to dispel the charges of racism that continue to haunt the school and, in doing so, resigns the Johnny Bright incident and any attendant racialized issues to the past.

Public apologies are curious phenomena that vibrate on multiple frequencies. They can have a therapeutic effect for those wronged, for the wrongdoers, and for those affected by either side of the trauma. They can assuage lingering guilt and help individuals and communities begin to heal and move forward. But historian Robert Weyeneth maintains, public apologies "provide more than symbolic restitution; they can also ignite vigorous debate about history. Apologizing offers a vehicle by which societies as a whole can think about the relevance of the past, particularly about events that remain controversial. . . . An apology, then, may derive power from the ability to compel the present to think about the past."[3]

As a form of cultural memory, apologies offer occasions to reconcile with the past. Reconciliation can also assume a celebratory cast, as it does with certain place names or monuments. It might also take on a didactic quality, educating a community and reminding it not to repeat its former sins. But there is another consequence to consider, one that may be unintended but nonetheless dangerous: attempts to redress past racial wrongs may define racism as a historical relic. In other words, offering some type of recompense may give the "illusion of substantive racial progress," argues legal scholar Angelique Davis, without all the dirty work necessary to acknowledge continued racial inequities.[4]

The commemorative efforts associated with Jack Trice, Ozzie Simmons, and Johnny Bright have not occurred in isolation. What philosopher Janna Thompson calls an "epidemic of apology" began after World War II as the world started to realize the magnitude of the Holocaust and other wartime atrocities.[5] Since that time, argues human rights scholar Elazar Barkan, "questions of morality and justice are receiving growing attention as political questions. As such, the need for restitution to past victims has become a major part of national politics and international diplomacy."[6] In particular, a considerable number of individuals, institutions, organizations, corporations, and governments have worked to make amends for past injustices perpetrated against minority groups.

It was evident as imperialist regimes issued formal apologies for wrongs committed against indigenous peoples: England's Queen Elizabeth II to New Zealand Maori, South African officials to citizens for apartheid, the Canadian government to First Nations, France to Algerians. Between 1997 and 2001, heads of Australian state and territory governments apologized to the Aboriginal and Torres Strait Islander communities, particularly to those of the "Stolen Generations," for the government's forced removal and assimilation policies (though Prime Minister Kevin Rudd did not issue a federal edict until 2008). In 2009 President Barack Obama signed a bill that, in part, expressed regret "on behalf of the people of the United States to all Native Peoples for the many instances of violence, maltreatment, and neglect inflicted on Native Peoples by citizens of the United States."[7]

Obama joined a growing presidential "apology phenomenon," set in motion when Ronald Reagan signed the Civil Liberties Act of 1988, offering restitution to the nearly 120,000 Japanese Americans interned by the U.S. government during World War II.[8] This act bolstered activists seeking social and financial restitution for African American slavery. It sparked the formation of the National Coalition of Blacks for Reparations in America and of "H.R. 40, a bill calling for the federal government to study the impact of slavery and make recommendations for reparations to the 35 million American descendants," explains historian Martha Biondi.[9] In a letter to the editor of the *New York Times*, one man wrote: "The United States has finally apologized to its Japanese-Americans for the racially based horrors visited upon them for four years and awarded them financial compensation. May we hope that this consciousness-raising exercise has helped sensitize the body politic to addressing the far greater injustices inflicted on Africans and their descendants on this continent over more than three centuries?"[10] These debates continue, and, in turn, a number of groups have expressed public regret for their connections to that "peculiar institution."

President Bill Clinton was not among those who officially apologized for the government's role in slavery. It was somewhat surprising, given the "politics of contrition" that came to characterize his time in office (1993–2001).[11] In fact, one of his first official White House acts was to sign the "Apology Resolution" addressing the United States' 1893 overthrow of the Kingdom of Hawaii. Clinton later awarded seven black World War II servicemen the Medal of Honor and issued presidential pardons to several African Americans dealt unjust incarcerations, dishonorable discharges, and other punishments attributed to little more than racial antipathy. He apologized for Western indifference to the genocide in Rwanda and for the U.S. Public Health Service's "Tuskegee Study of Untreated Syphilis in the Negro Male," a forty-year program that withheld medical treatment from those infected with the disease. "To our African-American citizens," he intoned, "I am sorry that your Federal Government orchestrated a study so clearly racist. . . . What was done cannot be undone, but we can end the silence."[12]

Clinton sought to end additional racialized silences. Notable among these campaigns was his 1997–98 "One America in the 21st Century: The President's Initiative on Race," in which he pledged to lead "the American people in a great and unprecedented conversation" to promote racial respect and accord. He formed a blue-ribbon advisory panel of experts to survey the status of race in the United States and arranged for a series of town hall meetings across the country, including an ESPN-televised forum on race and sport.[13] The president, who participated in ESPN's discussion, explained that "America, rightly or wrongly, is a sports-crazed country, and we often see games as a metaphor for what we are as a people."[14] Although many Americans perceive the overrepresentation of black athletes in a few high-profile sports as evidence of a colorblind ethos and a post-racial society, the panel's discussants drew attention to persistent inequalities that continued to plague sports and society, emphasizing the dangers of classifying racism as a bygone phenomenon.

A number of critics were skeptical about the motivations behind Clinton's gestures. Some believed they were a way to curry favor with black voters. Others speculated they were designed to deflect attention from the president's sex scandals. Political scientist Claire Jean Kim asserts that his actions risked glossing over lasting problems. She classifies the "One America" enterprise as "a high-profile example of how superficial multiculturalist rhetoric could be used to simultaneously grant minorities symbolic recognition and distract attention from the impact of racism on their material existence."[15] It may be that public commemorations do the same type of cultural work—that is, granting symbolic recognition to the contributions of people of color and to the racism they endured while concurrently distracting public consciousness from real and continued inequalities in both sport and society.

Sport, Race, and the Politics of Commemoration

In addition to those involving Trice, Simmons, and Bright, a number of other racialized, sports-related events occurred within the larger "politics of regret" that characterize the turn of the twenty-first century.[16] Taken in isolation, each initiative may seem august, penitent, or noble. Taken together, however, cultural efforts to remember the accomplishments and tribulations of black athletes raise questions about their underlying motivations.

At nearly the same time that Iowa State dedicated Jack Trice Stadium, the United States Tennis Association unveiled Arthur Ashe Stadium, honoring the pioneering African American tennis player, scholar, and activist. Yet, as sport sociologist Nancy Spencer argues, it may have been orchestrated to "ward off allegations that [the association] had not done enough for minorities."[17] The stadium not only venerates Ashe and secures his name in public history but also shields the tennis organization from criticism regarding racial deficiencies, in much the same way that Jack Trice Stadium does for Iowa State University.

Arthur Ashe Stadium, along with a controversial statue of the man in his hometown of Richmond, Virginia (situated among monuments dedicated to white "heroes" of the Confederacy), came in the wake of his untimely death.[18] The passing of track-and-field great Wilma Rudolph likewise motivated a spate of memorials. At the dedication of a statue in her birthplace of Clarksville, Tennessee, her former coach, Ed Temple, expressed that the tribute was "almost 40 years too late" and should "have happened many years ago."[19]

Sociologist Harry Edwards similarly commented on the San Jose State University statue for Tommie Smith and John Carlos, two athletes initially condemned for protesting American racism during the 1968 Summer Olympic Games. "It's 40 years late," Edwards told reporters at the statue's 2005 dedication ceremony, "but it's right on time."[20] These observations should encourage us to think about the historical context in which commemoration occurs. Why didn't these tributes happen decades earlier? What changed in the past four decades to generate commemorative interest? What makes a particular historical moment "right on time"?

Time may not heal all wounds, but it can have an analgesic effect. In 1968 many white Americans saw threatening hostility, disrespectful arrogance, and anti-American acrimony in the demonstrations of Smith and Carlos. But hindsight, presentism, and racial progress have transformed the men's "silent gestures" from signifiers of militancy to emblems of activism, from menacing black power salutes to dignified commentaries on the state of contemporary race relations. Sport studies scholar Maureen M. Smith reads the San Jose State statue as a form of "reparation"— as a way for the school to make amends for its failure to support its athletes during their Olympic fallout.[21]

A number of cultural forms, including the statue, re-narrativized the 1968 protest as one of romance. The media launched commemorative vehicles marking the twenty-fifth, thirtieth, and fortieth anniversaries of the 1968 Games, offering "revisionist" histories that "reinterpreted" and "rehabilitated" the legacy of Smith and Carlos, according to sociologist Douglas Hartmann.[22] In these tributes, as well as in films such as *Fists of Freedom* (1999), *Black Power Salute* (2008), and *Salute* (2008); in academic histories including Hartmann's *Race, Culture, and the Revolt of the Black Athlete* (2003) and Amy Bass's *Not the Triumph but the Struggle* (2004); and in ESPN's awarding Smith and Carlos its 2008 Arthur Ashe Courage Award, the athletes' once-maligned reputations have been redeemed.[23]

The same is true for boxing great Muhammad Ali, who in recent history has become a hero and cultural icon. But there was a time—in the late 1960s and early 1970s—when many Americans denounced his outspokenness, his race pride, his opposition to the Vietnam War, and his membership in the Nation of Islam. By 1996 with his once-controversial voice all but silenced by the ravages of Parkinson's disease, Ali became the subject of public veneration as his tremorous hand raised the Olympic torch at the opening ceremony in Atlanta. That moment, according to scholars Trevor B. McCrisken and Andrew Pepper, sealed Ali's "social and political rehabilitation" and "completed his transformation into a 'safe' all-American hero."[24] Confronted with the boxer's illness, asserts cultural critic Gerald Early, the public now "wants to drown him in a bathos of sainthood and atone for its guilt."[25] Stripped of his oppositional clout and absolved of his transgressions by time, disease, and popular culture, Ali has ascended to the highest ranks of America's sporting pantheon.

Jack Johnson, a predecessor and idol of Ali's, is also the focus of compensatory efforts. In the course of making his 2005 documentary *Unforgivable Blackness: The Rise and Fall of Jack Johnson*, acclaimed filmmaker Ken Burns, backed by Senators John McCain and Orrin Hatch and Representative Jesse Jackson Jr., sought a posthumous presidential pardon for the former heavyweight champion of the world. Johnson's 1913 conviction for violating the Mann Act, which forbade the transportation of women across state lines for immoral purposes, is routinely acknowledged today as a racially motivated act.[26] "We can never completely right the wrong perpetrated against Jack Johnson during his lifetime," McCain explained, "but this pardon is a small, meaningful step toward acknowledging his mistreatment before the law and celebrating his legacy of athletic greatness and historical significance."[27]

Several colleges and universities have similarly attempted to amend racialized grievances. The University of Maryland, for instance, apologized for insisting that Syracuse University bench its African American quarterback, Wilmeth Sidat-Singh, during the 1937 football contest. Maryland representatives invited Sidat-Singh's surviving family members to join them on the field between the first and second quarters of the 2013 Maryland-Syracuse football game, and the Syracuse team, which included "dozens" of African American players, wore helmet decals with Sidat-Singh's number 19 as a tribute. Syracuse coach Scott Shafer told the press that the event was "a teaching moment and an opportunity for our kids to look backwards and look at the history of our country and the history of our country's ugliness at times in the past and be part of righting a situation that was horribly wrong just 75, 76 years ago."[28]

Another benching, that of New York University (NYU) football player Leonard Bates in 1940, also generated institutional consideration. When NYU officials capitulated to the "gentlemen's agreement" with the University of Missouri, a group of students initiated a "Bates must play!" campaign. Still Bates stayed home when the team traveled to Missouri. The students redoubled their efforts later that school year after a basketball player and several track athletes likewise suffered the indignity of NYU's discriminatory practices. Administrators suspended the protest leaders in 1941. Sixty years later the university hosted a banquet to honor those leaders, the so-called Bates Seven. NYU representatives were careful to call the event a "tribute" and not an "apology."[29] Said spokesman John Beckman, "Fundamentally, what we want to do is embrace these members of our community and hold them up as models of people who fight for an important cause. I would call it an acknowledgment of good work and courage shown by members of our community."[30] Put differently, in honoring the Bates Seven, NYU honored itself.

The "gentlemen's agreement" tapered off in the "romantic era" of desegregation, but new inequities soon took its place.[31] As the civil rights movement gained steam and more black athletes joined the college ranks, they replaced the earlier ethos of assimilation with outspokenness and even militancy, banding together to correct a system that continued to disenfranchise them. Their efforts advanced into what Edwards called the "Revolt of the Black Athlete," and the late 1960s saw a number of racial protests in college sports.[32]

In 1969 African American players on the University of Wyoming's football team told their coach, Lloyd Eaton, they planned to wear black armbands during the game against Brigham Young University in protest of the Church of Jesus Christ of Latter-day Saints' policy that barred blacks from the priesthood. Eaton summarily dismissed the "Black 14" from his squad; university officials and the governor of Wyoming upheld Eaton's decision. In 1993 four of the athletes returned to campus for "recognition from school officials."[33] Nine years later as a symbol of institutional remorse, Wyoming administrators unveiled a bronze sculpture of a football player's arm encircled by an armband and extending into a raised fist, the symbol of black protest and pride so strikingly articulated by Olympic athletes Smith and Carols. A plaque bearing the name of each member of the Black 14 accompanies the monument.

Syracuse University officials similarly discharged nine black football players (though they were called the Syracuse 8) who, in 1970, boycotted spring practice as a way to show their discontent with Coach Ben Schwartzwalder and what they considered the "racist behavior" of the coaching staff.[34] Schwartzwalder suspended them from the team in what an investigative committee later determined to be "an act of institutional racism unworthy of a great university."[35] In recent years the school has offered the Syracuse 8 Scholarship Fund, awarded the spurned players letterman's jackets during the halftime of a football game, and bestowed them with the Chancellor's Medal for courage, one of the institution's highest honors.[36]

Allegations of Coach Schwartzwalder's racial offenses were largely absent from the 2008 film *The Express* that dramatizes the story of Syracuse University's Ernie Davis, who, in 1961, became the first African American to win the Heisman Trophy. In fact with the new millennium have come a number of historical sport films that work to reconcile the country's racist past. Among them was Disney's 2006 *Glory Road*, which tells the story of Texas Western College's 1966 national championship men's basketball team that started, for the first time in NCAA tournament history, five African American players. Upon the film's release, the Wheaties cereal box paid tribute to that momentous Texas Western team—an accolade (and commodification) not granted to them in the 1960s.[37] The movie also garnered the team's former members an invitation to the White House. Both honors, one might argue (as with Rudolph, Smith, and Carlos), came forty years past due.

Yet *Glory Road* and other celebratory sport films that revisit the civil rights era, argues critic Christopher Kelly, raise additional problems, for they seem "content to congratulate moviegoers (look how far we've come!) instead of unsettle them (look how much work is still left to be done!)."[38] As commemorative vehicles they present a progressive view of history that imagines racism as a discrete, finished phenomenon and that "allows us," according to one reviewer, "to grow misty-eyed without ever really contemplating the depth of this country's racist heritage or the considerable work still needed to overcome it."[39]

Sport historian Charles Martin took a more sanguine view of *Glory Road*: "That the Disney Corporation would release such a hard-hitting story in our conservative age, when many white Americans claim that all racial problems were solved decades ago, is a remarkable development."[40] To the contrary, it is precisely these types of narratives that appeal to audiences living in the conser-

vative age, for the film constructs the past as something temporally dislocated from the here and now. Audiences can watch *Glory
Road* and its depiction of the virulent racism of the 1960s and praise
themselves for the racial progress of the past fifty years, thereby
supporting the belief that "all racial problems were solved decades
ago." Sport films, like other commemorative vehicles, may actually create historical and contemporary blind spots.

Cultural Memory and "New Racism"

What begins as a cursory glance at recent commemorative efforts
designed to redress racial wrongs quickly becomes an exercise
in cataloging an overwhelming number of events. This is more
than mere coincidence. Clearly something about the turn of the
twenty-first century facilitates racialized memory. Part of it has
to do with the general "surfeit of memory" that surrounds us. For
a culture often accused of historical amnesia, American lives are
littered with references to the past. We are steeped in a heritage
industry that fertilizes the ground on which any number of cultural memories might begin to sprout.[41]

Still other ways of thinking about the currency of racialized
memory in fin de siècle America connect with the undeniable
changes since the era of Jim Crow racism. Landmark antidiscrimination legislation precipitated great progress in terms of segregation, hiring practices, schooling, voting rates, home ownership,
and political office, among other cultural institutions and practices. This transition happened on structural and ideological levels, and polls show that Americans from all walks of life report
improvements in race relations.[42] These changes not only make
it "safe" to travel back in time and confront the legacies of racism but also contribute to an abiding desire to gauge just how far
we've come.

Some observers interpret these shifts as indicative of our transformation to a "post-racial" society, characterized, according to
social psychologist Thomas F. Pettigrew, by the claim "that we
are now entering a new era in America in which race has sub-
stantially lost its special significance."[43] Nothing buttressed this

position more than the 2008 election of Barack Obama as the forty-fourth president of the United States. Certainly the momentous occasion signaled real and symbolic significance, yet critics have cautioned against getting swept up in a wave of "uncritical optimism" that may engender a "false sense of hope, masking the realities of gross racial/ethnic disparities."[44]

Although it may seem safe to revisit the past because of the racial progress in sport and society, legal scholar Roy L. Brooks argues to the contrary: "The great majority of African Americans are beset by a dearth of financial-, human-, and social-capital deficiencies inherited from slavery and the Jim Crow Era."[45] Imagining a color-blind society might even cause additional damage, for "political proponents of postracial thinking are agitating for the end to all race- and ethnicity-centered social policy mechanisms aimed at reducing social inequities," as critical race scholars Martell Teasley and David Ikard argue.[46]

The illustrious historian John Hope Franklin, who served on President Clinton's Advisory Board to the Initiative on Race, issued a related assessment. Although the early twenty-first century is no longer rife with the "open, blatant racism" of the past, he reflected, it is nevertheless "characterized by subtle, elusive, and even discreet forms of racism equally sinister and more difficult to handle."[47] Scholars have devised different theories to explain this line of thinking, promoting theories of "symbolic racism," "modern racism," "color-blind racism," "laissez-faire racism," and "new racism."[48]

The terms have their own unique and clever meanings, but at their core, summarizes sociologist Lawrence Bobo, contemporary racism "is a more covert, sophisticated, culture-centered, and subtle racist ideology, qualitatively less extreme and more socially permeable than Jim Crow racism with its attendant biological foundations and calls for more overt discrimination." This "new racism," he continues, "yields a powerful influence in our culture and politics," of which sport plays a prominent role.[49]

In describing her conceptualization of "new racism," sociologist Patricia Hill Collins explains, "recognizing that racism even exists remains a challenge for most White Americans, and increas-

ingly for American Americans as well. They believe that the passage of civil rights legislation eliminated racially discriminatory
practices and that any problems that Blacks may experience now
are of their own doing."[50] The perpetuation of this ideology aligns
with what critical race scholars Hernán Vera and Andrew Gordon call "a sincere fiction"; these ideas are "sincere" because many
people believe them to be true and simultaneously are "fictions"
because they ignore the legacy and continued presence of white
privilege and racial prejudice in America.[51]

One might cite any number of statistics to support the enduring
presence of systemic racism in the United States, including racial
differences in education, unemployment, housing, the criminal justice system, health care, life expectancy, infant mortality, wealth,
and poverty. As social theorist Joe R. Feagin summarizes, "Being
black means living with racial oppression from cradle to grave."[52]
Even though issues have unquestionably improved as a result of
civil rights struggles, iniquitous gaps persist. For instance, in 1967
the black unemployment rate was approximately double the white
unemployment rate, a ratio that has remained constant over time.
In 1967, black households earned 55 percent of what white households earned; by 2013 that discrepancy narrowed slightly, with
black households earning, on average, 59 percent of that of white
households. Constituting 12 percent of the U.S. population, African Americans hold just 3 percent of U.S. wealth. Data from 2010
determined that black men were six times more likely than white
men to be incarcerated in federal and state prisons, a rate that has
actually increased since the mid-twentieth century.[53] Meanwhile
attacks on affirmative action and other racially ameliorative programs continue. In 2013, for example, the U.S. Supreme Court ruled
unconstitutional key aspects of the 1965 federal Voting Rights Act.
Critics argue the finding will undermine African Americans' significant socio-political gains of the past four decades.

Sport also indicates the long residuals of racial discrimination.
The prevailing mythologies of meritocracy, egalitarianism, and
color blindness, along with the overrepresentation of black athletes in a handful of socially prominent sports, too often obscures

structural inequalities.[54] Thus as sociologist Abby Ferber gauges, "The mainstream spectacle of sport does nothing to encourage an interrogation of White supremacy and racism."[55] One need only look at the significant *under*representation of athletes of color in most sports—including "country club" sports, those contested at the Winter Olympics, the X Games, the Paralympic Games, and so on—to debunk the idea of black athletic "dominance." Collegiate graduation rates for African American males, especially those in big-time, revenue-producing sports, lag behind their white teammates. Few African Americans achieve those leadership positions that wield the most power, privilege, and prestige: owner, coach, manager, athletic trainer, and so forth. Successful athletes can make millions of dollars over the course of their careers, but those careers are scarce, are limited, and exploit and destroy their bodies. All athletes, but particularly athletes of color, furthermore, face difficulty parlaying athletic success into subsequent careers. A successful sports career is tough for anyone to realize, and athletes of color must contend with the complications of race, despite the dominant mythology perpetuated by the popular press.[56]

So what are the connections between new racism; the racialized memories of Trice, Simmons, and Bright; and their associated expressions of material culture? My primary concern is that symbolic acts, such as naming Jack Trice Stadium and Johnny Bright Field, become icons of racial progress. They simultaneously remind us of past racial injustice and stand as testaments to the end of an era. Without question, they also perform important pedagogical tasks and commemorate the achievements and adversities of athletes of color—experiences that might be too easily relegated to the dustbin of history without some tangible, prominent type of remembrance. But we should be careful about regarding them as emblematic of some type of end point, as a romantic conclusion to what is, in effect, an open-ended narrative.

Illustrative of this argument is the 2005 dedication for the statue of Tommie Smith and John Carlos at San Jose State. Carlos describes his incredible sense of pride at the ceremony, yet he "couldn't help but notice at the same time that the media kept trying to put a divide between what we did then and its application to today. They wanted it to be all about 'those tumultuous days way back when.' I wanted to say that . . . we still have battles to fight. I wanted to say that this was a problem that needs to be addressed. But with only a few exceptions, that's when they turned off the cameras."[57]

Material formations of cultural memory may also, paradoxically, encourage historical amnesia. Neal Rozendaal opens his biography of Iowa football great Duke Slater by confessing, "As a student at the University of Iowa, I must have passed Slater Hall hundreds of times and never given it much thought."[58] Although the dormitory ensures the community remembers Slater's name, it does little to flesh out the details of his life (including the fact that he could not live on the Iowa campus in the early 1900s). How often do we enter a building, stadium, or arena; walk down a street; pass by a statue; or settle beside some monument emblazoned with an individual's name? Do we take the time to investigate? To learn? To even read an accompanying plaque, should one exist? We could, but we too often lack the interest, the time, or the inclination.

I finished writing this book just as the United States commemorated the fiftieth anniversary of the 1963 March on Washington for Jobs and Freedom. Standing on the same spot where Martin Luther King Jr. delivered his now iconic "I Have a Dream" speech, President Obama told those who assembled at the Lincoln Memorial that "to dismiss the magnitude of this progress—to suggest, as some sometimes do, that little has changed—that dishonors the courage and the sacrifice of those who paid the price to march in those years. . . . But we would dishonor those heroes as well to suggest that the work of this nation is somehow complete."[59] At the risk of sounding grandiose, I remain convinced that the same is true when it comes to the memories of Jack Trice, Ozzie Simmons, and Johnny Bright. To suggest that their accomplishments, experiences, and misfortunes did not matter, did not make a difference, is no less an affront than the physical assaults they encountered in 1923, 1934, and 1951. Attempts to recognize the men, in any type of commemorative form, is better than allowing their legacies to drift into the ether of neglect. And yet, as we remember, we should not fall victim to utopian visions that posit some post-racist, post-racial society. Rather, the racialized memories of these three men and the injuries and insults they sustained while playing college football best serve contemporary society by reminding us that coming to terms with the past must also include efforts to engage with the present.

NOTES

Introduction

1. Between 1920 and 1950 the total number of African American Iowa residents was fewer than twenty thousand and did not reach 1 percent of the total population until 1970. Goudy, "Selected Demographics," in Silag, *Outside In*, 28.

2. There has been something of a "memory boom" in recent academic history. See, as examples, Halbwachs, *Collective Memory*; Nora, *Rethinking France*; Nora, "Between History and Memory," 7–25; Kline, "Emergence of *Memory*," 127–50; Winter, "Memory Boom," 52–67; Thelen, "Memory and American History," 1117–29; Shackel, *Memory in Black and White*; Kammen, *In the Past Lane*; and Shackel, *Myth, Memory*. Sport studies scholars have also begun to pay significant attention to the concept of memory. See especially Nathan, *Saying It's So*; Wieting, *Sport and Memory*; and Schultz, "Jack Trice Stadium," 715–48.

3. I use the term "racialized memory" for two important reasons. First, I want to distinguish it from "racial memory," particularly as it is used in the study of literature to signify the idea "that individuals can 'remember' events that were not personally experienced because they share an often mystical or genetic connection with first-hand witnesses." Second, I adapt sociologist Eduardo Bonilla-Silva's understanding of the term "racialization" to refer to "societies in which economic, political, social and ideological levels are partially structured by the placement of actors in racial categories or races." In the case of *racialized memory*, I simply mean the process by which historical actors instill racial character on the memories they forge about the past. Su, "Ghosts of Essentialism," 362; and Bonilla-Silva, "Rethinking Racism," 469.

4. Brooks, *When Sorry Isn't Enough*.

5. Williamson, "In Defense of Themselves," 93.

6. Wynn, "Impact of the Second World War," 42–53; and Franklin and Moss, *From Slavery to Freedom*, 363.

7. Henderson, *Negro in Sport*, 6; and Ashe, *Hard Road to Glory*, 1:92.

8. Wiggins, "'Strange Mix,'" 99.

9. Ashe, *Hard Road to Glory*, 2:92.

10. Wallace, "Good Lynching," 94.

11. Roberts, *Papa Jack*, 144.

12. Nevada senator Harry Reid quoted in Jim Litke, "Now Is the Time to Pardon Jack Johnson," *Pittsburgh Post-Gazette*, March 6, 2013, A6.

13. See Roberts, *Papa Jack*; Bederman, *Manliness and Civilization*; and Gilmore, "Jack Johnson," 496–506.

14. See, for example, Henderson, "Negro Women in Sports," 55; Gissendanner, "African-American Women," 81–92; and Cahn, *Coming on Strong*.

15. Ed Nace, "Negro Grid Stars, Past and Present," *Opportunity*, September 1930, 274.

16. Strode and Young, *Goal Dust*, 29. See also Watterson, *College Football*, 308–9.

17. Wiggins, "Prized Performers," 164–77.

18. Stewart, *Negro in America*, 18; Hawkins, *New Plantation*; and Spivey and Jones, "Intercollegiate Athletic Servitude," 939–47.

19. Wiggins, "Prized Performers"; and Spivey and Jones, "Intercollegiate Athletic Servitude."

20. Spivey, "Black Athlete," 117.

21. See, for example, Rampersand, *Jackie Robinson*; Strode and Young, *Goal Dust*; Tunnell, *Footsteps of a Giant*; Walker, *Long Time Coming*; Cahn, *Coming on Strong*; Moore, *All Things Being Equal*; and Edwards, *Revolt of the Black Athlete*, 15.

22. Wendell Smith, "Sports Beat: The Color Line Stops Caroline," *Pittsburgh Courier*, December 12, 1953, 24.

23. Breaux, "Facing Hostility," 14–15; and Jenkins, "Negro Student."

24. Behee, *Hail to the Victors!*, 68.

25. Ashe, *Hard Road to Glory*, 2:92.

26. Dalfiume, "'Forgotten Years,'" 103.

27. Stewart, *Negro in America*, 1.

28. Lamb, *Blackout*, 56.

29. Lamb, *Blackout*, 15.

30. Franklin, "Presidential Race Initiatives," 229.

31. Bonds, "President's Commission," 427, 429.

32. Quoted in Bonds, "Some Recommendations," 382.

33. Myrdal, *An American Dilemma*.

34. Clement, "Racial Integration," 224.

35. Wiggins, "Prized Performers."

36. Grundman, "Image of Intercollegiate Sports," 17–24.

37. Grundman, "Image of Intercollegiate Sports," 18.

38. Henderson, *Negro in Sport*, 121.

39. Quoted in Martin, "Racial Change," 560.

40. Schmidt, *Shaping College Football*, 150.

41. "Yale Threatens to Drop Harvard for Using Negro," *Philadelphia Press*, November 22, 1904, quoted in Schmidt, *Shaping College Football*, 150.

42. "Football," *Time*, October 28, 1934, 46. When New York University announced it would withhold Leonard Bates from the 1940 University of Missouri game, a black alumnus commented that if Bates were to play "it will be the first instance of legal-

ized lynching" of an African American athlete. Quoted in Spivey, "'End Jim Crow in Sports,'" 289.

43. Behee, *Hail to the Victors!*, 29–30.

44. Ashe, *Hard Road to Glory*, 2:94; and Chalk, *Black College Sport*, 193. See also Carroll, "Fritz Pollard," in Ross, *Race and Sport*, 14.

45. *Daily Worker*, October 18, 1939, quoted in Ashe, *Hard Road to Glory*, 2:97. See also Smith, "Outside the Pale," 255–81.

46. William G. Nunn, "Sports Talk," *Pittsburgh Courier*, November 19, 1932, A4.

47. Quoted in Henderson, *Negro in Sport*, 77.

48. Quoted in Henry Beach Needham, "The College Athlete: His Amateur Code: Its Evasion and Administration," *McClure's*, July 1905, 276–77 (emphasis in original).

49. Watterson, *College Football*, 64–79; and Smith, "Harvard and Columbia," 5–19.

50. Rader, *American Sports*, 183.

51. Strode and Young, *Goal Dust*, 152.

52. See, as examples, Gems, *For Pride*; Oriard, *King Football*; Smith, "Outside the Pale"; Carroll, *Fritz Pollard*, 37, 181; and Chalk, *Black College Sport*, 143–65.

53. Behee, *Hail to the Victors!*, 32.

54. Quoted in Carroll, *Fritz Pollard*, 37, 181. On violence and "sluggings" in the early history of college football, see Chalk, *Black College Sport*, 143–65.

55. Quoted in Spivey, "End Jim Crow," 289. An account of intentional assaults on Kenny Washington, the first to desegregate the National Football League (NFL) in 1946, can be found in Rathet and Smith, *Their Deeds*, 213.

56. Joseph C. Nichols, "Unscored-on Duke Tops Syracuse, 21–0," *New York Times*, November 13, 1938, 1. Duke broke its contract forbidding competition against black athletes in this case and gave Syracuse "permission" to use Sidat-Singh in the game. "Sidat-Singh to Face Duke," *New York Times*, October 22, 1938, 11.

57. "Notre Dame Rally Sets Back Illinois," *New York Times*, October 29, 1944, S1.

58. Childers, *In the Deep South*, 63, 5–6.

59. Fishman, "Paul Robeson's Student Days," 221–29. See also Yeakey, "Student without Peer," 491; Duberman, *Paul Robeson*; Robert Van Gelder, "Robeson Remembers," *New York Times*, January 16, 1944; and Berryman, "Early Black Leadership," 17–28.

60. Quoted in Ira Berkow, "A Black Star Long, Long Ago," *New York Times*, November 24, 1990, 39.

61. See Ashe, *Hard Road to Glory*, vol. 2; Behee, *Hail to the Victors!*, 32; McMahon, "Remembering the Black and Gold," in Wieting, *Sport and Memory*, 72; McMahon, "Pride to All," in Silag, *Outside In*, 61–98; Rampersand, *Jackie Robinson*, 70; and Oriard, *King Football*, 299, 305.

62. Matt Trowbridge, "The Man behind Floyd of Rosedale," *Iowa City Press Citizen*, November 25, 1989, 10F.

63. Behee, *Hail to the Victors!*, 92.

64. Smith, "Sports Beat," 24.

65. Carroll, *Fritz Pollard*, 101.

66. Quoted in Harold Parrott, "Daily Scribe Lets 'Cat' out of Bag on Grid Jim Crow," *Chicago Defender*, November 23, 1935, 15.

67. Miller, "Muscular Assimilationism," in Ross, *Race and Sport*, 151.

68. Nunn, "Sports Talk," A4.

69. Pride, "Negro Newspaper," 146; and Detweiler, "Negro Press Today," 399.

70. Ed Harris, "Simmons Inc., Harris Hot," *Philadelphia Tribune*, November 26, 1936, 11.

71. Evelyn Cunningham, "The Women: Baseball Is Bugging 'Em!!" *Pittsburgh Courier*, June 7, 1952, 29.

72. Randy Dixon, "All American Fame Beckons to Sepia Aces," *Philadelphia Tribune*, September 9, 1937, 11.

73. Miller, "Muscular Assimilationism," 146–82.

74. *The Crisis*, August 1935, 241.

75. Henderson, *Negro in Sport*, 123.

76. Rader, *American Sports*, 190.

77. Quoted in Grady, "Hawkeyes," in Dukes and Schrader, *Greatest Moments*, 13.

78. Maury White, "100 Years of Black Athletes in Iowa," *Des Moines Register*, September 3, 1995, 13D. See also Bergmann, *Negro in Iowa*, 82, 88; Bender, *Iowa Sports Heroes*, 31; Dahl, *In Celebration of a Century*, 73; and Steward, *Cyclone Memories*.

79. Chase, "'You Live What You Learn,'" in Silag, *Outside In*, 135.

80. Schwieder, "Life and Legacy of Jack Trice," 379–417. See also Johnson, "Ku Klux Klan in Iowa."

81. Rozendaal, *Duke Slater*, 7; and McMahon, "Remembering the Black and Gold," in Wieting, *Sport and Memory*, 77.

82. Willis Ward quoted in Behee, *Hail to the Victors!*, 68.

83. Butler, *Memory*, 16. See also Connerton, "Seven Types of Forgetting," 59–71.

1. Resurrecting Jack Trice

1. Quoted in L. A. Fung, "ISU Pays a Belated Tribute to Jack Trice," *Iowa State Daily*, November 5, 1984, 1.

2. Kuhn, "Memory Texts," 298 (emphasis in original).

3. White's work draws on Frye's *Anatomy of Criticism* in which he asserts that there are four "pre-generic" skeletal plots and narrative elements, or "mythoi," upon which all literature, including romance, satire, tragedy, and comedy, is built.

4. Burke, *What Is Cultural History?*, 125.

5. White, *Metahistory*, 8.

6. White, *Metahistory*, 9.

7. Gaylord Bates to Hiram Township (Ohio) Historical Society, Records, October 16, 1956, in Jack Trice Papers, Special Collections and University Archives, Parks Library, Iowa State University, Ames (hereafter Jack Trice Papers).

8. Gaylord Bates to Hiram Township (Ohio) Historical Society, Records, October 16, 1956, Jack Trice Papers.

9. Dorothy Schwieder contends that a photo of Trice's East Technical football team shows two African American athletes. See her "Life and Legacy of Jack Trice," 382.

10. "Iowa State Mourns Death of Trice, Football Fighter," *Iowa State Student*, October 10 1923, 3.

11. Hal Lebovitz, "Who Was Jack Trice?" *Cleveland Plain Dealer*, June 3, 1979, sec. 3, p. 2. See Ashe, *Hard Road to Glory*, vol. 2; Carroll, *Fritz Pollard*; Gems, *For Pride*; Edwin Bancroft Henderson, "The Negro Athlete and Race Prejudice," *Opportunity*, March 1936, 77–79; Henderson, *Negro in Sport*; Henderson, *Black Athlete*; Martin, "Color Line," 85–112; Oriard, *King Football*; Wiggins, "Prized Performers," 164–77; and Yeakey, "Student without Peer," 489–503.

12. The legislature of the state of Iowa established the Iowa State College of Agriculture and Mechanic Arts in 1858. In 1959 it became the Iowa State University of Science and Technology or, more commonly, Iowa State University (ISU). For consistency, I will refer to the school throughout this book as Iowa State University or ISU.

13. Willis Goudy, "Total Population for Iowa's Incorporated Places: 1850–2010," State Library of Iowa, State Data Center Program, 1988, http://www.iowadatacenter.org.

14. Tischauser, *Race Relations*, 5.

15. Pride, "Negro Newspaper," 145.

16. Quoted in Charles Bullard, "Trice Best Person to Name Stadium After, Says Ex-Classmate," *Des Moines Register*, June 4, 1976, Jack Trice Papers. This number was indicative of national trends. In 1920 African American students earned 396 bachelor's degrees, and 118 (about 30 percent) of them were from northern, integrated colleges. By 1925 that number had grown to 832, though just 224 (27 percent) of those black students graduated from PWCUs. See Aptheker, "Negro College Student," 152.

17. See, for example, "Jack Trice Has Finished His Fight," *The Alumnus (Iowa State College)*, October 18, 1923, 6.

18. The enduring narrative is that Jack Trice married Cora Mae Starland in 1923. However, someone who researched the story uncovered a copy of the Trices' marriage certificate and sent it to Charles Sohn, a former Iowa State professor and longtime champion of the Trice Stadium cause. The document lists their date of marriage as July 27, 1922, or the summer before Trice's first year at Iowa State. Charles Sohn, personal correspondence, October 1, 2013.

19. "Football Card Opens on State Field Saturday," *Iowa State Student*, September 26, 1923, 1.

20. "Cyclones Play Opening Game with Minnesota," *Iowa State Student*, October 3, 1923, 1, 6.

21. Harry Schmidt, interview by Bill Walsh, December 4, 1972, transcript, Jack Trice Papers.

22. Ashe, *Hard Road to Glory*, 2:94; and Wiggins, "Prized Performers," 169.

23. "Gophers Boast of Heavy Line on Grid Team," *Iowa State Student*, October 3, 1923, 1.

24. "Memories of Trice Don't Fade," *Iowa State Daily*, November 8, 1976, 4, 9.

25. Cora Mae Trice to David Lendt, August 3, 1988, Jack Trice Papers. The Department of Hygiene issued a statement concerning Jack Trice's official cause of death: "Traumatic Peritonitis, following injury to abdomen in football game, October 6,

1923. (Autopsy showed severe contusion of intestines upper portion of abdomen. This causes stasis or paralysis of intestines followed by peritonitis)." The statement, from October 16, 1923, is in the Jack Trice Papers.

26. "Jack Trice's Creed," *Pittsburgh Courier*, October 27, 1928, 6.

27. "Jack Trice Wrote Creed on Eve of Death from Injuries," *New York Age*, October 20, 1923, 2.

28. "Iowa State Students Revere Memory of Football Player," *Iowa State Student*, October 10, 1923, 1.

29. "Contributions Swell Jack Trice Fund," *Iowa State Student*, October 10, 1923, 1.

30. "Death Claims Football Player," *New York Amsterdam News*, October 12, 1923, 4.

31. See, for example, Tom S. Emmerson, "Jack Trice: Victor on the Fatal Field," *Iowa State Scientist*, November 7, 1957, 20.

32. C. A. W., "Trice," 102; and "Minnesota Writer, 'C.A.W.' Pens Beautiful Poem on Trice," *Iowa State Student*, October 15, 1923, 1. David K. Wiggins and Patrick B. Miller maintain that newspaper verse was widely popular through the interwar years. See their *Unlevel Playing Field*, 175.

33. Jones, *Football's Fallen Hero*; and Emmerson, "Jack Trice," 19–20.

34. "Death Scores a Touchdown," *Minnesota Alumni Weekly*, October 18, 1923, 64.

35. From the *Seattle Post-Intelligencer*, quoted in Emmerson, "Jack Trice," 19.

36. William Thompson, interview by Gary Stowe, July 29, 1974, transcript, Jack Trice Papers.

37. L. D. Coffman to R. A. Pearson, October 18, 1923, Jack Trice Papers.

38. See, for example, "Jack Trice Dies from Injuries; Hurt Saturday," *Iowa State Student*, October 8, 1923, 1; and Albert S. Tousley, "His Last Game Is Played," *Minnesota Daily*, October 9, 1923, 2.

39. John L. Griffith to S. W. Beyer, October 9, 1923, Jack Trice Papers.

40. S. W. Beyer to John L. Griffith, October 24, 1923, Jack Trice Papers.

41. "Football Claimed 18 Victims in 1923," *New York Times*, December 2, 1923, S1.

42. Harrison, *Colored Girls and Boys' Inspiring*, 203.

43. A number of sources identify Mitchell as the "father of intramurals," including Erin Rothwell and Philip Theodore in "Intramurals and College Student Development," 46–52.

44. Mitchell, "Racial Traits in Athletics," 93–99.

45. *Iowa State Student*, November 26, 1923, Jack Trice Papers.

46. John McCormick, "Once upon a Time in Iowa," *Newsweek*, September 17, 1984, 12–13.

47. Emmerson, "Jack Trice," 19–20; and Tom Emmerson, interview by author, July 15, 2004, tape recording, Ames IA.

48. Williamson, "In Defense of Themselves," 94; and Urban Research Corporation, *Student Protests, 1969*.

49. Williamson, "In Defense of Themselves," 95.

50. Brown and Brown, "Moo U," in Gilbert, *Vietnam War on Campus*, 121; and Wells, *War Within*, 425.

51. *The Bomb* 78 (1971): 42.

52. Brown and Brown, "Moo U," 135.

53. Brown and Brown, "Moo U," 132.

54. Steven Sullivan, "Home Improvement: BCC Repairs Restore House, Spirits," *Iowa Stater*, February 1997, http://www.iastate.edu/IaStater/1997/sept/bcc .html (accessed January 20, 2004).

55. Quoted in Schwieder, "Life and Legacy of Jack Trice," 402.

56. In 1963 President Parks established a committee designed to advise the university's administration on "problems arising from injustices based on race, creed, or color prejudice." He also established a controversial pilot program in 1968 to increase minority enrollment by lowering ISU's admission requirements for targeted individuals from disadvantaged geographical locations. In a later effort to increase the number of minority students, Parks established the position of director of minority affairs at Iowa State and hired William Bell, a physical education professor, coach, and athletic director from North Carolina A&T College at Greensboro, to fill the new position. In Underhill, *Alone among Friends*, 157.

57. Quoted in Underhill, *Alone among Friends*, 158.

58. It was a complicated chain of events, including an incident in which a handcuffed Roby, with the assistance of "a group of more than a dozen blacks," escaped the police. Ten hours later, Roby surrendered to police. Jerry Dickinson, "Student Sought after Escaping Arrest," *Ames Daily Tribune*, April 15, 1970, 1; and Nick Lamberto, "I.S.U. Student Surrenders," *Des Moines Register*, April 16, 1970, 8.

59. "Right On!" *Iowa State Daily*, April 10, 1970, Jack Trice Papers; Jim Healey, "Athletes under Fire," *Iowa State Daily*, April 10, 1970, Jack Trice Papers; and Nick Lamberto, "Some I.S.U. Blacks, Wrestlers Clash," *Des Moines Register*, April 10, 1970, Jack Trice Papers.

60. Quoted in Jim Healey, "BSO Head: Bomb a 'Hoax'; Judge a 'Racist,'" *Iowa State Daily*, April 29, 1970, Jack Trice Papers.

61. Ray Greene, letter to the editor, *Iowa State Daily*, April 30, 1970, Jack Trice Papers.

62. Quoted in "ISU Administrator Injured during Confrontation," *Ames Daily Tribune*, May 17, 1974, Jack Trice Papers; and "ISU Blacks Say Ames Like South 10 Years Ago," *Ames Daily Tribune*, May 18, 1974, Jack Trice Papers.

63. Quoted in Swan, "From Vietnam to Don Smith," 60.

64. William Kunerth, interview by author, July 19, 2004, tape recording, Belle Fourche SD.

65. Jim Smith, "Rusted Fading Plaque Last Jack Trice Remembrance," *Iowa State Daily*, February 7, 1974, Jack Trice Papers; Jack Trice Memorial Foundation, Jack Trice Scrapbook (1974), Jack Trice Papers; and Gus Schrader, Red Peppers, *Cedar Rapids Gazette*, June 6, 1972, cited in Rozendaal, *Duke Slater*, 181.

66. Jim Smith and Alan Beals, "Trice: A Forgotten Story Remembered," *Iowa State Daily*, October 5, 1973, Jack Trice Papers.

67. Charles Sohn, email message to author, August 16, 2004.

68. Charles Sohn, email message to author, August 16, 2004. In 1975 the Jack Trice Memorial Stadium Committee disbanded, but the group was reformed in 1976 under the title of the Jack Trice Memorial Foundation.

69. Buttons in Jack Trice Papers.

70. Supporters of the Trice campaign were disappointed, however, when the banners were not televised and outraged when an ABC correspondent repeatedly referred to the venue as the "new Cyclone Stadium." "Contest: Let's Banner Together," *Iowa State Daily*, October 15, 1975, Jack Trice Papers.

71. Gerry Forge, "'Jack Trice Stadium' Proposed by Students," *Iowa State Daily*, February 6, 1974, Jack Trice Papers.

72. Smith, "Rusted Fading Plaque."

73. Quoted in "Want Field Named Trice: ISU Black Died after Game," *Des Moines Register*, June 1, 1974, Jack Trice Papers.

74. "Want Field Named Trice."

75. "How about Jack Trice?" *Iowa State Daily*, May 10, 1974, Jack Trice Papers.

76. Chuck Offenburger, "Name for ISU Stadium Something to Rave About," *Des Moines Register*, March 4, 1978, Jack Trice Papers. The following year student support for naming the stadium after Trice on the GSB-sponsored referendum question remained high, scoring nearly twice as many votes as the second-place choice of Cyclone Stadium. "GSB Calls Football Stadium 'Jack Trice' Unofficially," *Iowa State Daily*, October 20, 1978, Jack Trice Papers.

77. Joni Hass, "Poll: Students Oppose Plus-Minus, Favor Trice," *Iowa State Daily*, November 13, 1975, 1, 15.

78. "Editorial: Clean It Up," *Iowa State Daily*, September 1, 1981, News clippings, 1977–82, Jack Trice Papers.

79. Jerry Dickinson, "Parks Doesn't Know What to Do about Stadium Name Controversy," *Ames Daily Times*, May 17, 1976, Jack Trice Papers.

80. W. Robert Parks, "Ad Hoc Advisory Representatives on the Naming of the Stadium," March 12, 1976, Jack Trice Papers.

81. "ISU Committee Recommends 'Cyclone Stadium,'" Iowa State University Press Release, May 7, 1976, Jack Trice Papers.

82. See, for example, Edna Y. Clinton, letter to the editor, *Iowa State Daily*, June 24, 1976, Jack Trice Papers.

83. See Rozendaal, *Duke Slater*, 178–83; and Wine, *Black and Gold Memories*.

84. Schrader, Red Peppers, in Rozendaal, *Duke Slater*, 181.

85. White, "Legend of Jack Trice," 49.

86. Frederick McConico, "Urges 'Jack Trice Stadium,'" *Iowa State Daily*, October 9, 1974, Jack Trice Papers.

87. Merl Ross quoted in Jeff Burkhead, "A Day to Remember Jack Trice," *Ames Daily Times*, September 15, 1989, Jack Trice Papers.

88. Donald Kaul, Over the Coffee, *Des Moines Register*, September 17, 1975, Jack Trice Papers; and Donald Kaul, "Let's Just Call It Trice Field," *Des Moines Register*, September 28, 1975, Jack Trice Papers. Harry Schmidt, Trice's teammate, called the "stomping" charge "totally untrue." See Buck Turnbull, "Recalls the Courage, Talent of Jack Trice," *Des Moines Register*, October 31, 1975, Sports 1, 14.

89. Chuck Offenburger, "Iowa Boy," *Des Moines Register*, March 26, 1981, Jack Trice Papers.

90. Ashe, *Hard Road to Glory*, 1:93; and Whittingham, *Rites of Autumn*, 198.

91. "How about Jack Trice?"; and Tom Hansen, "Point of View: Give Jack a Chance," *Iowa State Daily*, September 8, 1977, Jack Trice Papers. See also Rose Marie King, "Trice Kin Finds Name Well-Known," *Iowa State Daily*, September 15, 1978, Jack Trice Papers.

92. This account of the narrative is widely retold. See, for example, Donald Kaul, Over the Coffee, *Des Moines Register*, October 16, 1981, 15A; King, "Trice Kin"; Patrick Koffman, "Jack Trice: ISU's Unsung Hero Remembered," *Iowa State Daily*, October 20, 1983, Jack Trice Papers; Schrader, Red Peppers, in Rozendaal, *Duke Slater*; "Want Field Named Trice"; and Scott Dominiak, "The Honor of My Race, Family, and Self Is at Stake," *College Football Historical Society Newsletter*, February 1990, 12–13.

93. I have been unable to determine whether Trice played these teams as a member of the freshmen football team or track and field team. Over the years others have picked up on the idea that ISU benched him. For instance, in writing on the 1923 season with "Death of a Racial Pioneer," *The Journal of Blacks in Higher Education* reported, "Some of Iowa State's opponents that year objected to playing against a team with a black player. As a result, Trice sat out the team's first scheduled game" (43).

94. Harry Schmidt, interview by Bill Walsh, December 4, 1972, transcript, Jack Trice Papers.

95. Thompson, interview by Stowe.

96. Michael Keller, letter to the editor, *Iowa State Daily*, October 5, 1983; and "The Story of the Man Who Did 'Big Things,'" *Iowa State Daily*, October 2, 1975, Jack Trice Papers.

97. Bob Dolgan, "Big Man, Large Legacy," *Cleveland Plain Dealer*, October 13, 1997, Jack Trice Papers.

98. Behee, *Hail to the Victors!*, 68.

99. Behee, *Hail to the Victors!*, 68.

100. See Spangler, *Negro in Minnesota*, 92, 152, 155; and Delton, "Labor, Politics," 419–34.

101. White, *Content of Form*, 24.

102. Irwin-Zarecka, *Frames of Remembrance*, 18. The official stance against naming the stadium for Trice was that the structure should reflect the entire athletic program, not just one individual. Gary Richards, "Trice and Others Considered as Possible Stadium Names," *Iowa State Daily*, February 19, 1974, Jack Trice Papers.

103. Quoted in "Trice Stadium Would Be 'Suitable,' Ray Says," undated clipping, News clippings, 1977–82, Jack Trice Papers.

104. In 1928 the Missouri Valley Intercollegiate Athletic Association split into two factions—the Big 6, which included Iowa State, Kansas State, and the Universities of Oklahoma, Missouri, Kansas, and Nebraska; and the Missouri Valley Conference, which comprised Drake University, Grinnell College, Washington University, and Oklahoma A&M.

105. Quoted in "Denies Big Six Has Bias Clause," *Philadelphia Tribune*, November 29, 1947, 11. It was not until 1960 that every school in the conference fielded integrated teams.

106. As historian Samuel Zebulon Baker reasons, "Why recruit black athletes if they couldn't play in every game or in every venue?" See Baker, *Fields of Contest*, 43. It was not

until 1952, when Al Stevenson and Hank Philmon joined the Iowa State football team, that any conference member fielded a black athlete. Stevenson did not return for the 1953 season. Philmon went on to a stellar career with the Cyclones. A second African American player, Harold R. E. Potts, joined Philmon in 1954. In 1956 John Crawford joined the Iowa State basketball team, making him the first black conference player in the sport.

107. Kunerth, interview by author.

108. Emmerson, interview by author.

109. Quoted in Jane Zajec, "Billboard Touts 'Trice' as Name of Stadium," *Iowa State Daily*, August 27, 1981, 3; and Kevin Boone, "The Trice Issue: Dead or Sleeping?" *Iowa State Daily*, March 21, 1979, Jack Trice Papers.

110. "Banner 'Christens' No-Name Stadium," *Iowa State Daily*, October 29, 1980, News clippings, 1977–82, Jack Trice Papers.

111. Susan Caslin, "KRNT Balks at GSB Radio Ad," *Iowa State Daily*, December 2, 1980, Jack Trice Papers.

112. Zajec, "Billboard Touts 'Trice,'" 3.

113. Cecelia M. Comito, "Trice Honored at Game with Moment of Silence," *Iowa State Daily*, October 11, 1983, Jack Trice Papers.

114. Cecelia M. Comito, "Administration Nixes Trice Tribute," *Iowa State Daily*, October 5, 1983, 1, 13; and Barbara Musfeldt, "ISU Intercepts Halftime Honor for Gridder Trice," *Des Moines Register*, October 4, 1983, Jack Trice Papers.

115. Comito, "Trice Honored at Game."

116. Donald Kaul, *Jack Trice Field Dedication*, sound recording 001 734 (audiocassette), 1984, Special Collections and University Archives, Parks Library, Iowa State University, Ames.

117. McCormick, "Once upon a Time," 12–13.

118. Melinda Mooty, "Trice Statue in Place for Veisha," *Iowa State Daily*, April 22, 1988, Jack Trice Papers.

119. Finn Bullers, "Jack Trice Finally Gets a Campus Statue," *Ames Dispatch Tribune*, May 9, 1988, Jack Trice Papers. There was also a $600 Jack Trice Memorial Scholarship created at this time.

120. "Art on Campus Information: Jack Trice Stadium," December 20, 2004, www.museums.iastate.edu/AOCFactSheetsPDF/jacktrice.pdf (accessed January 20, 2004).

121. David Speer, "Making Jack Trice Larger than Life," *Ames Daily Times*, April 1, 1988, Jack Trice Papers.

122. "Statue Commemorates Jack Trice Legacy to ISU," undated clipping, News clippings, Jack Trice Papers.

123. Quoted in Susan Oberlander, "Iowa State U. Honors Its First Black Athlete, Ending Long Controversy," *Chronicle of Higher Education*, June 22, 1988, A29–30.

124. Lou Ransom, "White University Rights 65-Year Wrong Done to Black Athlete," *Jet*, May 30, 1988, 49–52.

125. "Death Scores a Touchdown."

126. Jack Hovelson, "Stadium Compromise Disappoints Trice Backers," *Des Moines Register*, December 16, 1983, Jack Trice Papers.

2. Commemorative Balancing Act

1. Farwell T. Brown, "Closing Chapter in the Jack Trice Story," *Ames Intelligencer*, Spring 1987, 1.

2. Dolgan, "Big Man, Large Legacy," D1.

3. Hodgkin and Radstone, *Contested Pasts*, 11.

4. Bodnar, *Remaking America*.

5. Adam Gold, interview by author, August 31, 2004, tape recording, Iowa City.

6. "ISU President to Recommend Making It Jack Trice Stadium," *Omaha World Herald*, February 4, 1997, 21.

7. Tim Frerking, "Jack Trice Plays On," *Iowa State Daily*, February 4, 1997, 1.

8. Schwartz, "Social Context of Commemoration," 395.

9. Gold, interview by author.

10. Fowler, *Carrie Catt*.

11. Catt had no affiliation with the Old Botany building, but "it was the only major building without a namesake and was architecturally interesting." Iowa State University, Government of the Student Body, (Carrie Chapman) Catt Hall Review Committee Records, RS 22/1/8, Special Collections and University Archives, Iowa State University Library.

12. "The Catt Is out of the Bag: Was She Racist?" *uhuru!*, September 29, 1995, 1.

13. See, for example, Thomas R. O'Donnell, "Protesters: Rename Catt Building," *Des Moines Register*, March 7, 1996, M2.

14. Quoted in Sara Ziegler, "Protest against Catt Hall Continues in Full Force," *Iowa State Daily*, September 10, 1997, 1–2.

15. Quoted in Loewen, *Lies across America*, 41. The September 29th Movement summarized many of Catt's writings, especially those containing prejudicial remarks, in September 29th Movement Records, RS 22/3/3, Special Collections and University Archives, Parks Library, Iowa State University, Ames. See also Cohen, "Nationalism and Suffrage," 712, 721–22.

16. See Meron Wondwosen, "White Woman's Burden: Carrie Chapman Catt and Racism within the Suffrage Movement," *uhuru!*, August 1996, 1–7.

17. Amanda Fier, "Another Catt Letter Circulated," *Iowa State Daily*, October 9, 1996, 2.

18. Amy Houser, "Media Blitz for Catt?" *Iowa State Daily*, September 29, 1996, 1; and Troy McCullough and Jennifer Holland, "Controversy Gains Momentum," *Iowa State Daily*, April 12, 1996, 1–2.

19. See, for example, Van Voris, *Carrie Chapman Catt*, 201.

20. Fowler, *Carrie Catt*, 83–90. See also Amidon, "Carrie Chapman Catt," 305–28; Davis, *Women, Race and Class*, 122; Giddings, *When and Where I Enter*; Catt and Shuler, *Woman Suffrage and Politics*; Finnegan, *Selling Suffrage*; Graham, *Woman Suffrage*; and Cott, *Grounding of Modern Feminism*.

21. Quoted in "Suffragette's Racial Remark Haunts College," *New York Times*, May 5, 1996, 30.

22. Milton McGriff, "An Open Letter to President Jischke," *UHURU!*, September 9, 1996, 8.

23. Milton McGriff, "In My View," *Iowa State Daily*, October 24, 1996, 7.

24. Derrick Rollins, "Rename Catt Hall," *Iowa State Daily*, September 15, 1996, 1; and Arianna Layton, "Catt Protest Continues," *Iowa State Daily*, September 8, 1997, 1–2. See also Tim Frerking, "Jischke: Catt Agreement May Never Be Possible," *Iowa State Daily*, September 9, 1996, 1–2; and Diane Heldt, "Student Idea: Recognize Catt's Racism," *Ames Daily Times*, April 5, 1996, A1.

25. Wallace and Bell, "Being Black," 307–27.

26. Wallace and Bell, "Being Black," 307.

27. Alice Lukens, "Catt Hall Dispute Is about More than the Building," *Ames Daily Times*, April 13, 1996, A1, A7; and Sara Ziegler, "September 29th Movement Tells Regents Call Hall Case Is Being 'Ignored,'" *Iowa State Daily*, June 17, 1998, 1. See also Underhill, *Alone among Friends*, 149–72; and Swan, "From Vietnam to Don Smith."

28. Lukens, "Call Hall Dispute," 320.

29. Dobbs, "Strategic Focus and Accountability," in Schwieder and van Houten, *Sesquicentennial History*, 135.

30. "News and Views," 73.

31. Quoted in Lukens, "Catt Hall Dispute," A7.

32. Derrick Rollins quoted in Amanda Fier, "Catt Debate Heats Up with Memo," *Iowa State Daily*, September 19, 1996, 1.

33. Tracy Lucht, "Minority Leaders: 'We're Being Silenced,'" *Iowa State Daily*, February 3, 1997, 1.

34. See Sigelman and Welch, *Black American's Views.*

35. Thurgood Marshall, "We Must Dissent," in Smith, *Supreme Justice*, 313.

36. Quoted in Kim, "Managing the Racial Breach," 77.

37. Fuller, "Debating the Present," in Romano and Raiford, *Civil Rights Movement*, 167–96.

38. Mashon, "Losing Control," 12.

39. PBS, "Riot Results," *NewsHour: Online Focus*, April 28, 1997, http://www.pbs.org/newshour/bb/social_issues-jan-june97-riot_4-28/ (accessed December 21, 2004).

40. Enomoto, "Public Sympathy," 245–46.

41. R. Price and J. T. Lovitt, "Poll: More Now Believe O. J. Is Guilty," *USA Today*, October 4, 1996, A3.

42. David R. Carlin Jr., "Why Farrakhan Repels," *Commonweal*, November 17, 1995, 7.

43. Tucker, "Black, White, and Read All Over," 316–17.

44. See Lusane, *Race in the Global Era*, 55–68.

45. See, as examples, Bill Maxwell, "We Can't Look at Nation's Past in Today's Mirror," *Rocky Mountain Times* (Denver CO), August 13, 1995, accessed September 9, 2006, from the LexisNexis database; and Lederman, "Old Times Not Forgotten," in Eitzen, *Sport in Contemporary Society*, 115–20.

46. Kevin Sack, "Symbols of Old South Feed a New Bitterness," *New York Times*, February 8, 1997, 1.

47. Herrnstein and Murray, *Bell Curve*.

48. Vera, Feagin, and Gordon, "Superior Intellect?," 295.

49. Rainbow Rowell, "ISU Weighs New Tribute to Tragic Football Hero," *Omaha World Herald*, February 19, 1997, 1.

50. Keesia Wirt, Rhaason Mitchell, and Tara Deering, "University Reaction Is One of Concern," *Iowa State Daily*, September 23, 1997, 4; and Luke Dekoster, "Two Groups Begin 24-Hour Hunger Strike Today," *Iowa State Daily*, September 30, 1997, Jack Trice Papers.

51. Tracy Lucht, "University Charges 20 from Last Week's Protest," *Iowa State Daily*, November 13, 1996, 1–2.

52. Kunerth, interview by author.

53. Quoted in "Faculty Members Join in Protest," *Iowa State Daily*, January 31, 1997, 2.

54. Iowa State University, "Plaza of Heroines," http://www.Ias.iastate.edu /archive/plaza.

55. Tim Frerking, "Two More Asking University to Remove Catt Hall Bricks," *Iowa State Daily*, September 25, 1996, 1–2.

56. Heather Wiese, "New Bricks to Be Placed in Plaza," *Iowa State Daily*, April 12, 1996.

57. Phyllis Harris quoted in Jenny Hykes, "Two Women Cover Their Bricks," *Iowa State Daily*, April 17, 1996, Jack Trice Papers.

58. Matthew T. Seifert, "Investigation Sought in Name Uncoverings," *Iowa State Daily*, July 2, 1996, 1–2.

59. Kristin Kernen and Matthew T. Seifert, "University to Remove Bricks," *Iowa State Daily*, July 25, 1996, 1–2.

60. Thomas R. O'Donnell, "Bid to Rename ISU's Catt Hall Is Quashed," *Des Moines Register*, March 28, 1996, M8.

61. "Catt Hall Sparks Controversy," *The Iowa Stater*, February 1997, http://www .ur.iastate.edu/IaStater/1997/feb/catt.html (accessed January 21, 2005).

62. Ziegler, "September 29th Movement," 1, 12.

63. Carrie Tett, "GSB Votes to Lay Catt Hall Issue to Rest," *Iowa State Daily*, March 3, 1998, 1, 16.

64. Committee for the Review of the Catt Controversy, *Official Report*, Special Collections and University Archives, Parks Library, Iowa State University, Ames.

65. Committee for the Review of the Catt Controversy, "Committee Statement," *Official Report*, Special Collections and University Archives, Parks Library, Iowa State University, Ames.

66. An ISU brochure titled "Catt Hall and the Plaza of the Heroins [*sic*]" mentions, "The Plaza of Heroines has not escaped controversy, however. After members of the Iowa State community disputed the renaming of Old Botany Hall to Catt Hall, a small group of donors who purchased bricks in the Plaza covered the names of their heroine in protest." There is no explanation about the controversy and why donors covered their bricks. Available at https://bjfeltes.files.wordpress .com/2012/11/catt-hall-brocheur.pdf.

67. Kaul, *Jack Trice Field Dedication*, sound recording.

68. Martin Jischke, "Remarks: Jack Trice Stadium Dedication," Iowa State University, Ames, August 30, 1997, Jack Trice Papers.

69. Jischke's speech at the dedication for Jack Trice Stadium was reprinted in "Honor Trice's Sacrifice, Inspiration," *Des Moines Register*, September 6, 1997, 9A.

70. Theresa Wilson, "Beardshear Eight Needs a Lesson in Civil Disobedience," *Iowa State Daily*, February 13, 1997. Catt Hall in the Carrie Chapman Catt Papers, S 21/7/3, Special Collections and University Archives, Parks Library, Iowa State University, Ames.

71. Tara Deering, "One for the Books," *Iowa State Daily*, September 2, 1997, 2.

72. Rowell, "ISU Weighs New Tribute," 1.

73. Iowa State University, "Jack Trice Sculpture Finished on East Concourse," October 16, 2009, http://www.cyclones.com/ViewArticle.dbml?DB_OEM_ID=10700&ATCLID=204814735.

74. See Joshua Kagavi, "Jack Trice's Jersey Number Mystery Solved," kagavi.com, http://www.kagavi.com/jack-trices-jersey-number-mystery-solved/.

75. Jamie Pollard email to Tom Emmerson, July 15, 2013.

76. "Football: Jack Trice Era Throwback Uniform Announcement," Cyclones TV, Iowa State University, August 2013, http://www.cyclones.com/mediaPortal/player.dbml?db_oem_id=10700&id=2826905&catid=1006.

77. Quoted in Dan Greenspan, "Iowa State Will Wear Throwback Jerseys to Honor Jack Trice," College Football 24/7, nfl.com, August 6, 2013, http://www.nfl.com/news/story/0ap1000000227083/article/iowa-state-will-wear-throwback-jerseys-to-honor-jack-trice.

78. Randy Peterson, "Portrayal of Jack Trice Challenged Des Moines-Based Actor," *Des Moines Register*, August 10, 2013, http://archive.indystar.com/article/D2/20130810/SPORTS020602/308100062/Portrayal-Jack-Trice-challenged-Des-Moines-based-actor.

79. Emmerson, "Jack Trice," 19–20.

80. Jones, *Football's Fallen Hero*; and Emmerson, "Jack Trice," 19–20.

81. Zaslow, *Girls from Ames*, 85.

82. Iowa State University, "Jack Trice Sculpture Finished."

83. King and Springwood, *Beyond the Cheers*, 18.

3. A Tale of Two Governors

1. Steve Harvey, "Floyd the Pig and Gertie the Goose: Trophies or Booby Prizes?" *Los Angeles Times*, December 14, 1990, 11.

2. "Iowa Football: Iowa Hawkeye Traditions," Hawkeye Sports, http://hawkeyesports.collegesports.com/sports/m-footbl/stats/061004aac.html (accessed April 23, 2013). For additional examples, see Carpenter and Lyon, *Between Two Rivers*, 183–84; and "Iowa Swings to G.O.P. (Grab onto the Pig)," *Chicago Daily Tribune*, November 8, 1962, D2.

3. See Connerton, "Seven Types of Forgetting," 59–71.

4. Oriard, *King Football*, 303.

5. Ches Washington, "Ches Recalls Our Golden Sports Era," *Pittsburgh Courier*, September 17, 1960, A17.

6. Baker, *Jesse Owens*.

7. Wiggins, "Prized Performers," 169.

8. Ashe, *Hard Road to Glory*, 2:94.

9. Miller, "Slouching toward a New Expediency," 7.

10. Martin, "Color Line," 100.

11. Other schools included Ohio State, Cincinnati, Indiana, and Michigan. Martin, *Benching Jim Crow*, 30. See also Oriard, *King Football*, 301–2.

12. Wolters, *New Negro on Campus*, 113–14. See also Levine, *American College*, 159; and Miller, "Slouching toward a New Expediency."

13. Trowbridge, "Man behind Floyd of Rosedale," 10F.

14. "Simmons Heads Race Stars in White Colleges," *Pittsburgh Courier*, October 3, 1936, A5.

15. Quoted in "English Go 'Off Their Nut' in Praising Owens and Mates on Olympic Squad," *Philadelphia Tribune*, August 27, 1936, 10.

16. "Black Auxiliaries," *Crisis*, September 1936, 273.

17. Howard, *Lynchings*. Stuart E. Tolnay and E. M. Beck speculate that the upsurge was due to frustrations from the economic depression in *A Festival of Violence*. See also Zangrando, NAACP *Crusade*; and Shay, *Judge Lynch*.

18. "Can the States Stop Lynching?" *Crisis*, January 1936, 6–7, 18.

19. Ashe, *Hard Road to Glory*, 2:95.

20. Throughout his career journalists saddled Ozzie Simmons with an exhaustive supply of nicknames. They included the Black Bullet, the Hula-Hipped Hawkeye, the Hula-Hipped Hide Handler, the Sepia Sprite, the Wizard of Oz, the Dancing Dervish, the Ebony Express, Joe Louis of the Gridiron, Dusky Demon, Galloping Ghost, and the Texas Tornado, to name a few. See, for example, F. M. Davis, "Davis Says It Looks Bad for Oze Simmons," *Philadelphia Tribune*, October 15, 1936, 12; "Cornhuskers to Aid Ozzie against Minn.," *Chicago Defender*, November 9, 1935, 1; and "As Iowa's 'Texas Tornado' Withered Northwestern," *Pittsburgh Courier*, October 13, 1934, A5.

21. "Simmons Holds Sprint Record, That's Why He's Poison on Touchdowns," *Baltimore Afro-American*, November 30, 1935, 19.

22. *Pittsburgh Courier*, February 15, 1936, quoted in Ashe, *Hard Road to Glory*, 2:94–95.

23. Al Monroe, "Speaking of Sports," *Chicago Defender*, November 10, 1934, 16.

24. Trowbridge, "Man behind Floyd of Rosedale."

25. Monroe, "Speaking of Sports." An obituary for Simmons stated that a "white man he didn't know encouraged" Simmons to play at Iowa. See Letitia Stein, "Ozzie Simmons, 87: Early Black All-American Football Player," *Chicago Tribune*, October 4, 2001, 2C. Throughout his life journalists alternately spelled his name "Ozzie" and "Oze." According to his widow he preferred "Ozzie," and that spelling appeared on his death certificate. Eutopia Morsell-Simmons, phone interview by author, September 1, 2003, Iowa City.

26. Jack Gurwell, "Don and Ozzie Simmons, Two Brothers Hailing from Texas," *Daily Iowan*, August 12, 1934, S1.

27. Trowbridge, "Man behind Floyd of Rosedale."

28. See Petersen, *Slater of Iowa*; and Rozendaal, *Duke Slater*. Other Iowa black footballers in the pre-Simmons era include Ledrue Galloway, Arlington Daniels, Harold Bradley, and Wendell Benjamin.

29. Art Snider, "Oze Simmons Dances Way down Gridiron Past Opposing Tacklers to Football Fame," *The Daily Iowan*, August 2, 1935, 6. The *New York Times* similarly reported that when Solem asked what he could do for the team, Ozzie Simmons replied, "I kin fetch them touchdowns." See Allison Danzig, "On College Gridirons," *New York Times*, October 11, 1945, 30.

30. Boskin, *Sambo*, 169.

31. Oriard, *King Football*, 299.

32. Dick Bolin, phone interview by author, January 18, 2003, Iowa City.

33. Dick Bolin, phone interview by author, January 18, 2003, Iowa City.

34. Gurwell, "Don and Ozzie Simmons," S1.

35. Papas, *Gophers Illustrated*, 66.

36. Iowa ruled eleven of the athletes in question ineligible and apparently placated the conference enough for reinstatement. See Schmidt, "1929 Iowa Football Scandal," 343–51.

37. Monroe, "Speaking of Sports," 16.

38. Bill Gibson, "Hear Me Talkin' to Ya," *Baltimore Afro-American*, October 20, 1934, 20.

39. "Iowa Speedster 'Tops' to NU Grid Mentor," *Daily Iowan*, October 6, 1934, 6. In a scathing editorial, the *Chicago Defender*'s Al Monroe chastised the *Chicago Tribune* for failing to give credit to Simmons for the win against Northwestern and instead focusing on those white "blocking backs and linemen who 'made Simmons's runs possible.'" Al Monroe, editorial, *Chicago Defender*, October 13, 1934, 16.

40. See Gibson, *Golden Gophers*.

41. "What Happened to Ozzie Simmons Comes out at Last as Coach Solem of Iowa Tells of His Great Star," *Pittsburgh Courier*, November 17, 1934, A4.

42. Mitchell, "Racial Traits in Athletics," 93–99.

43. "Simmons, a Star to Others," *Chicago Defender*, October 27, 1934, 17.

44. Henderson, *Negro in Sport*, 114, 116.

45. "Prepare for Simmons and Crayne," *Minneapolis Tribune*, October 25, 1935, 19; and "Hawkeyes Will Take to Air in Hope of Upset," *Minneapolis Tribune*, October 27, 1934, 20.

46. "Minnesota Stops Iowa Eleven, 48–12," *New York Times*, October 28, 1934, S6.

47. Edward Burns, "Iowa Fans Get Up Full Steam for Minnesota," *Chicago Daily Tribune*, October 26, 1934, 27.

48. "3,500 Students Storm Iowa Practice Field and Call on Team to Turn Back Minnesota," *New York Times*, October 26, 1934, 27.

49. Edward Burns, "Minnesota Beats Iowa 48–12," *Chicago Daily Tribune*, October 28, 1934, A1.

50. "Oz Simmons Knock'd out Twice Sat.," *Philadelphia Tribune*, November 1, 1934, 12.

51. Writing about the *Chicago Defender*, Ottley argues that "with the exception of the Bible, no publication was more influential among the Negro Masses." See Ottley, *Lonely Warrior*, 8. See also Suggs, *Black Press*, 40.

52. Detweiler, "Negro Press Today," 396.

53. David K. Kellum, "Simmons Injured; Iowa Drubbed by Minnesota," *Chicago Defender*, November 3, 1934, 17. It was reported that Grange "was tackled so hard by the Minnesota ends that he was forced out of the game." See "Illinois Loses, 20–27; Grange Badly Hurt," *New York Times*, November 16, 1924, S1.

54. Earl, "Red Peppers: Hot Sport Chatter," *Cedar Rapids Gazette*, November 29, 1934, 10.

55. Jack Quinlan, "Sounding Board," *Minneapolis Journal*, November 6, 1935, 23.

56. "Comments by the Editor," *St. Paul (MN) Recorder*, December 20, 1935, 1.

57. Hoffbeck, "Bobby Marshall." See also Soderstrom, "Weeds in Linnaeus's Garden."

58. "Page Definitely Out; Iowa Off to Bloomington," *Chicago Daily Tribune*, November 2, 1934, 35.

59. "Hundreds Go to Iowa for Grid Games," *Chicago Defender*, November 16, 1935, 13.

60. "Simmons and Crayne Will Be Dangerous," *Minneapolis Journal*, November 3, 1935, 6.

61. "Gluek's Pilsner Pale Beer," *Minneapolis Tribune*, November 9, 1935, 22.

62. The Associated Press reported Governor Herring's comment, and newspapers throughout the country printed it. See, for example, "Governor Herring Starts Furore with Warning Gophers against Rough Play," *Minneapolis Journal*, November 9, 1935, 1–2.

63. "Governor Herring Starts Furore," 1–2. More than fifty years later, former U.S. president Ronald Reagan, who announced Iowa football games for Des Moines radio station W HO from 1932 to 1936, also commented on the hits Simmons received. "I remember," said Reagan, "there were some really hard, and often late, tackles aimed at Ozzie." Quoted in Trowbridge, "Man behind Floyd of Rosedale," F10.

64. "Cornhuskers to Aid Ozzie," 1.

65. "Speech by Gov. Herring May Cause Break with Minnesota," *Daily Iowan*, November 9, 1935, 1.

66. McGrath and Delmont, *Floyd Björnsterne Olson*; Mayer, *Floyd B. Olson*; and Haynes, *Dubious Alliance*, 11–12.

67. Floyd Olson to Clyde Herring, November 9, 1935, Clyde Herring Papers, Special Collections and University Archives, University of Iowa, Iowa City (hereafter Herring Papers).

68. See Schultz, "'Wager Concerning a Diplomatic Pig,'" 1–21.

69. "Iowa's Executive to Pay Up for His Bet on Hawkeyes," *Des Moines Register*, November 10, 1935, 1; and "Gophers Win Pig for Olson," *Minneapolis Tribune*, November 10, 1935, 1.

70. "Gopher Second Half Comeback Squelches Hawkeyes 13 to 6," *Minneapolis Tribune*, November 10, 1935, 1.

71. "Herring Loses Bet, Will Give Hog to Olson," *Minneapolis Journal*, November 10, 1935, 1.

72. "More Trouble for Herring: Warrant out for Gambling," *Minneapolis Tribune*, November 14, 1935, 4.

73. "Laughter and Reform," *New York Times*, November 15, 1935, 10.

74. Quoted in "BET: Governor Herring Loses on Pigskin and Pays with a Pig," *Newsweek*, November 23, 1935, 14.

75. Clyde Herring to Floyd Olson, November 12, 1935, Herring Papers.

76. Floyd of Rosedale—the actual hog—was awarded to a fourteen-year-old winner of a Minnesota 4-H Club essay-writing contest on "Opportunities for Youths on the Farm." Later Floyd of Rosedale was sold to a breeder and eventually died of hog cholera. See "Floyd of Rosedale—Minnesota vs. Iowa," Minnesota Football, http://www.gophersports.com/sports/m-footbl/spec-rel/rosedale.html (accessed September 29, 2002).

77. "Sidelights of the Week," *New York Times*, February 23, 1936, E2; and Kammen, *Mystic Chords of Memory*, 13.

78. Harvey Woodruff, "N.U. Defeats Iowa, 18–7," *Chicago Tribune*, October 4, 1936, B1. See also "Simmons Lays Prejudice to His Teammates," *New York Amsterdam News*, November 14, 1946, 1; and Sec Taylor, "Sittin' In," *Des Moines Register*, November 22, 1934, 7. Likewise, the *New York Times* reported that while Simmons was the "most brilliant running back in football" during the 1934 season, his "blocking fell off and he was left unprotected against tacklers who had eyes and hands for no one else." Allison Danzig, "Defeats of Four Major Gridiron Powers on Same Day Came as a Shock," *New York Times*, October 14, 1935, 25.

79. Certainly Simmons was injured in other incidents, though discerning the extent to which his race played a role is impossible. For instance, in the 1935 game against Illinois, the *New York Times* reported that "the Illini were guilty of roughing him in the fourth period. Once with Tom Wilson, fullback, charging into Simmons after the ball had been declared dead and knocking him flat on his back from an upright position." See "Simmons' Long Run Leads Iowa to 19–0 Triumph over Illinois," *New York Times*, October 27, 1935, S6.

80. Al Monroe, "The Lad Who Ran Alone," *Chicago Defender*, November 30, 1935, 13.

81. "Iowa Stars Get Bad Break," *Philadelphia Tribune*, November 15, 1936, 12.

82. "Iowa Team for Simmons, Says Capt. Dick Crayne," *Baltimore Afro-American*, September 21, 1935, 21.

83. Wilfred Smith, "Coach Defends Oze Simmons and Iowa Team," *Chicago Daily Tribune*, November 9, 1934, 29.

84. Hyman and White, *Big Ten Football*, 268.

85. "Simmons Heads Race Stars," A5; and "Oze Simmons Topped Best Work in 1936," *Chicago Defender*, December 19, 1936, 13.

86. "Oze Simmons Wins Iowa Amateur Poll," *Philadelphia Tribune*, January 30, 1936, 12.

87. "Simmons, Iowa's Grid Ace, Feted," *Chicago Defender*, April 20, 1935, 16.

88. Quoted in "Crayne Rates Simmons America's No. 1 Back," *Pittsburgh Courier*, November 14, 1936, A5.

89. Davis, "Davis Says It Looks Bad," 12.

90. R. W. Houston, "Refuses to Apologize," *Chicago Tribune*, November 12, 1936, 31.

91. Quoted in "Simmons Will Return to Squad," *Iowa City Press Citizen*, November 12, 1936, 1; and Houston, "Refuses to Apologize," 31.

92. Harris, "Simmons Inc.," 11.

93. Morsell-Simmons, interview by author.

94. Ed Harris, "Locals to See Star as Iowa Clashes with Temple Sat.," *Philadelphia Tribune*, November 19, 1936. 11.

95. "Oze Simmons Brilliant in Iowa Victory," *New York Amsterdam News*, November 28, 1936, 18.

96. "Southern Colleges Ban Football Stars," *Chicago Defender*, November 5, 1932, 8.

97. "Homer Harris Gets Call over Simmons," *New York Amsterdam News*, December 5, 1936, 20.

98. "Iowa to Pick Game Captain," *Des Moines Register*, December 12, 1935, 11. The *Philadelphia Tribune* reported that Simmons "only received four votes. Two of them were cast by white boys who have not played this season." See "Iowa Stars Get Bad Break," 12. Conversely, the *New York Amsterdam News* reported that Simmons received eleven votes to Harris's twelve. "Homer Harris Gets Call," 20. See also "Oze Simmons Brilliant," 16.

99. "Iowa to Pick Game Captain," 11; and "Homer Harris Iowa Captain," *New York Amsterdam News*, December 5, 1946, 16.

100. "What Happened to Ozzie Simmons," A4.

101. The *New York Amsterdam News*, however, placed Simmons on its first Negro All-America Team from the "abundance of backfield men" who though "unsung . . . nobly acquitted themselves in white institutions." Roi Ottley, "The *Amsterdam News* Picks First Negro All-American Team," *New York Amsterdam News*, December 5, 1936, 19.

102. Fritz Pollard, "All-American Lowdown," *New York Amsterdam News*, January 8, 1938, 15.

103. F. M. Davis, "Let's Make Oze Simmons First Negro All-Star," *Philadelphia Tribune*, July 22, 1937, 12.

104. Ashe, *Hard Road to Glory*, 2:94. See also Wiggins, "Prized Performers," 169. For a possible explanation of these omissions, see Carroll, *Fritz Pollard*, 271. There is a long list of "All-America" football teams. In 1935 Simmons was selected as a first-team All-American by *The Sporting News* and second-team All-American by News Enterprise Association and the Associated Press. The American Football Coaches Association All-America Team, perhaps the most respected All-America Team, never named Simmons as a first-team selection.

105. Quoted in "Simmons Scores Once in Professional Grid Debut," *Philadelphia Tribune*, December 3, 1936, 11.

106. David W. Kellum, "Simmons in Pro Football Debut Here," *Chicago Defender*, December 5, 1936, 14.

107. Rozendaal, *Duke Slater*, 142. Simmons may have been just a few years ahead of his time, for Henderson, in *Negro in Sport*, found that many of the "college stars of the 1938–1948 decade went into the professional ranks" (138).

108. Carroll, *Fritz Pollard*, 203–4.

109. Houston, "Refuses to Apologize," 31.

110. Wilfrid Smith, "Gophers Bury Hawkeyes under 8 Touchdowns before 63,200," *Chicago Daily Tribune*, November 8, 1936, B1.

111. "Oze Simmons Plays with Pro Grid Team," *Chicago Defender*, September 25, 1937, 7.

112. "Star Negro Team to Battle Chicago Bears at Soldiers Field," *Pittsburgh Courier*, August 6, 1938, 17.

113. "Believe Our Football Players Can Whip Chicago Bears Eleven," *Chicago Defender*, August 6, 1938, 8.

114. William G. Nunn, "All-Stars Fall before Battering Chicago Bears," *Pittsburgh Courier*, October 1, 1938, 17.

115. See Levy, *Tackling Jim Crow*, 66–67.

116. Fowler, "Collective Memory and Forgetting," 61. See also Connerton, *How Societies Remember*; and Hume, *Obituaries in American Culture*.

117. Associated Press, "Simmons Was among First Black All-Americans," espn *Classic*, October 4, 2001, http://espn.go.com/classic/obit/s/2001/1004/1259620.html. See also Stein, "Ozzie Simmons, 87"; "Pioneer All-American Football Player, Ozzie Simmons, Dies in Chicago," *Jet*, October 22, 2001, 57; and Michael Oriard, "All-American Boy," *Village Voice*, November 13, 2001, http://www.villagevoice.com/2001–11–13/news/all-american-boy/.

118. Foucault, *Language, Counter-Memory, Practice*.

119. Trowbridge, "Man behind Floyd of Rosedale," 10F.

120. Mark Steil, "The Origin of Floyd of Rosedale," Minnesota Public Radio, November 17, 2005, http://news.minnesota.publicradio.org/features/2005/11/14_steilm_floydofrosedale/.

121. Pat Borzi, "Trophy Tells a Tale of Rivalry and Race," *New York Times*, November 25, 2010, http://www.nytimes.com/2010/11/26/sports/ncaafootball/26rosedale.html?_r=2&ref=sports&. Borzi references a 1988 interview with Simmons, in which he recalled the 1934 Minnesota game: "'I really had the feeling they were after me because I was good,' he said. 'Oh, I think me being black added a little oomph to it.'"

122. Morsell-Simmons, interview by author. Mrs. Simmons passed away in 2010.

4. Photographic Memory

1. Moore, *All Things Being Equal*, 57.

2. Moore, *All Things Being Equal*, 58. For a biography of Bright, see Barrett, *Johnny Bright, Champion*.

3. Maury White, "Mugging of Bright Made History," *Des Moines Register*, undated clipping, Johnny Bright Files, Cowles Library, Drake University, Des Moines, Iowa (hereafter Johnny Bright Files).

4. Irwin-Zarecka, *Frames of Remembrance*, 163; and Ultang, *Holding the Moment*, 111.

5. "Jaw Closed Affair Here—Not at Drake," *Stillwater News Press*, October 23, 1951, 7.

6. See Ross, *Outside the Lines*; Levy, *Tackling Jim Crow*; and Lomax, "African American Experience," 163–78.

7. Miller, "Muscular Assimilationism," in Ross, *Race and Sport*, 166–7.

8. Berghorn, Yetman, and Hanna, "Racial Participation and Integration," 107–24.

9. Harris, "African American Predominance," in Brooks and Althouse, *Racism in College Athletics*, 55.

10. Spivey, *Fire from the Soul*, 247; and Spivey, "Black Athlete," 123.

11. Wiggins, "Prized Performers," 164–77.

12. See Kemper, *College Football*, 80–115.

13. Blake Sebring, "Johnny Bright Could Do It All," *Fort Wayne News-Sentinel*, December 30, 1999, 1S.

14. Quoted in Sebring, "Johnny Bright Could Do It All."

15. See Ritchey, *Drake University*; and Dahl, *In Celebration of a Century*.

16. Dahl, *In Celebration of a Century*, 19; and Chase, "'You Live What You Learn,'" in Silag, *Outside In*, 135.

17. Dahl, *In Celebration of a Century*, 73.

18. "Star Prep Gridder Quits Drake's Jim Crow Setup," *Chicago Defender*, September 6, 1947, 11.

19. Quoted in Adam Buckley Cohen, "Photos Taught a Lesson," *Los Angeles Times*, July 18, 1999, D7.

20. Buck Turnbull, "Bright Joins Iowa 'Hall,'" *Des Moines Register*, March 24, 1970, 1, 4.

21. Ken Fuson, "Drake Great Johnny Bright Is Dead at 53," *Des Moines Register*, December 15, 1983, 1.

22. "Johnny Bright Honored Today as Drake's Best Ever," *Bulldog Bulletin* (Drake University), September 13, 1969, 3, 7.

23. The entire Bulldog team amassed 3,154 yards in 1949, and Bright accounted for more than half of those yards. See Kaley, "History of Intercollegiate Football at Drake," 182.

24. "Bright Offensive Leader," *New York Times*, December 11, 1950, 33.

25. Quoted in Bob Spiegel, "Here's How A&M Campus Reacts to Bright Case Now," *Des Moines Register*, October 30, 1951, 1; and Cohen, "Photos Taught a Lesson," D7. While it was usually reported that Bright was the first black athlete on Lewis Field, the all-black Langston University played Western University of Kansas City there in 1934. Kopecky, *History of Equal Opportunity*, 265.

26. "Bright Lauds Oklahoma Grid Foes," *Pittsburgh Courier*, October 29, 1949, 24.

27. Frank N. Gardner to C. H. McElroy, October 1949, quoted in C. H. McElroy to the Investigating Committee of the Missouri Valley Intercollegiate Athletic Con-

ference, November 10, 1951, Athletics Files, "Johnny Bright Case—Reactions, 1951," Special Collections and University Archives, Edmon Low Library, Oklahoma State University Library, Stillwater (hereafter referenced as JBC—R, 1951).

28. Interview with Ray Eiland in Rubin, *Moment of Impact*.

29. Quoted in Beeson, "Desegregation and Affirmative Action," 26.

30. Richards, "Negro Higher and Professional Education," 341–49.

31. See Hubbell, "Desegregation of the University of Oklahoma."

32. In 1953 A&M admitted black undergraduate students to all semesters. Kopecky, *History of Equal Opportunity*, 271–78.

33. See Demas, *Integrating the Gridiron*, 49–71. Interestingly, however, students at Kansas University persuaded conference leaders to reject A&M's 1947 bid to enter the MVIAA "on the ground that the schools discriminates against Negroes in intercollegiate athletics." Cited in Baker, "Fields of Contest," 48.

34. "Bright a Marked Man on Saturday," *Stillwater News Press*, October 18, 1951, 17.

35. "Bright Top Target in Mo-Valley Tilt," *Stillwater News Press*, October 19, 1951, 7.

36. "Bright a Marked Man," *Stillwater News Press*, 17.

37. A&M's student paper, the *Daily O'Collegian*, did not use similar imagery to discuss Bright, reporting only that "'Stop Bright' has been the Aggies' theme song this week." "Crucial Offensive Game Looms in Cowboy-Drake Tilt Saturday," *Daily O'Collegian*, October 19, 1951, 7.

38. Don Ultang, interview by Brian Thomas, June 5, 1999, transcript, Iowa Journalists Oral History Project, State Historical Society of Iowa, Iowa City.

39. Ultang interview by Thomas.

40. Ultang interview by Thomas.

41. Ultang interview by Thomas.

42. John Abrams, "Bright out Early after Quick TD Pass," *Stillwater News Press*, October 21, 1951, 7.

43. "Bright 'Slugged' Drake Men Claim," *New York Times*, October 22, 1951, 37.

44. Jack McClelland, "Preliminary Statement to the Missouri Valley Investigating Committee," October 1951, Johnny Bright Files.

45. McClelland, "Preliminary Statement."

46. "Oklahoma Aggies Halt Drake, 27–14," *New York Times*, October 21, 1951, 156; and "Drake Players Say Aggies Deliberately Slugged Bright," *Stillwater News Press*, October 21, 1951, 7.

47. Maury White, "Aggies Outlast Drake," *Des Moines Register*, October 21, 1951, S8.

48. Quoted in Trachtenberg, "Through a Glass, Darkly," 117–18.

49. Ultang interview by Thomas.

50. Quoted in "Caught by the Camera," *Life*, November 5, 1951, 121.

51. "Incident Explained," *Times-Delphic* (Drake University), December 11, 1951, 1. Footage of the incident can be found in Rubin, *Moment of Impact*.

52. "Bright's Final Play: Four-Yard Gain, Then Down and Out," *Des Moines Register*, October 22, 1951, S1.

53. Edwards, *Raw Histories*, 14.

54. See, for example, "Injury to Johnny Bright Draws Protest from Drake," *Chicago Tribune*, October 22, 1951, C1.

55. "Caught by the Camera," *Life*, November 5, 1951, 124.

56. Fulton, *Eyes of Time*, 106–7.

57. Meeting Minutes, Drake University's Athletic Council, October 23, 1951, Johnny Bright Files.

58. Complete letters are reprinted in "Whitworth Is 'Very Sorry' about Bright," *Des Moines Register*, October 25, 1951, 6. See also George M. Daniels, "Bright to Finish Season Despite Aggie Injuries," *Baltimore Afro-American*, November 3, 1951, 17; and "Drake Studies A&M Apologies; Bright Drills," *Stillwater News Press*, October 25, 1951, 1.

59. Quoted in "Movies Show Half-Dozen Plays Could Be Jaw-Breaker," *Stillwater News Press*, October 23, 1951, 1. See also "Apology Offered by Aggies' Coach," *New York Times*, October 23, 1951, 39. A Kansas man asked an astute question concerning this statement in his letter to A&M officials: "How could a college man, who has played so much football as he says he has, lose his head on the first play of the game?" S. G. Unger to President, [Athletic Director] Iba, and J. B. Whitworth, no date, JBC—R, 1951. Oklahoma City's *Black Dispatch* similarly questioned how Smith might have lost his temper before the competition had even started. "Whitworth Admits Player Illegally Hit John Bright," *Black Dispatch*, October 27, 1951, 12.

60. Norm Coder, "Ags: 'No Action unless Protest Made," *Des Moines Register*, October 23, 1951, 13.

61. "Jaw Closed Affair Here," *Stillwater News Press*, 7.

62. "Bright's Jaw Still Leading Valley Talk," *Stillwater News Press*, October 22, 1951, 5.

63. Frank N. Gardner, "Preliminary Statement to the Missouri Valley Investigating Committee," October 1951, Johnny Bright Files (emphasis in original).

64. "Statement of Jerry Start, Defensive Linebacker," quoted in "Preliminary Statement to the Missouri Valley Investigating Committee," October 1951, Johnny Bright Files.

65. Statements from Charles Lanphere, Jerry Stark, George Smith, and Jim Peterson, quoted in "Preliminary Statement to the Missouri Valley Investigating Committee," October 1951, Johnny Bright Files.

66. Spiegel, "Here's How A&M Campus Reacts," 1. Nearly half a century later, Gene Aldridge, a member of the 1951 squad, remembered that Coach Whitworth had observed that when Bright was not carrying or throwing the ball he tended to stand in the backfield and watch the play unfold. Whitworth instructed the Aggies' defensive linemen to keep Bright "moving around." According to Aldridge, that "meant he didn't want Bright resting. So if you don't want somebody resting, you're going to go back there and put a hit on him." Cohen, "Photos Taught a Lesson," D7. In 1955 Whitworth took over the football program at the University of Alabama, a school that actively resisted integration. See Kemper, *College Football*, 122.

67. President Harmon's Report to the Drake Board of Trustees, December 14, 1951, Johnny Bright Files.

68. C. H. McElroy to the Investigating Committee of the Missouri Valley Inter-collegiate Athletic Conference, November 10, 1951, JBC—R, 1951.

69. "Bright Incident Revived," *New York Times*, November 24, 1951, 21.

70. Henry Harmon to Jack McClelland, November 15, 1951, Johnny Bright Files.

71. "Drake University News Bureau Statement of Withdrawal from the MVC," Johnny Bright Files. Joining the MVC in 1908, Drake was the league's oldest member at the time. The university rejoined the conference in 1957 when Oklahoma A&M left for the Big 8 Conference; however, Drake's football team would not reenter the MVC until 1972.

72. "Bradley, Following Drake's Suit, Quits Conference on Bright Issue," *New York Times*, November 29, 1951, 59. Bradley's withdrawal left the MVC with six members: Oklahoma A&M, Houston, Detroit University, Tulsa University, St. Louis University, and the University of Wichita. Later that year, Cornell College in Mt. Vernon, Iowa, canceled a wrestling meet with Oklahoma A&M. Cornell's dean said the action was taken "in recognition of the fact that as yet no disciplinary action has been taken either by Oklahoma A&M or the Missouri Valley Conference regarding the Bright incident." "Cancel Aggie Mat Meet," *New York Times*, December 5, 1951, 63.

73. "Bright Selected for East-West Tilt," *Times-Delphic* (Drake University), December 7, 1951, 1.

74. "Play My Way, or I'll Quit," *Daily O'Collegian*, November 29, 1951, 2.

75. Rulon, *Oklahoma State University*, 292.

76. Kopecky, *History of Equal Opportunity*, 278.

77. "Letters Ask Detroit to 'Rough Up' Aggies," *New York Times*, October 23, 1951, 33.

78. Quote is from "It's Just a Game," *Time*, November 5, 1951, 100. See also Sperber, *Onward to Victory*, 474, 480–81; and Oriard, *King Football*, 334–35.

79. "Dartmouth Roughs Star," *Chicago Daily Tribune*, November 30, 1951, C1.

80. Sperber, *Onward to Victory*, 304. See also Figone, "Gambling and College Basketball," 44–61.

81. "Trouble at West Point," *Time*, August 13, 1951, 17–18.

82. Hill, "Anecdotal Evidence," in Phillips, *Deconstructing Sport History*, 126–27 (emphasis in original).

83. Thousands of people must have written letters about the incident. *Life* magazine reported receiving more than three hundred pieces of mail on the issue. The University of Detroit football players received "scores" of letters, urging them to "even the score against Oklahoma A. and M." in their upcoming game. Critics and supporters inundated Drake University, Bright, and A&M with correspondence. "Letters Ask Detroit," *New York Times*, 33.

84. Robert McDowell to Oklahoma A&M, JBC—R, 1951.

85. Herbert M. Jones to Oklahoma A&M President, November 2, 1951, JBC—R, 1951.

86. Stanley M. Richmond to Oklahoma A&M President, November 2, 1951, JBC—R, 1951.

87. Edward Luby to Oklahoma A&M President, October 23, 1951, JBC—R, 1951.

88. Mrs. Eugene Dauchent to Oklahoma A&M President, November 5, 1951; and Laura S. Carpluter, Intercultural Chairman for Sacramento United Church Women, to Oklahoma A&M President, no date, JBC—R, 1951.

89. Donald A. Eagle to Henry G. Bennett, October 21, 1951, JBC—R 1951.

90. F. J. Tiptor to Oklahoma A&M, November 3, 1951, JBC—R, 1951.

91. Nelson A. Schmidt to Oklahoma A&M President, November 5, 1951, JBC—R, 1951.

92. "Drake and Johnny Bright," *Chicago Defender*, December 8, 1951, 10. For a notable exception, see "Assault on Bright Laid to Racial Intolerance," *Des Moines Tribune*, October 26, 1951, 12.

93. "Why Are They Afraid?" *Chicago Defender*, November 10, 1951, 10.

94. "Wichita Honors Bright," *New York Times*, November 9, 1951, 34.

95. In 1951 Princeton's Dick Kazmaier won both the offensive title and the Heisman Trophy. Bright finished ninth in total offense, and it was not until 1961 that the first African American, Ernie Davis, received the Heisman Trophy.

96. Jeff Olson, "The Day Dignity Defeated Dirty Play," *Des Moines Register*, October 14, 2001, C1.

97. In addition to his many records, Johnny Bright was selected for the prestigious East-West Shrine Game and participated in two Hula Bowl games in Hawaii. After his senior season at Drake, the Iowa Amateur Athletic Association named him the outstanding athlete of 1951. The midwestern chapter of the Football Writers Association of America declared him the outstanding back of the 1951 season, the *Pittsburgh Courier* named him athlete of the year, and the Gridiron Club of Boston presented him the 1951 prestigious Nils V. "Swede" Nelson Award for sportsmanship.

98. Rathet and Smith, *Their Deeds and Dogged Faith*, 221.

99. Bill Nunn, "Pgh. Steelers on Look Out for Tan Football Players," *Pittsburgh Courier*, January 5, 1952, 14.

100. Quoted in Frank Fitzpatrick, "The Scars of Hatred," *Philadelphia Inquirer*, May 20, 2003, D1. The Eagles chose two other black athletes, taking Youngstown College's Ralph Goldston and Don Stevens as their tenth and thirtieth picks, respectively.

101. Quoted in "Bright Signs up for 'Fabulous Sum' with Canadian Team," *Times-Delphic* (Drake University), March 11, 1951, 3.

102. See Schultz, "Photography, Instant Memory," 221–43.

103. Quoted in Maury White, "Bright Joins Iowa 'Hall,'" *Des Moines Register*, undated clipping, Johnny Bright Files.

104. Brian Bergman, "Bright's Revenge," *Maclean's*, October 4, 2004, 43.

105. Valentine and Darnell, "Football and 'Tolerance,'" in Joseph, Darnell, and Nakamura, *Race and Sport in Canada*, 63.

106. Longley, Crosset, and Jefferson, "Migration of African-Americans," 1374–97.

107. Longley, Crosset, and Jefferson, "Migration of African-Americans," 1374–97.

108. Quoted in Cohen, "Photos Taught a Lesson," D7.

109. Gordon S. White Jr., "Taking a Look Back at Drake," *New York Times*, November 13, 1985, B14.

110. "Apology Offered," 39.

111. Phil Mushnick, "Racism Has No Gray Area: Drake RB Experienced the Real Thing in '51," *New York Post*, July 23, 1999, 112.

112. Olson, "Day Dignity Defeated Dirty Play," C1.

113. Quoted in Frank Fitzpatrick, "Bright Story Offers a Lesson to NFL Owners," *Philadelphia Inquirer,* May 19, 2003.

114. Quoted in Barb Dietrick, "Bright—Return of a Legend," *Times-Delphic* (Drake University), November 11, 1980, 1.

115. Quoted in Dave Hanson, "Bright Not Bitter: Blow Helped Clean Up Sports," *Des Moines Tribune*, November 13, 1980, 21 (emphasis in original).

116. Moore, *All Things Being Equal*, 58.

Afterword

1. David J. Schmidly to David E. Maxwell, September 28, 2005; and David E. Maxwell to David J. Schmidly, October 21, 2005, Drake University Archives, Cowles Library, Des Moines.

2. Berry Tramel, "'The Right Thing To Do': 55 Years Later, Scars from Bright Incident May Be Fading," *Knight Ridder Tribune Business News*, February 24, 2006, ProQuest.

3. Weyeneth, "Power of the Apology," 30, 32.

4. Davis, "Racial Reconciliation or Retreat?," 42.

5. Thompson, *Taking Responsibility*, viii.

6. Barkan, *Guilt of Nations*, xvi.

7. "S.J. Res. 14," 111th Cong., 1st sess., Library of Congress, April 30, 2009, http:// thomas.loc.gov/cgi-bin/query/z?c111:S.J.RES.14.IS:.

8. Lazare, *On Apology.*

9. Biondi, "Rise of the Reparations Movement," 8.

10. Robert S. Browne, "Let's Talk about Reparations for Slavery," *New York Times*, January 7, 1991, A16.

11. Weyeneth, "Power of the Apology," 36.

12. Allison Mitchell, "Clinton Regrets 'Clearly Racist' U.S. Study," *New York Times*, May 16, 1997, A10.

13. Quoted in Kim, "Managing the Racial Breach," 77. See also Peter Baker and Michael A. Fletcher, "Clinton's Town Hall Taking Discussion of Race into Sports Arena," *Washington Post*, April 14 1998, A2.

14. Quoted in James Bennett, "President Leads TV Discussion on Role of Race in Sports," *New York Times*, April 15, 1998, http://www.nytimes.com/1998/04/15/us /president-leads-tv-discussion-on-role-of-race-in-sports.html.

15. Kim, "Clinton's Race Initiative," 196.

16. Olick and Coughlin, "Politics of Regret," in Torpey, *Politics and the Past*, 37–62.

17. Spencer, "From 'Child's Play' to 'Party Crasher,'" in Andrews and Jackson, *Sports Stars*, 90.

18. Schultz, "Contesting the Master Narrative," 1235–51.

19. Marc Ira Hooks, "Olympic Athlete Honored," *Leaf-Chronicle*, July 19, 1996, A1, A6.

20. John Crumpacker, "Olympic Protest: Smith and Carlos Statue Captures Sprinters' Moment," *San Francisco Gate*, October 18, 2005, http://www.sfgate.com/sports/article/OLYMPIC-PROTEST-Smith-and-Carlos-Statue-2601229.php.

21. Smith, "Mapping America's Sporting Landscape," 1252–68.

22. Hartmann, *Race, Culture*, 265–66.

23. Roy, *Fists of Freedom*; Small, *Black Power Salute*; Norman, *Salute*; Hartmann, *Race, Culture*; and Bass, *Not the Triumph*.

24. McCrisken and Pepper, *American History*, 175.

25. Early, *Muhammad Ali Reader*, viii.

26. "Cowan Joins Effort to Pardon Boxing Great Jack Johnson," *Boston Globe*, March 5, 2013, http://www.bostonglobe.com/news/politics/2013/03/05/massachusetts-senator-william-cowan-joins-effort-pardon-boxing-great-jack-johnson/xpI8KmjAFadQ89M0pSe1FI/story.html.

27. "Cowan Joins Effort." See also Antoniazzi, "'(Un)Forgivable Blackness' and the Oval Office," 9–18.

28. Michael Cohen, "Scott Shafer Relays Wilmeth Sidat-Singh Story to Syracuse Players Leading up to Game with Maryland," *Syracuse Post-Standard*, November 6, 2013, http://www.syracuse.com/orangefootball/index.ssf/2013/11/scott_shafer_relays_wilmeth_si.html. In 2005 Syracuse University retired Sidat-Singh's number.

29. The suspended students were Naomi Bloom, Jean Borstein, Mervyn Jones, Robert Schoenfeld, Argyle Stoute, Anita Kreiger, and Evelyn Maisel. See Spivey, "'End Jim Crow in Sports,'" 282–303.

30. Quoted in Edward Wong, "College Football: NYU Honors Protesters It Punished in '41," *New York Times*, May 4, 2001, http://www.nytimes.com/2001/05/04/sports/college-football-nyu-honors-protesters-it-punished-in-41.html?pagewanted=all&src=pm. The banquet came as a result of the efforts of one of the Bates Seven, Evelyn Maisel Witkin, and historians Donald Spivey and Jeffrey Sammons.

31. Wiggins, "Prized Performers."

32. Edwards, *Revolt of the Black Athlete*.

33. "Ousted Black Athletes Honored," *Philadelphia Tribune*, October 1, 1993, 7C.

34. Quoted in C. Gerald Fraser, "8 Black Syracuse Football Players Continue Boycott," *New York Times*, September 28, 1970, 61.

35. Quoted in Neil Amdur, "Syracuse Athletics Charged with 'Chronic Racism' in Report on Football Suspension of 8 Blacks," *New York Times*, December 9, 1970, 70.

36. See William C. Rhoden, "Syracuse Honors Nine Players Who Took a Stand," *New York Times*, October 22, 2006, H10; and "'Syracuse Eight' to Receive Chancellor's Medal for Courage," cuse.com, October 20, 2006, http://www.suathletics.com/news/2006/10/20/syracuseeightpressconf.aspx. In a related story, former University of Washington football coach Jim Owens apologized to black players he dismissed in 1969 after they refused to pledge their loyalty to the team. Owens's 2003 apology took place just before Washington officials dedicated a statue in his honor. John Iwasaki, "A Controversial Statue Creates Dissent, Healing," *Seattle Post-Intelligencer*, October 24, 2003, http://www.seattlepi.com/sports/article/A-controversial-statue-creates-dissent-healing-1127965.php.

37. So what motivated General Mills to bestow the same honor to the multitalented Jim Thorpe in 2001, sixty-six years after his death and eighty-nine years after he won Olympic gold in the decathlon and pentathlon? Film played a role in the University of Michigan's 2012 decision to honor 1930s football star Willis Ward, who, seventy-eight years earlier, sat out the Georgia Tech game as a result of the schools' gentlemen's agreement. The ceremony came as the result of the efforts of third-grader Genna Urbain, who, upon seeing the documentary *Black and Blue: The Story of Gerald Ford, Willis Ward, and the 1934 Michigan-Georgia Tech Football Game*, lobbied university and state officials. Popular history provides new and varied occasions for the public to engage with the past.

38. Christopher Kelly, "We Shall Overreach," *Texas Monthly*, January 2009, 48. See also Schultz, "*Glory Road*," 205–13; and Schultz, "Truth about Historical Sport Films," 29–45.

39. Jason Byassee, "Not a Slam Dunk: Race and Redemption in *Glory Road*," *Christian Century*, February 7, 2006, 8.

40. Martin, review of *Glory Road*, 444.

41. Maier, "A Surfeit of Memory?," 136–52; Phillips, O'Neill, and Osmond, "Broadening Horizons in Sport History," 271–93; de Groot, *Consuming History*; and Doss, *Memorial Mania*.

42. CBS, "Poll: Blacks See Improved Race Relations," April 29, 2008, www.cbsnews.com/news/poll-blacks-see-improved-race-relations/.

43. Pettigrew, "Post-Racism?," 279.

44. Teasley and Ikard, "Barack Obama," 419–20.

45. Brooks, "Making the Case for Atonement," 678.

46. Teasley and Ikard, "Barack Obama," 413.

47. Franklin, "Presidential Race Initiatives," 236.

48. Tarman and Sears, "Conceptualization and Measurement," 731–61; Bonilla-Silva, *Racism without Racists*; Bonilla-Silva, *White Supremacy and Racism*; Bonilla-Silva and Dietrich, "Color-Blind Racism in Obamerica," 190–206; Bobo, Kluege, and Smith, "Laissez-Faire Racism," in Tuch and Martin, *Racial Attitudes in the 1990s*, 15–42; and Collins, *Black Sexual Politics*.

49. Bobo, "Jim Crow and Post-Racialism," 15.

50. Collins, *Black Sexual Politics*, 5.

51. Vera and Gordon, *Screen Saviors*.

52. Feagin, *Racist America*, 173.

53. Pew Research Center, "King's Dream Remains an Elusive Goal; Many Americans See Racial Disparities," August 13, 2013, http://www.pewsocialtrends.org/2013/08/22/kings-dream-remains-an-elusive-goal-many-americans-see-racial-disparities/. See also Feagin, *Systemic Racism*; Oliver and Shapiro, *Black Wealth/White Wealth*; Massey, *Categorically Unequal*; Western, *Punishment and Inequality in America*; Sampson and Sharkey, "Neighborhood Selection," 1–29; Gee and Ford, "Structural Racism," 115–32; and Davis and Bent-Goodley, *The Color of Social Policy*.

54. Leonard, "Next M. J. or the Next O. J.?," 284–313.

55. Ferber, "Construction of Black Masculinity," 12.

56. See Lapchick et al., "The 2012 Racial and Gender Report Card: College Sport"; Bimper, Harrison, and Clark, "Diamonds in the Rough," 107–30; Dubrow and Adams, "Hoop Inequalities," 43–59; Day and McDonald, "Not So Fast, My Friend," 138–58; and Harrison, "Critical Race Analysis," 270–96.

57. Carlos, *John Carlos Story*, 170.

58. Rozendaal, *Duke Slater*, 3.

59. Barack Obama, "Remarks by the President at the 'Let Freedom Ring' Ceremony Commemorating the 50th Anniversary of the March on Washington" (Washington DC: Office of the Press Secretary, White House, August 28, 2013), http://www.whitehouse.gov/the-press-office/2013/08/28/remarks-president-let-freedom-ring-ceremony-commemorating-50th-anniversa.

BIBLIOGRAPHY

Archival Sources

Athletic Files. Special Collections. University of Iowa, Iowa City.

Athletics Files. Special Collections and University Archives. Edmon Low Library, Oklahoma State University, Stillwater.

Carrie Chapman Catt Papers. Special Collections and University Archives, Parks Library, Iowa State University, Ames.

Clyde Herring Papers. Special Collections. University of Iowa, Iowa City.

Committee for Review of the Catt Hall Controversy. Special Collections and University Archives. Parks Library, Iowa State University, Ames.

Iowa Journalists Oral History Project. State Historical Society of Iowa, Iowa City.

Jack Trice Papers. Special Collections and University Archives. Parks Library, Iowa State University, Ames.

Johnny Bright Files. Cowles Library, Drake University, Des Moines, Iowa.

September 29th Movement Records. Special Collections and University Archives. Parks Library, Iowa State University, Ames.

Published Sources

Amidon, Kevin S. "Carrie Chapman Catt and the Evolutionary Politics of Sex and Race." *Journal of the History of Ideas* 68, no. 2 (2007): 305–28.

Antoniazzi, Barbara. "'(Un)Forgivable Blackness' and the Oval Office: Jack Johnson and Henry Louis Gates at the Postracial White House." *Race, Gender and Class* 17, no. 3–4 (2010): 9–18.

Aptheker, Herbert. "The Negro College Student in the 1920s—Years of Preparation and Protest: An Introduction." *Science and Society* 33 (1969): 150–67.

Ashe, Arthur R. *A Hard Road to Glory: A History of the African-American Athlete.* Vol. 1, *1619–1918.* New York: Warner Books, 1988.

———. *A Hard Road to Glory: A History of the African-American Athlete.* Vol. 2, *1919–1945.* New York: Warner Books, 1988.

Baker, Samuel Zebulon. *Fields of Contest: Race, Region, and College Football in the U.S. South, 1945–1975.* PhD diss., Emory University, 2009.

Baker, William J. *Jesse Owens: An American Life.* New York: Free Press, 1986.

Barkan, Elazar. *Guilt of Nations: Restitution and Negotiating Historic Injustices.* New York: W. W. Norton, 2000.

Barrett, Warrick Lee. *Johnny Bright, Champion.* Lincoln NE: toExcel, 1996.

Bass, Amy. *Not the Triumph but the Struggle: The 1968 Olympics and the Making of the Black Athlete.* Minneapolis: University of Minnesota Press, 2004.

Bederman, Gail. *Manliness and Civilization: A Cultural History of Gender and Race in the United States, 1880–1917.* Chicago: University of Chicago Press, 1995.

Beeson, Ronald Max. "Desegregation and Affirmative Action in Higher Education in Oklahoma: A Historical Case Study." PhD diss., Oklahoma State University, 1972.

Behee, John. *Hail to the Victors! Black Athletes at the University of Michigan.* Ann Arbor MI: Ulrich's Books, 1974.

Bender, Jack. *A Gallery of Iowa Sports Heroes: Five Decades of Cartoons.* Cedar Rapids IA: Voice of the Hawkeyes, 1989.

Berghorn, Forrest J., Norman R. Yetman, and William E. Hanna. "Racial Participation and Integration in Men's and Women's Intercollegiate Basketball: Continuity and Change, 1958–1985." *Sociology of Sport Journal* 5, no. 2 (1988): 107–24.

Bergmann, Leola Nelson. *The Negro in Iowa.* Iowa City: State Historical Society, 1948. Reprint, 1969.

Berryman, Jack. "Early Black Leadership in Collegiate Football: Massachusetts as a Pioneer." *Historical Journal of Massachusetts* 9 (1981): 17–28.

Bimper, Albert Y., Jr., Louis Harrison Jr., and Langston Clark. "Diamonds in the Rough: Examining a Case of Successful Black Student Athletes in College Sport." *Journal of Black Psychology* 39, no. 2 (2012): 107–30.

Biondi, Martha. "The Rise of the Reparations Movement." *Radical History Review* 87, no. 1 (2003): 5–18.

Bobo, Lawrence D. "Somewhere between Jim Crow and Post-Racialism: Reflections on the Racial Divide in America Today." *Daedalus* 140, no. 2 (2011): 15.

Bobo, Lawrence, James R. Kluege, and Ryan A. Smith. "Laissez-Faire Racism: The Crystallization of a Kinder, Gentler Antiblack Ideology." In *Racial Attitudes in the 1990s,* edited by Steven Tuch and Jack K. Martin, 15–42. Westport CT: Praeger, 1997.

Bodnar, John. *Remaking America: Public Memory, Commemoration, and Patriotism in the Twentieth Century.* Princeton NJ: Princeton University Press, 1992.

Bonds, Alfred B. "The President's Commission on Higher Education and Negro Higher Education." *Journal of Negro Education* 17, no. 3 (1948): 426–36.

———. "Some Recommendations of the President's Commission on Higher Education." *Science* 107, no. 2781 (1948): 379–83.

Bonilla-Silva, Eduardo. *Racism without Racists: Color-blind Racism and the Persistence of Racial Inequality in the United States.* Lanham MD: Rowman & Littlefield, 2003.

———. "Rethinking Racism: Toward a Structural Interpretation." *American Sociological Review* 62, no. 3 (1997): 465–80.

———. *White Supremacy and Racism in the Post–Civil Rights Era.* Boulder CO: Lynne Rienner, 2001.

Bonilla-Silva, Eduardo, and David Dietrich. "The Sweet Enchantment of Color-Blind Racism in Obamerica." *The Annals of the American Academy of Political and Social Science* 634, no. 1 (2011): 190–206.

Boskin, Joseph. *Sambo: The Rise & Demise of an American Jester.* New York: Oxford University Press, 1986.

Breaux, Richard Melvin. "Facing Hostility, Finding Housing: African American Students at the University of Iowa, 1920s–1950s." *Iowa Heritage Illustrated* 83 (2000): 14–15.

Brooks, Roy L., ed. "Making the Case for Atonement in 'Post-Racial America.'" *Journal of Gender, Race and Justice* 14, no. 3 (2011): 678.

———. *When Sorry Isn't Enough: The Controversy over Apologies and Reparations for Human Injustice.* New York: New York University Press, 1999.

Brown, Clyde, and Gayle K. Pluta Brown. "Moo U and the Cambodian Invasion: Nonviolent Anti–Vietnam War Protest at Iowa State University." In *The Vietnam War on Campus: Other Voices, More Distant Drums,* edited by Marc Jason Gilbert, 119–41. Westport CT: Praeger, 2000.

Burke, Peter. *What Is Cultural History?* Malden MA: Polity Press, 2004.

Butler, Thomas, ed. *Memory: History, Culture and the Mind.* Oxford: Blackwell Publishers, 1989.

Cahn, Susan K. *Coming on Strong: Gender and Sexuality in Twentieth-Century Women's Sport.* Cambridge MA: Harvard University Press, 1994.

Carlos, John. *The John Carlos Story: The Sports Moment That Changed the World.* With Dave Zirin. Chicago: Haymarket Books, 2011.

Carpenter, Allan, and Randy Lyon. *Between Two Rivers: Iowa Year by Year, 1846–1996.* 3rd ed. Ames: Iowa State University Press, 1997.

Carroll, John M. "Fritz Pollard and Integration in Early Professional Football." In Ross, *Race and Sport,* 3–25.

———. *Fritz Pollard: Pioneer in Racial Advancement.* Urbana: University of Illinois Press, 1992.

Catt, Carrie Chapman, and Nettie Rogers Shuler. *Woman Suffrage and Politics: The Inner Story of the Suffrage Movement.* New York: Charles Scribner's Sons, 1923.

C. A. W. "Trice." *The Bomb* 31 (1924): 102.

Chalk, Ocania. *Black College Sport.* New York: Dodd, Mead, 1976.

Chase, Hal S. "'You Live What You Learn': The African-American Presence in Iowa Education, 1838–2000." In Silag, *Outside In,* 134–65.

Childers, James Saxon. *In the Deep South: A Novel about a White Man and a Black Man.* New York: Farrar & Rinehart, 1936. Reprint, Tuscaloosa: University of Alabama Press, 1988.

Clement, Rufus E. "Racial Integration in the Field of Sports." *Journal of Negro Education* 23, no. 3 (1954): 222–30.

Cohen, Philip N. "Nationalism and Suffrage: Gender Struggle in Nation-Building America." *Signs* 21, no. 3 (Spring 1996): 707–27.

Collins, Patricia Hill. *Black Sexual Politics: African Americans, Gender, and the New Racism.* New York: Routledge, 2005.

Connerton, Paul. *How Societies Remember.* Cambridge: Cambridge University Press, 1989.

———. "Seven Types of Forgetting." *Memory Studies* 1, no. 1 (2008): 59–71.

Cott, Nancy F. *The Grounding of Modern Feminism.* New Haven CT: Yale University Press, 1987.

Dahl, Orin L. *In Celebration of a Century: Drake University, 1881–1981.* Des Moines IA: Drake University, 1980.

Dalfiume, Richard M. "The 'Forgotten Years' of the Negro Revolution." *The Journal of American History* 55, no. 1 (1968): 90–106.

Davis, Angela. *Women, Race and Class.* New York: Vintage Books, 1983.

Davis, Angelique M. "Racial Reconciliation or Retreat? How Legislative Resolutions Apologizing for Slavery Promulgate White Supremacy." *Black Scholar* 42, no. 1 (2012): 37–48.

Davis, King E., and Tricia B. Bent-Goodley. *The Color of Social Policy.* Alexandria VA: Council on Social Work Education, 2004.

Day, Jacob C., and Steve McDonald. "Not So Fast, My Friend: Social Capital and the Race Disparity in Promotions among College Football Coaches." *Sociological Spectrum* 30, no. 2 (2010): 138–58.

"The Death of a Racial Pioneer in College Football." *The Journal of Blacks in Higher Education* 61 (2008): 43.

De Groot, Jerome. *Consuming History: Historians and Heritage in Contemporary Popular Culture.* New York: Routledge, 2009.

Delton, Jennifer. "Labor, Politics, and African American Identity in Minneapolis, 1930–1950." *Minnesota History* 57, no. 8 (2001–2): 419–34.

Demas, Lane. *Integrating the Gridiron: Black Civil Rights and American College Football.* New Brunswick NJ: Rutgers University Press, 2010.

Detweiler, Frederick G. "The Negro Press Today." *American Journal of Sociology* 44, no. 3 (1939): 391–400.

Dobbs, Charles M. "Strategic Focus and Accountability: The Eaton-Jischke Years." In *A Sesquicentennial History of Iowa State University: Tradition and Transformation,* edited by Dorothy Schwieder and Gretchen van Houten, 111–38. Ames: Iowa State University Press, 2007.

Doss, Erika. *Memorial Mania: Public Feeling in America.* Chicago: University of Chicago Press, 2012.

Duberman, Martin B. *Paul Robeson.* New York: Knopf, 1988.

Dubrow, Joshua Kjerulf, and Jimi Adams. "Hoop Inequalities: Race, Class and Family Structure Background and the Odds of Playing in the National Basketball Association." *International Review for the Sociology of Sport* 47, no. 1 (2012): 43–59.

Early, Gerald, ed. *The Muhammad Ali Reader*. New York: Rob Weisbach Books, 1998.

Edwards, Elizabeth. *Raw Histories: Photographs, Anthropology and Museums*. Oxford: Berg, 2001.

Edwards, Harry. *The Revolt of the Black Athlete*. New York: Free Press, 1969.

Enomoto, Carl E. "Public Sympathy for O. J. Simpson: The Roles of Race, Age, Gender, Income, and Education." *American Journal of Economics and Sociology* 58, no. 1 (1999): 145–61.

Feagin, Joe. *Racist America: Roots, Current Realities, and Future Reparations*. New York: Routledge, 2001.

———. *Systemic Racism: A Theory of Oppression*. New York: Routledge, 2006.

Ferber, Abby L. "The Construction of Black Masculinity: White Supremacy Now and Then." *Journal of Sport and Social Issues* 31, no. 1 (2007): 11–24.

Figone, Albert J. "Gambling and College Basketball: The Scandal of 1951." *Journal of Sport History* 16 (Spring 1989): 44–61.

Finnegan, Margaret. *Selling Suffrage*. New York: Columbia University Press, 1999.

Fishman, George. "Paul Robeson's Student Days and the Fight against Racism at Rutgers." *Freedomways* 9 (1969): 221–29.

Foucault, Michel. *Language, Counter-Memory, Practice: Selected Essays and Interviews*. Edited by Donald F. Bouchard. Translated by Donald F. Bouchard and Sherry Simon. Ithaca NY: Cornell University Press, 1977.

Fowler, Bridget. "Collective Memory and Forgetting: Components for a Study of Obituaries." *Theory, Culture and Society* 22, no. 6 (2005): 53–72.

Fowler, Robert Booth. *Carrie Catt: Feminist Politician*. Boston: Northeastern University Press, 1986.

Franklin, John Hope. "A Half-Century of Presidential Race Initiatives: Some Reflections." *Journal of Supreme Court History* 24, no. 2 (2011): 226–37.

Franklin, John Hope, and Alfred A. Moss, Jr. *From Slavery to Freedom: A History of African Americans*. 6th ed. New York: Alfred A. Knopf, 1988.

Frye, Northrop. *Anatomy of Criticism: Four Essays*. Princeton NJ: Princeton University Press, 1957.

Fuller, Jennifer. "Debating the Present through the Past: Representations of the Civil Rights Movement in the 1990s." In *The Civil Rights Movement in American Memory*, edited by Renee Christine Romano and Leigh Raiford, 167–96. Athens: University of Georgia Press, 2006.

Fulton, Marianne, ed. *Eyes of Time: Photojournalism in America*. Boston: Little, Brown, 1988.

Gee, Gilbert C., and Chandra L. Ford. "Structural Racism and Health Inequities: Old Issues, New Directions." *Du Bois Review* 8, no. 1 (2011): 115–32.

Gems, Gerald R. *For Pride, Profit, and Patriarchy: Football and the Incorporation of American Cultural Values*. Lanham MD: Scarecrow Press, 2000.

Gibson, William S. *The Golden Gophers: A Record of the Achievements of the Undefeated Football Teams of 1933, 1934, and 1935 of the University of Minnesota*. Minneapolis: General Alumni Association of the University of Minnesota, 1935.

Giddings, Paula. *When and Where I Enter: The Impact of Black Women on Race and Sex in America*. New York: William Morrow, 1996.

Gilbert, Marc Jason. *The Vietnam War on Campus: Other Voices, More Distant Drums*. Westport CT: Praeger, 2000.

Gilmore, Al-Tony. "Jack Johnson, the Man and His Times." *Journal of Popular Culture* 6, no. 3 (1973): 496–506.

Gissendanner, Cindy Himes. "African-American Women and Competitive Sport, 1920–1960." In *Women, Sport, and Culture*, edited by Susan Birrell and Cheryl L. Cole, 81–92. Champaign IL: Human Kinetics, 1994.

Goudy, Willis. "Selected Demographics: Iowa's African-American Residents, 1840–2000." In Silag, *Outside In*, 23–41.

Grady, Al. "Hawkeyes: The Pride of Iowa." In *Greatest Moments in Hawkeyes Football History*, by Mark Dukes and Gus Schrader and edited by Francis J. Fitzgerald, 6–13. Chicago: Triumph Books, 1998.

Graham, Sara Hunter. *Woman Suffrage and the New Democracy*. New Haven CT: Yale University Press, 1996.

Grundman, Adolph H. "Image of Intercollegiate Sports and the Civil Rights Movement: A Historians' View." *Arena Review* 3 (1979): 17–24.

Halbwachs, Maurice. *The Collective Memory*. Translated by Francis J. Ditter Jr. and Vida Yazdi Ditter. New York: Harper & Row, 1980.

Harris, Othello. "African American Predominance in Collegiate Sport." In *Racism in College Athletics: The African-American Athlete's Experience*, edited by Dana Brooks and Ronald Althouse, 51–74. Morgantown WV: Fitness Information Technology, 1993.

Harrison, Keith. "A Critical Race Analysis of the Hiring Process for Head Coaches in NCAA College Football." *Journal of Intercollegiate Sport* 3, no. 2 (2010): 270–96.

Harrison, William Henry. *Colored Girls and Boys' Inspiring United States History*. Allentown PA: Searle & Dressler, 1921.

Hartmann, Douglas. *Race, Culture, and the Revolt of the Black Athlete: The 1968 Olympic Protests and Their Aftermath*. Chicago: University of Chicago Press, 2003.

Hawkins, Billy. *The New Plantation: Black Athletes, College Sports, and Predominantly White NCAA Institutions*. New York: Palgrave Macmillan, 2010.

Haynes, John Earl. *Dubious Alliance: The Making of Minnesota's DFL Party*. Minneapolis: University of Minnesota Press, 1984.

Henderson, Edwin Bancroft. *The Black Athlete: Emergence and Arrival*. Cornwells Heights PA: Publishers Agency, 1976.

——. *The Negro in Sport*. 1939. Reprint, Washington DC: Associated Publishers, 1949.

——. "Negro Women in Sports." *Negro History Bulletin* 15, no. 3 (December 1951): 55.

Herrnstein, Richard J., and Charles Murray. *The Bell Curve: Intelligence and Class Structure in American Life*. New York: Free Press, 1994.

Hill, Jeffrey. "Anecdotal Evidence: Sport, the Newspaper Press, and History." In *Deconstructing Sport History: A Postmodern Analysis*, edited by Murray G. Phillips, 117–30. Albany: State University of New York Press, 2006.

Hodgkin, Katherine, and Susannah Radstone, eds. *Contested Pasts: The Politics of Memory.* London: Routledge, 2003.

Hoffbeck, Steven R. "Bobby Marshall: Pioneering African American Athlete." *Minnesota History* 59, no. 4 (2004–5): 158–74.

Howard, Walter T. *Lynchings: Extralegal Violence in Florida during the 1930s.* Cranbury NJ: Associated University Presses, 1995.

Hubbell, John T. "The Desegregation of the University of Oklahoma, 1946–1950." *The Journal of Negro History* 57, no. 4 (1972): 370–84.

Hume, Janice. *Obituaries in American Culture.* Jackson: University Press of Mississippi, 2000.

Hyman, Mervin D., and Gordon S. White, Jr. *Big Ten Football: Its Life and Times, Great Coaches, Players, and Games.* New York: Macmillan, 1977.

Irwin-Zarecka, Iwona. *Frames of Remembrance: The Dynamics of Collective Memory.* London: Transaction Publishers, 1994.

Jenkins, Herbert Crawford. "The Negro Student at the University of Iowa: A Sociological Study." Thesis, University of Iowa, 1933.

Johnson, Kay. "The Ku Klux Klan in Iowa: A Study in Intolerance." Thesis, University of Iowa, 1967.

Jones, Steven L. *Football's Fallen Hero: The Jack Trice Story.* Logan IA: Perfect Learning, 2000.

Kaley, Jack Warren. "A History of Intercollegiate Football at Drake University from 1893–1954." Thesis, Drake University, 1956.

Kammen, Michael. *In the Past Lane: Historical Perspectives on American Culture.* New York: Oxford University Press, 1997.

———. *Mystic Chords of Memory: The Transformation of Tradition in American Culture.* New York: Alfred A. Knopf, 1991.

Kemper, Kurt Edward. *College Football and American Culture in the Cold War Era.* Urbana: University of Illinois Press, 2009.

Kim, Claire Jean. "Clinton's Race Initiative: Recasting the American Dilemma." *Polity* 33, no. 2 (2000): 175–97.

———. "Managing the Racial Breach: Clinton, Black-White Polarization, and the Race Initiative." *Political Science Quarterly* 117 (2002): 55–79.

King, C. Richard, and Charles Frueling Springwood. *Beyond the Cheers: Race as Spectacle in College Sport.* Albany: State University of New York Press, 2001.

Kline, Kerwin Lee. "On the Emergence of *Memory* in Historical Discourse." *Representations* 69 (2000): 127–50.

Kopecky, Pauline W. *A History of Equal Opportunity at Oklahoma State University.* Stillwater: Oklahoma State University, 1990.

Kuhn, Annette. "Memory Texts and Memory Work: Performances of Memory in and with Visual Media." *Memory Studies* 3, no. 4 (2010): 298–313.

Lamb, Chris. *Blackout: The Untold Story of Jackie Robinson's First Spring Training.* Lincoln: University of Nebraska Press, 2004.

Lapchick, Richard, Robert Augusta, Nathaniel Kinkopf, and Frank McPhee. "The 2012 Racial and Gender Report Card: College Sport." Orlando FL: The Institute for Diversity and Ethics in Sport, July 10, 2013.

Lazare, Aaron. *On Apology*. New York: Oxford University Press, 2004.

Lederman, Douglas. "Old Times Not Forgotten." In *Sport in Contemporary Society: An Anthology*, edited by D. Stanley Eitzen, 115–20. Boulder CO: Paradigm Publishers, 2005.

Leonard, David J. "The Next M. J. or the Next O. J.? Kobe Bryant, Race, and the Absurdity of Colorblind Rhetoric." *Journal of Sport and Social Issues* 28, no. 3 (2004): 284–313.

Levine, David O. *The American College and the Culture of Aspiration, 1915–1940*. Ithaca NY: Cornell University Press, 1986.

Levy, Alan H. *Tackling Jim Crow: Racial Segregation in Professional Football*. Jefferson NC: McFarland, 2003.

Loewen, James W. "The African American Experience in Professional Football." *Journal of Social History* 33, no. 1 (1999): 163–78.

———. *Lies across America: What Our Historic Sites Get Wrong*. New York: New Press, 1999.

Lomax, Michael E. "The African American Experience in Professional Football." *Journal of Social History* 33, no. 1 (1999): 163–78.

Longley, Neil, Todd Crosset, and Steve Jefferson. "The Migration of African-Americans to the Canadian Football League during the 1950s: An Escape from Racism?" *International Journal of the History of Sport* 25, no. 10 (2008): 1374–97.

Lusane, Clarence. *Race in the Global Era: African Americans at the Millennium*. Boston: South End Press, 1997.

Maier, Charles S. "A Surfeit of Memory? Reflections on History, Melancholy and Denial." *History and Memory* 5, no. 2 (1993): 136–52.

Martin, Charles H. *Benching Jim Crow: The Rise and Fall of the Color Line in Southern College Sports, 1890–1980*. Urbana: University of Illinois Press, 2010.

———. "The Color Line in Midwestern College Sports, 1890–1960." *Indiana Magazine of History* 98, no. 2 (2002): 85–112.

———. "Racial Change and 'Big-Time' College Football in Georgia: The Age of Segregation, 1892–1957." *Georgia Historical Quarterly* 79, no. 3 (1996): 532–62.

———. Review of *Glory Road*, directed by James Gartner (Walt Disney Pictures). *Journal of Sport History* 32, no. 3 (2005): 443–44.

Mashon, Mike. "Losing Control: Popular Reception(s) of the Rodney King Video." *Wide Angle: A Film Quarterly of Theory, Criticism, and Practice* 15, no. 2 (1993): 7–18.

Massey, Douglas S. *Categorically Unequal: The American Stratification System*. New York: Russell Sage Foundation, 2007.

Mayer, George H. *The Political Career of Floyd B. Olson*. Minneapolis: University of Minnesota Press, 1951.

McCrisken, Trevor B., and Andrew Pepper. *American History and Contemporary Hollywood Film*. New Brunswick NJ: Rutgers University Press, 2005.

McGrath, John S., and James J. Delmont. *Floyd Björnsterne Olson: Minnesota's Greatest Liberal Governor, a Memorial Volume.* St. Paul MN: McGrath & Delmont, 1937.

McMahon, David R. "Pride to All: African-Americans and Sports in Iowa." In Silag, *Outside In*, 61–98.

———. "Remembering the Black and Gold: African-Americans, Sport Memory, and the University of Iowa." In *Sport and Memory in North America*, edited by Stephen G. Wieting, 61–98. London: Frank Cass, 2001.

Miller, Patrick B. "Muscular Assimilationism: Sport and the Paradoxes of Racial Reform." In Ross, *Race and Sport*, 146–82.

———. "Slouching toward a New Expediency: College Football and the Color Line during the Depression Decade." *American Studies* 40 (1999): 5–30.

Mitchell, Elmer D. "Racial Traits in Athletics." *American Physical Education Review* 27, no. 3 (1922): 93–99.

Moore, Lenny. *All Things Being Equal: The Autobiography of Lenny Moore.* With Jeffrey Jay Ellish. Champaign IL: Sports Publishing, 2006.

Myrdal, Gunnar. *An American Dilemma: The Negro Problem and Modern Democracy.* New York: Harper & Bros., 1944.

Nathan, Daniel A. *Saying It's So: A Cultural History of the Black Sox Scandal.* Urbana: University of Illinois Press, 2003.

"News and Views: Catt Fight at Iowa State." *The Journal of Blacks in Higher Education* 18 (1997–98): 73–74.

Nora, Pierre. "Between Memory and History: Les Lieux de Mémoire." *Representations* 26 (1989): 7–25.

———, ed. *Rethinking France: Les Lieux de Mémoire.* Translated by Mary Trouille. Chicago: University of Chicago Press, 2001.

Norman, Matt, dir. *Salute.* Film. Wingman Pictures, Australia, 2008.

Olick, Jeffrey K, and Brenda Coughlin. "The Politics of Regret: Analytical Frames." In *Politics and the Past: On Repairing Historical Injustices*, edited by John Torpey, 37–62. Lanham MD: Rowman & Littlefield, 2003.

Oliver, Melvin L., and Thomas M. Shapiro. *Black Wealth/White Wealth: A New Perspective on Racial Inequality.* New York: Routledge, 2006.

Oriard, Michael. *King Football: Sport and Spectacle in the Golden Age of Radio and Newsreels, Movies and Magazines, the Weekly & the Daily Press.* Chapel Hill: University of North Carolina Press, 2001.

Ottley, Roi. *Lonely Warrior: The Life and Times of Robert S. Abbott.* Chicago: Henry Regency, 1955.

Papas, Al. *Gophers Illustrated: The Incredible Complete History of Minnesota Football.* Minneapolis: University of Minnesota Press, 2009.

Petersen, James A. *Slater of Iowa.* Chicago: Hinckley & Schmitt, 1958.

Pettigrew, Thomas F. "Post-Racism? Putting President Obama's Victory in Perspective." *Du Bois Review* 6, no. 2 (2009): 279.

Phillips, Murray G., Mark E. O'Neill, and Gary Osmond. "Broadening Horizons in Sport History: Films, Photographs, and Monuments." *Journal of Sport History* 24, no. 2 (2007): 271–93.

Pride, Armistead Scott. "The Negro Newspaper in the United States." *International Communication Gazette* 2 (1956): 141–49.

Rader, Benjamin G. *American Sports: From the Age of Folk Games to the Age of Televised Sports.* 5th ed. Upper Saddle River NJ: Prentice-Hall, 2004.

Rampersand, Arnold. *Jackie Robinson: A Biography.* New York: Ballantine Books, 1997.

Rathet, Mike, and Don R. Smith. *Their Deeds and Dogged Faith.* New York: Rutledge Books, 1984.

Richards, Eugene S. "Negro Higher and Professional Education in Oklahoma." *The Journal of Negro Education* 17, no. 3 (1948): 341–49.

Ritchey, Charles J. *Drake University through Seventy-five Years, 1881–1956.* Des Moines IA: Drake University, 1956.

Roberts, Randy. *Papa Jack: Jack Johnson and the Era of White Hopes.* New York: Free Press, 1983.

Ross, Charles K. *Outside the Lines: African Americans and the Integration of the National Football League.* New York: New York University Press, 1999.

———, ed. *Race and Sport: The Struggle for Equality on and off the Field.* Jackson: University Press of Mississippi, 2004.

Rothwell, Erin, and Philip Theodore. "Intramurals and College Student Development: The Role of Intramurals on Values Clarification." *Recreational Sports Journal* 30 (2006): 46–52.

Roy, George, dir. *Fists of Freedom: The Story of the '68 Summer Games.* Film. HBO Sports, 1999.

Rozendaal, Neal. *Duke Slater: Pioneering Black NFL Player and Judge.* Jefferson NC: McFarland, 2012.

Rubin, Cyma, dir. *Moment of Impact: Stories of the Pulitzer Prize Photographs.* VHS. Palisades Park NJ: TNT, Haber Video, 1999.

Rulon, Philip Reed. *Oklahoma State University since 1890.* Stillwater: Oklahoma State University Press, 1975.

Sampson, Robert J., and Patrick Sharkey. "Neighborhood Selection and the Social Reproduction of Concentrated Racial Inequality." *Demography* 45, no. 1 (2008): 1–29.

Schmidt, Raymond. "The 1929 Iowa Football Scandal: Playing Tribute to the Carnegie Report?" *Journal of Sport History* 34, no. 4 (2007): 343–51.

———. *Shaping College Football: The Transformation of American Sport, 1919–1930.* Syracuse NY: Syracuse University Press, 2007.

Schultz, Jaime. "Contesting the Master Narrative: The Arthur Ashe Statue on Monument Avenue in Richmond, Virginia." *International Journal of Sport History* 28, no. 8–9 (2011): 1235–51.

―――. "*Glory Road* and the 'White Savior' Historical Sport Film." *Journal of Popular Film and Television* 42, no. 4 (2014): 205–13.

―――. "Jack Trice Stadium and the Politics of Memory." *International Journal of Sport History* 24, no. 6 (2007): 715–48.

―――. "The Legend of Jack Trice and the Campaign for Jack Trice Stadium, 1973–1984." *Journal of Social History* 41, no. 4 (2008): 997–1029.

―――. "Photography, Instant Memory and the Slugging of Johnny Bright." *Stadion* 32 (2006): 221–43.

―――. "The Truth about Historical Sport Films." *Journal of Sport History* 41, no. 1 (2014): 29–45.

―――. "'A Wager Concerning a Diplomatic Pig': A Crooked Reading of the Floyd of Rosedale Narrative." *Journal of Sport History* 32, no. 1 (2005): 1–21.

Schwartz, Barry. "The Social Context of Commemoration: A Study of Collective Memory." *Social Forces* 61 (1982): 374–402.

Schwieder, Dorothy. "The Life and Legacy of Jack Trice." *Annals of Iowa* 69, no. 4 (2010): 379–417.

Shackel, Paul A. *Memory in Black and White: Race, Commemoration, and the Post-Bellum Landscape*. Walnut Creek CA: AltaMira Press, 2003.

―――, ed. *Myth, Memory and the Making of the American Landscape*. Gainesville: University of Florida Press, 2001.

Shay, Frank. *Judge Lynch, His First Hundred Years*. New York: Ives Washburn, 1938.

Sigelman, Lee, and Susan Welch. *Black Americans' Views of Racial Inequality: The Dream Deferred*. New York: Cambridge University Press, 1991.

Silag, Bill, ed. *Outside In: African-American History in Iowa, 1883–2000*. Des Moines: State Historical Society of Iowa, 2001.

Small, Geoff, dir. *Black Power Salute*. Film. British Broadcasting Corporation, 2008.

Smith, Clay J., Jr., ed. *Supreme Justice: Speeches and Writings: Thurgood Marshall*. Philadelphia: University of Pennsylvania Press, 2003.

Smith, Maureen M. "Mapping America's Sporting Landscape: A Case Study of Three Statues." *International Journal of the History of Sport* 28, no. 8–9 (2011): 1252–68.

Smith, Ronald A. "Harvard and Columbia and a Reconsideration of the 1905–06 Football Crisis." *Journal of Sport History* 8, no. 3 (1981): 5–19.

Smith, Thomas G. "Outside the Pale: The Exclusion of Blacks from the National Football League, 1934–1946." *Journal of Sport History* 15, no. 3 (1989): 255–81.

Soderstrom, Mark. "Weeds in Linnaeus's Garden: Science and Segregation, Eugenics, and the Rhetoric of Racism at the University of Minnesota and the Big Ten, 1900–45." PhD diss., University of Minnesota, 2004.

Spangler, Earl. *The Negro in Minnesota*. Minneapolis: T. S. Denison, 1961.

Spencer, Nancy E. "From 'Child's Play' to 'Party Crasher': Venus Williams, Racism, and Professional Women's Tennis." In *Sports Stars: The Cultural Politics of Sporting Celebrity*, edited by David L. Andrews and Steven J. Jackson, 87–101. London: Routledge, 2001.

Sperber, Murray. *Onward to Victory: The Crisis that Shaped College Sports.* New York: Henry Holt, 1998.

Spivey, Donald. "The Black Athlete in Big-Time Intercollegiate Sports, 1941–1968." *Phylon* 22, no. 2 (1983): 116–25.

———. "'End Jim Crow in Sports': The Protest at New York University, 1940–1941." *Journal of Sport History* 15, no. 3 (1989): 282–303.

———. *Fire from the Soul: A History of the African-American Struggle.* Durham NC: Carolina Academic Press, 2003.

Spivey, Donald, and Thomas A. Jones. "Intercollegiate Athletic Servitude: A Case Study of the Black Illini Student-Athletes, 1931–1967." *Social Science Quarterly* 55, no. 4 (1975): 939–47.

Steward, Roger. *Cyclone Memories: 100 Years of Iowa State Football.* Webster City IA: S&RS Publishers, 1991.

Stewart, Maxwell S. *The Negro in America.* New York: Public Affairs Committee, 1944.

Strode, Woody, and Sam Young. *Goal Dust: The Warm and Candid Memoirs of a Pioneer Black Athlete and Actor.* New York: Madison Books, 1990.

Su, John J. "Ghosts of Essentialism: Racial Memory as Epistemological Claim." *American Literature* 81, no. 2 (2009): 361–86.

Suggs, Henry Lewis, ed. *The Black Press in the Middle West, 1865–1985.* Westport CT: Greenwood Press, 1996.

Swan, Michael Lee. "From Vietnam to Don Smith and Beyond: *The Iowa State Daily* and Its Portrayal of a Radical Decade, 1966–1975." PhD diss., Iowa State University, 1998.

Tarman, Christopher, and David O. Sears, "The Conceptualization and Measurement of Symbolic Racism." *Journal of Politics* 67, no. 3 (2005): 731–61.

Teasley, Martell, and David Ikard. "Barack Obama and the Politics of Race: The Myth of Postracism in America." *Journal of Black Studies* 40, no. 3 (2010): 419–20.

Thelen, David. "Memory and American History." *Journal of American History* 75, no. 4 (1989): 1117–29.

Thompson, Janna. *Taking Responsibility for the Past: Reparation and Historical Justice.* Cambridge: Polity, 2002.

Tischauser, Leslie V. *Race Relations in the United States, 1920–1940.* Westport CT: Greenwood Press, 2008.

Tolnay, Stewart Emory, and E. M. Beck. *A Festival of Violence: An Analysis of Southern Lynchings, 1882–1930.* Urbana: University of Illinois Press, 1995.

Trachtenberg, Alan. "Through a Glass, Darkly: Photograph and Cultural Memory." *Social Research* 75, no. 1 (2008): 111–32.

Tucker, Lauren R. "Black, White, and Read All Over: Racial Reasoning and the Construction of Public Reaction to the O. J. Simpson Criminal Trial Verdict by the *Chicago Tribune* and the *Chicago Defender.*" *Howard Journal of Communications* 8 (1997): 315–27.

Tunnell, Emlen. *Footsteps of a Giant.* With Bill Gleason. Garden City NY: Doubleday, 1966.

Ultang, Don. *Holding the Moment: Mid-America at Mid-Century.* Ames: Iowa State University Press, 1991.

Underhill, Robert. *Alone among Friends: A Biography of W. Robert Parks.* Ames: Iowa State University Press, 1999.

Urban Research Corporation. *Student Protests, 1969.* Chicago: Urban Research Corporation, 1970.

Valentine, John, and Simon C. Darnell. "Football and 'Tolerance': Black Football Players in 20th-Century Canada." In *Race and Sport in Canada: Intersecting Inequalities,* edited by Janelle Joseph, Simon Darnell, and Yuka Nakamura, 57–80. Toronto: Canadian Scholars' Press, 2012.

Van Voris, Jacqueline. *Carrie Chapman Catt: A Public Life.* New York: Feminist Press at the City University of New York, 1987.

Vera, Hernán, and Andrew M. Gordon. *Screen Saviors: Hollywood Fictions of Whiteness.* Lanham MD: Rowman & Littlefield, 2003.

Vera, Hernán, Joe R. Feagin, and Andrew Gordon. "Superior Intellect? Sincere Fictions of the White Self." *Journal of Negro Education* 64, no. 3 (1995): 295–306.

Walker, Chet. *Long Time Coming: A Black Athlete's Coming-of-Age in America.* With Chris Messenger. New York: Grove Press, 1995.

Wallace, David L., and Anissa Bell. "Being Black at a Predominantly White University." *College English* 61 (1999): 307–27.

Wallace, Michele Faith. "The Good Lynching and 'Birth of a Nation' Discourses and Aesthetics of Jim Crow." *Cinema Journal* 43, no. 1 (2003): 85–104.

Watterson, John Sayle. *College Football: History, Spectacle, Controversy.* Baltimore: Johns Hopkins University Press, 2000.

Wells, Tom. *The War Within: America's Battle over Vietnam.* Berkeley: University of California Press, 1994.

Western, Bruce. *Punishment and Inequality in America.* New York: Russell Sage Foundation, 2006.

Weyeneth, Robert R. "The Power of the Apology and the Process of Historical Reconciliation." *The Public Historian* 23, no. 3 (2001): 9–38.

White, Hayden. *The Content of Form: Narrative Discourse and Historical Representation.* Baltimore: Johns Hopkins University Press, 1987.

———. *Metahistory: The Historical Imagination in Nineteenth-Century Europe.* Baltimore MD: Johns Hopkins University Press, 1973.

White, Maury. "The Legend of Jack Trice." *The Iowan* 46 (Fall 1997): 49–50.

Whittingham, Richard. *Rites of Autumn: The Story of College Football.* New York: Free Press, 2001.

Wieting, Stephen G., ed. *Sport and Memory in North America.* London: Frank Cass, 2001.

Wiggins, David K. *Glory Bound: Black Athletes in a White America.* Syracuse NY: Syracuse University Press, 1997.

———. "Prized Performers, but Frequently Overlooked Students: The Involvement of Black Athletes in Intercollegiate Sports on Predominantly White University Campuses, 1890–1972." *Research Quarterly for Exercise and Sport* 62 (1991): 164–77.

————. "'Strange Mix of Entitlement and Exploitation': The African American Experience in Predominantly White College Sport." *Wake Forest Journal of Law and Policy* 2, no. 1 (2012): 95–113.

Wiggins, David K., and Patrick B. Miller, eds. *The Unlevel Playing Field: A Documentary History of the African American Experience in Sport.* Urbana: University of Illinois Press, 2003.

Williamson, Joy Ann. "In Defense of Themselves: The Black Student Struggle for Success and Recognition at Predominantly White Colleges and Universities." *Journal of Negro Education* 68, no. 1 (1999): 92–105.

Wine, George. *Black and Gold Memories: The Hawkeyes of the 20th Century.* Iowa City: University of Iowa Department of Intercollegiate Athletics, 2003.

Winter, Jay. "The Memory Boom in Contemporary Historical Studies." *Raritan* 21, no. 1 (2001): 52–67.

Wolters, Raymond. *The New Negro on Campus: Black College Rebellions of the 1920s.* Princeton NJ: Princeton University Press, 1975.

Wynn, Neil A. "The Impact of the Second World War on the American Negro." *Journal of Contemporary History* 6, no. 2 (1971): 42–53.

Yeakey, Lamont H. "A Student without Peer: The Undergraduate College Years of Paul Robeson." *Journal of Negro Education* 42, no. 2 (1973): 489–503.

Zangrando, Robert L. *The NAACP Crusade against Lynching, 1909–1950.* Philadelphia: Temple University Press, 1980.

Zaslow, Jeffrey. *The Girls from Ames: A Story of Women and a Forty-year Friendship.* New York: Gotham Books, 2009.

INDEX

Page numbers in italics refer to illustrations.

onciliation, 2–3, 132–33; significance of narrative in, 21–22. *See also* memory

Cunningham, Evelyn, 15

Curtis Hotel, 46–47

Dahl, Orin L., 107

Daily Iowan, 79–81, 92

Dalfiume, Richard M., 7

Darnell, Simon, 128

Dartmouth College, 11, 123

Davis, Angelique, 132–33

Davis, Ernie, 140, 171n95

Davis, Nancy Randolph, 112

Dean, Bob, 128, 129

deaths, 11, 34–35

Der Angriff, 75–76

desegregation, 6–9, 16, 104–5, 112

Des Moines Register, 45, 70, 113–18, 122

Detweiler, Frederick G., 84

Dickerson, Voris, 96

Dobbs, Charles M., 58

Dobson, Richard, 75

Doby, Larry, 104

Dolgan, Bob, 53

"Double V" campaign, 7

Drake University (Bulldogs): and 1951 Bulldogs-Aggies game, 103, 114–18; black students at, 107, 121; departure of, from the MVC, 121–22, 170n71; and Johnny Bright Field, 2–3, 131–32; Johnny Bright's athletic career at, 107–10, 126–27; and pre-1951 A&M games, 110–12; response of, to Johnny Bright incident, 118–22

Du Bois, W. E. B., 23

Duke University, 12, 149n56

Dwight, Ed, 66–67, 71

Eagles (Philadelphia), 127, 171n100

Early, Gerald, 137

East Technical High School (Cleveland), 22–23

Eaton, Lloyd, 139

Edmonton Eskimos, 103

Edmonton Journal, 129

Edwards, Harry, 50, 136, 139

Eiland, Ray, 112

Emmerson, Tom, 36, 49, 67

Eskimos (Edmonton), 103

The Express, 140

Farrakhan, Louis, 61

Feagin, Joe R., 61, 143

Ferber, Abby, 144

films, 137, 140–41, 174n37. *See also specific films*

Fisher, Robert, 46

Fists of Freedom, 137

Floyd of Rosedale, 2–3, 73, 74, 89–91, 95, 100–101, 164n76

football (college): deaths in, 11, 34–35; desegregation of, 4, 105–6; "gentlemen's agreements" in, 9–10, 75, 96, 98, 105; segregation in, 48; social significance of, 15, 16; violence in, 11–14, 34–35, 122–23. *See also* National Football League (NFL)

Ford, Jim, 107, 129

Fowler, Bridget, 100

Fowler, Robert, 57

Franklin, John Hope, 7, 142

Frye, Northrop: *Anatomy of Criticism*, 150n3

Fulton, Marianne, 117–18

Gaer, Warren, 108, 109, 115, 118, 119

Gallagher, Jim, 127

Gant, London "Brutus," 75

Gardner, Frank, 119

Garvey, Marcus, 23

Geary, Patrick, 53

"gentlemen's agreements," 9–10, 75, 96, 98, 105, 138–39

Georgia Tech, 10, 174n37

G.I. Bill, 8

The Girls from Ames (Zaslow), 71

Glory Road, 140–41

Goebbels, Joseph, 76

Gold, Adam, 54, 55

Goldman, Ron, 60

golf, 105–6

Gophers. *See* University of Minnesota (Gophers)

Gordon, Andrew, 61, 143

Government of the Student Body (GSB), 42, 49, 50, 54–55, 64–65

Graham, Henry, 46–47

Grange, Harold "Red," 85, 122

Great Depression, 76

King, C. Richard, 71
King, Martin Luther, Jr., 39, 62, 145
King, Rodney, 60
Kinnick, Nile, 43
Kinnick Stadium, 43–44
Kline, Laura, 55
Kopecky, Pauline W.: *A History of Equal Opportunity*, 122
Kraft, Walter, 48
Kunerth, William, 40, 48–49, 62
Kunh, Annette, 21

Layton, Wilbur, 40
Lewis, John Henry, 74, 99
Lewis, William H., 10, 16
Life, 117–18, 170n83
Lillard, Joe, 14
Long Island University, 124
Lookabaugh, Jim, 111
Los Angeles Times, 73
Louis, Joe, 15, 74, 86, 99
lynching, 4–5, 23, 76, 88

Macomber, Gene, 116
Major League Baseball (MLB), 104–5
Manhattan College, 123
Mann Act, 5, 138
Marshall, Robert, 86
Marshall, Thurgood, 58–59
Martin, Charles H., 75, 140
Mashon, Mike, 60
Matthews, William, 9–10
Maxwell, David E., 131
McCain, John, 137–38
McClelland, Jack, 119
McCrisken, Trevor B., 137
McCullough, Lou, 42
McElroy, C. H., 119
McGriff, Milton, 57, 64
McLaurin, George W., 112
media. *See* black press; white press
memorials. *See* commemorations
memory, 18, 46–47, 53–54, 72. *See also* cultural memory; racialized memory
Miller, Owen, 107
Miller, Patrick B., 15, 74
Million Man March (1995), 61
Minneapolis Journal, 85–86, 89

Minneapolis Tribune, 87, 88, 89
Minnesota Alumni Weekly, 33
Missouri Valley Conference (MVC), 119–22, 155n104, 170nn71–72
Mitchell, Elmer, 35; "Racial Traits in Athletics," 82
MLB. *See* Major League Baseball (MLB)
Monroe, Al, 77, 92, 162n39
Moore, Lenny, 103, 130
Morsell-Simmons, Eutopia, 96, 100–101
Motley, Marion, 11, 104
Mulhall, Gary, 42
Murray, Charles: *The Bell Curve*, 61
muscular assimilation, 15, 80, 81
MVC. *See* Missouri Valley Conference (MVC)
Myrdal, Gunnar: *An American Dilemma*, 8

NAACP. *See* National Association for the Advancement of Colored People (NAACP)
Nace, Ed, 5
narratives, 21–22, 47, 80, 140–41, 150n3
National Association for the Advancement of Colored People (NAACP), 7, 23, 63, 76
National Football League (NFL), 14, 75, 79, 98, 103, 104, 127
National Urban League, 7, 23
Nave, William, 28
Newcombe, Don, 104
"New Negro" movement, 23
"new racism," 142–44
newspapers. *See* black press; white press; *and specific newspapers*
Newsweek, 36, 50
New York Amsterdam News, 96, 97
New York Post, 129
New York Times, 89–90, 100, 122, 129, 164n79
New York University, 138–39, 148n42
NFL. *See* National Football League (NFL)
Nixon, Richard, 38
Northwestern University (Wildcats), 75, 81–82
Not the Triumph but the Struggle (Bass), 137
Nunn, William G., 11, 99

Obama, Barack, 133, 142, 145
obituaries, 100
Offenburger, Chuck, 45

Oklahoma A&M (Aggies): and 1951 Aggies-
Bulldogs game, 114–18; and the Big 7,
112–13; desegregation at, 112, 168n32;
official apology of, 131–32; and pre-1951
Bulldogs games, 110–12; and public reac-
tion to Johnny Bright incident, 124–25,
169n59, 170n83; response of, to Johnny
Bright incident, 118–22; and targeting
Johnny Bright, 103, 113, 116–18
Oklahoman, 132
Oklahoma State University. *See* Oklahoma
A&M (Aggies)
Oklahoma State University since 1890 (Rulon), 122
Olson, Floyd B., 73, 88–91, 91, 92
Olszewski, Johnny, 123
Olympic Games, 74, 75–76, 136–37
"One America" campaign, 134–35
Opportunity, 5, 11
Oriard, Michael, 73–74, 80
Owens, Jesse, 15, 74, 75
Owens, Jim, 173n36

Page, James, 81
Parks, W. Robert, 39, 40, 43, 48, 153n56
Pearson, Raymond, 30, 34
Pepper, Andrew, 137
Perry, Lincoln Theodore, 79
Pettigrew, Thomas F., 141
Philadelphia Eagles, 127, 171n100
Philadelphia Tribune, 15, 92, 94, 96, 97
Philmon, Hank, 155n106
Pilkington, Jim, 117
Pittsburgh Courier, 6, 11, 15, 77, 99, 127
Plaza of Heroines (ISU), 63–64, 159n66
Plessy v. Ferguson, 4
Pollard, Frederick Douglass "Fritz," 4, 12,
82, 97
Pollard, Jamie, 67, 70
post-racial societies, 141–43
Potts, Harold R. E., 156n106
Princeton University, 11, 123
Professional Golfers' Association, 105–6
Purdue University, 12
PWCUs (predominantly white colleges
and universities): black athletes at, 3–9,
74–75; civil rights movement in, 36–40;
desegregation of, 8–9; "gentlemen's

agreements" at, 9–10, 75; graduation
rates of, 151n116; racial statistics of, 4; and
racism on campuses, 5–6, 75

Quinlan, Jack, 85–86

*Race, Culture, and the Revolt of the Black
Athlete* (Hartmann), 137
racialized memory, 2–3, 104, 129–30, 141–42,
147n3. *See also* cultural memory; memory
"Racial Traits in Athletics" (Mitchell), 82
racism: during the 1920s, 23; during the
1990s, 59–61; black athletes' protest of, 139–
40; on college campuses, 6, 75; commemoration's impact on, 3, 71–72; and cultural
memories, 47–48, 129–30; at Drake University, 107, 121; and "gentlemen's agreements," 9–10, 75, 96, 98, 105; government
campaigns fighting, 134–35; in Iowa, 16–17;
at ISU, 57–58; and Jack Trice's death, 33–34,
45–47; and the Johnny Bright incident, 125–
26, 129–30; and Ozzie Simmons's injuries,
84–86; and racial progress, 131–33; silence
regarding, 13–14, 34–35, 130; in sports, 75–76,
105–6, 134; sports as challenge to, 15; and
stereotypes, 79–80, 82–83; subtle forms of,
142–44; twenty-first-century shifts in, 141–
44; at the University of Iowa, 96
Rader, Benjamin G., 16
Radstone, Susannah, 53
Ray, Robert, 48
Reagan, Ronald, 133, 163n63
Redskins (Washington), 106
Reed, Dwight, 75, 87
Rhoads, Paul, 70
Rice, Grantland, 10
Robeson, Paul, 4, 10, 13
Robinson, Jackie, 104
Robinson, John, 114–17
Robinson, Mack, 74
Roby, Roosevelt, 39, 153n58
Rollins, Derrick, 58
romance (narrative form), 21–22, 33, 52
Roosevelt, Theodore, 11
Rozendaal, Neal, 98, 145
Rudolph, Wilma, 136
Rulon, Philip Reed: *Oklahoma State Univer-
sity since 1890*, 122